Stylish
One-Dish Dinners

Stews,
Stir-Fries,
Roasts, Braises,
and more
for
Family Dinners
and
Entertaining
Friends

Stylish
One-Dish Dinners

Linda West Eckhardt

and

Katherine West DeFoyd

DOUBLEDAY

New York London Toronto Sydney Auckland

PUBLISHED BY DOUBLEDAY
a division of Random House, Inc.
1540 Broadway, New York, New York 10036

DOUBLEDAY and the portrayal of an anchor with a dolphin are
trademarks of Doubleday, a division of Random House, Inc.

BOOK DESIGN BY TERRY KARYDES
ILLUSTRATIONS BY MEREDITH HAMILTON

Library of Congress Cataloging-in-Publication Data
Eckhardt, Linda West, 1939–
Stylish one-dish dinners: stews, stir-fries, roasts, braises, and more
for family dinners and entertaining friends / Linda West Eckhardt
and Katherine West DeFoyd.
p.   cm.
Includes index.
1. Entrees (Cookery)   2. Casserole cookery.   3. Soups.   4. Salads.
5. Menus.   I. DeFoyd, Katherine West.   II. Title.
TX740.E355   1999
641.8′2—dc21
98-31915
CIP

ISBN 0-385-49179-4
Copyright © 1999 by Linda West Eckhardt
and Katherine West DeFoyd
All Rights Reserved
Printed in the United States of America
September 1999

1   2   3   4   5   6   7   8   9   10

FIRST EDITION

To
Lily and Noel,
who shared one pot
as this book
was being written
and are a
delicious addition
to our lives.

Combine disparate ingredients in one pot, stir it up, apply heat before serving, then take the first bite, and you begin to see how the final mix results from the contribution of each part.

Writing a book is a similar process. We could not have put this onto your bookshelf without the contributions of a number of people. First and foremost, we thank our editor, Judy Kern, for her unflagging energy and enthusiasm for the project. We thank especially Meredith Hamilton, who illustrated the book with wit and charm. We admire her mind and the way she illustrates the ideas presented to her. She took this book project to a higher plane.

To the people who made this book happen, Terry Karydes, who designed the interior; Jean Traina, who designed the jacket; and Christina Semmel, who managed the publicity, we say hats off for a job well done.

To Kathleen Hennessy, Denise Carlson, Jim Barnard, Jenny Johnson, Carol Smith, Mike Ryberg, Mike Ferrara, Kelly Thomala, Beth Zauhar, and the crew at Axiom, we say thank you for your continuing support in sending us around to shows across the country. To Don Stuart, KitchenAid Large Appliances, and Brian Maynard, KitchenAid Small Appliances, we say thank you for giving us the opportunity to share our ideas with America.

Marlys Bielunski of the National Cattlemen's Beef Association and Brenda McDowell of McDowell and Piasecki, Food Communications, Inc., have extended themselves to us in countless ways. We are grateful for all we have learned and for all the opportunities you have afforded us. We love that easy beef.

Thanks to Jill Melton, Senior Food Editor at *Cooking Light* magazine, for her wise head and good suggestions for recipes and menu ideas. Earlier versions of a number of these recipes began there.

Thanks also to Cynthia Nicholson Lagrone, Food Editor of *Country Living* magazine, for her excellent suggestions for this book.

Thanks to Wendy Burrell of the Burrell Group for sharing her vast knowledge of foods with us. Thanks to Lorraine Leong for teaching us some basic principles of Cantonese cooking and wok technique. Her good humor and knowledge sure spiced up our book. Thanks to Diana Butts for her good ideas and great recipe suggestions. Thanks to Debbie Pucci, who brought us a little bit of Brooklyn (and Queens). Love that White Bean Escarole Soup. Thanks Irena Gulyansky for instructing us about Russian specialties. Thanks to David Murray for his famous Yankee Dirty Rice. As Katherine's father-in-law, he's always being solicited to bring something to the potluck. He's that good a cook.

Thanks to the Italian Trade Commission and the Parmigiano Reggiano Cheese consortium for sending Linda to Italy. Thanks to Karen Harram for acting as her guide.

We thank the James Beard Foundation for generously awarding us their highest honor for our last book. The award sure motivated us to do our best another time.

To our families, Linda's husband Joe, who cheerfully ate his way through another book project, and Gordon, Katherine's husband, who not only eats but cooks and cleans as well as edits and types, we say many thanks. To Lily and Noel, the year-old twins who will eat anything (well almost) so long as it is mashed, we say thanks for waiting a few extra days before being born so your mother could finish the manuscript in peace.

Linda West Eckhardt
Katherine West DeFoyd

Contents

Introduction   xvii

part I
Off the Top of the Stove

ONE-DISH DINNERS COOKED
MOSTLY IN SKILLETS AND WOKS

Chapter 1   Stir-Fry It Fast   2

Stir-Fried Chicken Thighs with Sugar Snaps, Shiitakes,
    Carrots, and Broccoli   2
Chicken-Walnut Stir-Fry   6
Japanese Eggplant, Bell Pepper, and Lamb Stir-Fry   8
Chinese Sweet and Sour Pork with Eggplant   10
Stir-Fried Sirloin and Bitter Greens   12
Beef and Tomato Stir-Fry with Whiskey and
    Black Bean Sauce   14
Thai Curried Coconut Salmon and
    Spinach Stir-Fry with Basil   16
Stir-Fried Shrimp and Onions in a Catsup Sauce   20

Chapter 2   Skillet Sautés   22

Blueberry Chicken   22
Berkeley Panned Chicken with Polenta, Peppers,
    and Corn   24
Cinnamon Lamb Sauté   26
Spanish Steak with Sautéed Peppers and Walnuts   28
Grouper Veracruz   30
Martini Scallops on a Bed of Spinach   32
Mustard Salmon with Buttered Egg Noodles   34
Lamb and Mint Paella   36
Seafood Paella with Artichoke Hearts   38
Turkey and Cranberry Couscous   40
Dave's Yankee Dirty Rice   42
Quesadillas Primavera   44

Chapter 3   Basically Braised   46

Braised Bok Choy and Chicken in a Ginger Sauce   46
Braised Chicken with Artichokes and Greek Olives   48
Beer-Braised Pork Chops with Onions, Apples, Cabbage,
    and Currants   50
Broccoli Rabe with Italian Sausage, Tortellini, and Fresh
    Cherry Tomatoes   52
Stracotto (Parma Pot Roast with Pasta)   54
Braised Herbes de Provence Beef in Burgundy Wine   56
Zucchini Beef Bow-ties   58
Tequila-Braised Chicken with Two Kinds of Peaches   60

Chapter 4   The Fast and
                Fabulous Egg   62

Lox-Tarragon Omelet   62
Herbes de Provence Lettuce Frittata   64
Spring Frittata with Flat-Leaf Parsley, Baby Leeks, Green
    Onions, and a Touch of Balsamic Vinegar   66
Lemon Madras Egg Curry   68
Poblano Pepper Chilequiles   70

Chapter 5   And Don't Forget the Much
                Maligned Microwave   72

Asparagus, Ham, and Rice Casserole   72
Polenta with Chicken Apple Sausage, Apples, and
    Fontina Cheese   74
Risotto with Apples and Sausage   76
Risotto with Ham, Corn, and Red Peppers   78

part II

Out of the Dutch Oven

CHILIES, SOUPS, AND STEWS

Chapter 6 Chili from Texas, Cincinnati, and the White Breast of a Chicken   82

Real Texas Chili   82
Cincinnati-Style Chili   84
Kaki's White Chicken Chili for Sissies   86

Chapter 7 Soups and Stews Made from Real Red Meat   88

Tamarind Beef and Bean Stew with Pineapple and Bananas   88
Barbara Bradley's Green Chile Stew with Beef and Pork   90
Peppery Italian Beef Stew on Grilled Polenta Rounds   92
Beef Bigos   94
German Spiced Beef with Root Vegetables   96
Pork Paprikash over Rice   98
Uzbekistan Lamb Stew with Cilantro, Dried Fruit, and Pine Nuts   100
Lamb and Sweet Potato Curry Stew   102

Chapter 8 Seafood and Shellfish Soups and Stews   104

Fennel and Pernod Shellfish Stew   104
Shrimp and Ginger Soup   106
Oregon Bouillabaisse   108
Gulf Chowder   110
Caldo Mariscos y Chipotle   112
Louisiana Swampland Shellfish Gumbo   114

Chapter 9   Poultry in the Pot   116

Chicken Pot-au-Feu   116
Tortilla Chicken Soup   120
Tarragon-Smothered Chicken with Pearl Onions and
    Mushrooms   122
Jerry Thompson's Costa Rican Tropical Stew   126

Chapter 10   Beans, Rice, and Posole   128

Debra Pucci's Super-Quick White Bean and
    Escarole Soup   128
Red Beans and Rice   130
Spinach and Sugar Snap Risotto with
    Parmigiano-Reggiano   132
Barbara Bradley's Posole   134

Chapter 11   Noodles and Dumplings   136

Paprika Chicken with Saffron Dumplings   136
California Hot Pot   138

part III
**Vegetables onto
the Middle
of the Plate**

Chapter 12   Composed Salads and
    Vegetables Make a Meal   142

Baby Spinach and Strawberry Salad with Goat
    Cheese Disks   142
Bulgur, Tomato, and Feta Salad   144
Bulgur, Chick-pea, and Tomato Pilaf   146
Orecchiette Puttanesca   148

Orecchiette with Wild and Brown Mushrooms in a
    Balsamic Vinaigrette   150
Fresh Tomato, Ricotta, and Chopped Basil Salsa Cruda
    on Penne   152
Warm Penne and Pistachio Vegetable Salad   154
Warm Lima Bean, Mint, and Parsley Salad   156
Grilled Marinated Chicken and Vegetable Salad with
    Pine Nuts   158
Clam and Cheese Tortellini Salad   162
Crab with Vegetable Confetti Salad and a Lemon-Mustard
    Vinaigrette   164
Poached Salmon and Carrot Salad with a Blueberry
    Vinaigrette   166
Skewered Tomatoes and Shrimp with Roasted Red Peppers
    and Corn Salad on a Bed of Mesclun   168
Bay Shrimp, Tomato, and Basil Salad   170
Artichokes, Capers, Olives, Lemon Zest, and Italian Tuna
    on Pasta Shells   172
Seared Tuna with a Black and White Sesame Seed Crust
    on a Bed of Greens   174
Sun-Dried Tomatoes, Pancetta, Mushrooms, and Wilted
    Lettuce Salad   176
Fresh Figs, Nectarines, and Ham Tossed in a Red Wine
    Reduction   178
Couscous Summer Deli Salad   180
Roast Peppered Beef with Pears and Apples   182

part IV

Out of the Oven

ROASTS, CASSEROLES, PIZZA,
QUICHES, AND STRATAS

Chapter 13 Roasts, Fast and Slow   186

Slow-Roasted Barbecued Brisket and Southwestern
    Vegetables   186
Roasted Lemon Chicken with Fingerling Potatoes, Tomatoes,
    and Olives   188
Roasted Duck with Sweet Potatoes, Sage, Fruit, and Port   190
Roasted Monkfish with Garlic and Ginger on a Bed of Root
    Vegetables   192
Roasted Root Vegetables with Sirloin   194

Chapter 14 Casseroles and Other
Comfortable Dinners
from One Pot   196

Chipotle Chicken con Queso on a Bed of Lima Beans   196
Duck Sausage on a Bed of Lentils   198
Melinda's Sweet Hot Ham Balls with Yams and Red Onion   200
Joann's Spicy East Texas Pork Chop and Rice Casserole   202
Aunt Mary's Green Rice Custard   204
Not June Cleaver's Tuna Noodle, but Linguine with Sautéed
   Tuna and Mixed Peppers   206

Chapter 15 A Pizza, a Tart, a Couple
of Quiches, and a Strata   208

Onions, Onions, and More Onions Pizza   208
Shrimp and Crabmeat Quiche   212
Tortilla and Cilantro Quiche   214
Italian Country Strata   216
Asparagus-Tarragon Tart   218

Index   221

Introduction

One Pot Meals Throughout The Ages

Cave Dwellers
500 BC

Plains Indians
500 AD

Suburbs
1950 AD

Post Modern
2000 AD

Cooking and serving meals from one pot is hardly a new idea. Ever since cooks discovered fire, they have been composing meals that could be sizzled and served as simply as possible. What is new about this old idea is that it's okay to make these communal suppers into company fare as well as family meals. What has changed is the way we entertain. Nowadays, if we're going to entertain at all, we know we'd better keep it simple.

And why not? Millennium cooks aren't all that different from the hunters and gatherers who spent a lot of time away from camp, plucking berries and chewing on roots for sustenance while they hunted for the really big game. Once the big game was hauled into camp, it called for a celebration and everybody was invited to gather around the communal campfire.

So think about it. Men and women now charge out into the big world to hack a path through the post-modern jungle. When we indeed do collect the spoils for all that effort, we're still most likely to retreat home for rest and recreation. Statistics show we've begun to spend a lot more of our time and disposable income fashioning a home that says comfort, safety, security. We want our house to be our home, and we want to share it with family and friends.

Why do you think we have this explosion in home-as-fashion businesses? What are we all looking for in the Williams-Sonoma, Pottery Barn, and Home Depot stores? We're looking for home, that's what. And once we get our place all decked out to suit us, then what do we want to do? We want to invite the neighbors over, and perhaps even the boss and her husband. Even Mom and Dad.

What better way to celebrate that home than by having friends and family to gather round the dinner table for a meal. But now

What is old becomes new again.

the tension begins. Do we have three or four days to get ready for company? Can we create a party that will take days to clean up after? Get over it. This is the new age, for better and for worse. While we do have good intentions and a real yearning for the solace of family and friends, what we don't have is a whole lot of time and energy to devote to the effort.

And so, what is old becomes new again. We can devote our limited attention span to making one dish that not only gets cooked but also is served from one pan or plate. We can buy a great loaf of bread, compose a salad from prepared ingredients, and finish off our dinner with a terrific dessert that came from a good bakery. All we need to add to make this into a party is a bottle of wine, some candlelight, our favorite music. To complete the mix, we call up our friends and family. Perhaps we can even draft the guests into bringing the side dishes and drinks. Hey, sounds like a party doesn't it?

Our first collaboration, *Entertaining 101*, was given the James Beard Foundation Award for 1998 as the best cookbook about entertaining for the year. When we wrote that first book, our intent was to empower the new cooks coming along, to offer them a hand in making meals they'd be happy to serve to company. After teaching in cooking schools around the country and visiting twenty-five cities to promote that book, we've learned a lot about what people can and will do to entertain.

We learned from questions that came back to us that people want to know how to set up a party. How best to present food in a way that turns an ordinary meal into a celebration. And, at the bottom of it, cooks want foolproof recipes for brightly flavored meals they can make without catastrophe. Testing and cross-testing recipes and menus, we can make that happen for you.

This book will tell readers how to cook, serve, and present a meal so that it becomes a party. One thing is certain: We are convinced the greatest gift you can give to anyone is a home-cooked meal. Now that 50 percent of the American food dollar is spent eating out or ordering in, restaurant meals are no big deal to most of us. They are a part of our normal lives. When we really want to make a gift to people we love, there is simply nothing more meaningful than getting into the kitchen to cook for them.

Along with all our experience eating out has come a greater sophistication about the world's cuisines. We've all adored Italian food, Latin dishes, and Asian foods of all kinds. What we don't often realize is that these home-based cuisines can be re-created in our own home kitchens, and with ingredients from the neighborhood grocery store. Many of the best traditional ethnic dishes are made and served in one pot. This notion of fusion cooking has become so expected that we don't even give it a name anymore. We just follow our intuitive noses and cook and serve what we've first experienced in good restaurants. It's that simple.

What we need is some basic information and knowledge about how to put together these ethnic one-dish dinners. This book sets out to teach you just how to do that.

WHAT YOU'LL FIND IN THIS BOOK

Included are 101 one-dish dinners, each with one basic recipe you can make from scratch and a suggested menu that will offer ideas for how to complete the meal. Every menu also has a section

Many of the best traditional ethnic dishes are made and served in one pot.

called "All the Trimmings," which tells you how to present the meal. When is it better to serve from the pot you cooked in? Is it better to plate up the food in the kitchen or to serve it family style at the table? How do you add drama to the presentation so that the meal says "party"?

Finally, every menu contains a mini-cooking lesson that will teach you a basic cooking technique you can take with you to make other meals. We believe every cook needs some basic instruction, so think of this book as a cooking school-by-correspondence class. After all, that's how we learned to cook—by doing it.

Our goal is to empower people who love good food.

Our goal is to empower people who love good food, who care about their friends and family, and who want to invite people into their home to celebrate. We want to make these basic human tasks easy. Eating together as a family makes a house a home. We want to show you how.

Linda West Eckhardt
Maplewood, New Jersey

Katherine West DeFoyd
South Orange, New Jersey

Stylish
One-Dish Dinners

PART I

Off the Top of the Stove

One-Dish Dinners
Cooked Mostly in Skillets and Woks

Stir-Fry It Fast

Stir-Fried Chicken Thighs with Sugar Snaps, Shiitakes, Carrots, and Broccoli

Learn to whack chicken thighs into 3 pieces, holding the cleaver or knife at a slight angle, cook the pieces quickly, and you will have rendered not only the good flavor of the meat, but also the subtle flavor hidden in the bone marrow and skin. Yes, you can pick the chicken up with your fingers to eat it, and yes, we do give the bones to the dog. Everybody wins. Don't be startled by the addition of Korean kim chee to this menu. This fermented cabbage slaw is sold in the produce section of many grocery stores and adds a hot and spicy, vinegary salad that you don't have to make at home. If you can't find it in your market, a scoop of deli cole slaw also goes well as a side dish.

PREPARATION TIME: 20 MINUTES   COOKING TIME: 30–40 MINUTES
MARINATING TIME: 20 MINUTES   MAKES 6 SERVINGS

All the Trimmings

Serve the way most Asian dinners are served, all at once family style. Choose a big platter and form the rice into a moat. Fill the center with chicken thighs and vegetables. Pass the kim chee in another bowl and pour steaming hot tea all around. A bowl of fresh fruit is all the dessert you'll need.

Like all stir-fries, this is meant to be eaten as soon as it's made, but leftovers may be covered and refrigerated for a day or so, then reheated in a wok or microwave until bubbling. Still good.

MARINADE:

    2 tablespoons soy sauce
    1 teaspoon kosher salt
    1 teaspoon sugar
    1 teaspoon whiskey

5 LARGE CHICKEN THIGHS
(ABOUT 1½ POUNDS), EACH
THIGH WHACKED INTO 3
PIECES WITH A CLEAVER

¼ CUP PEANUT OIL

4 GREEN ONIONS
WITH TOPS, MINCED

2 TABLESPOONS OYSTER SAUCE

2½ TEASPOONS SUGAR,
OR TO TASTE

¾ CUP CHICKEN BROTH

1 OUNCE DRIED SHIITAKE
MUSHROOMS; OR 1 CUP
FRESH, CHOPPED

1 CUP SMALL CREMINI
MUSHROOMS, CUT INTO
QUARTERS

1 STALK BROCCOLI
(ABOUT ¼ POUND), STALK
PEELED AND FINELY CHOPPED,
FLORETS SEPARATED INTO
BITE-SIZE PIECES

1 TEASPOON KOSHER SALT, PLUS
ADDITIONAL TO TASTE

1 MEDIUM CARROT, PEELED
AND CUT INTO MATCHSTICK
JULIENNE

1 CUP SUGAR SNAP PEAS

4 CUPS COOKED WHITE RICE
(PAGE 7)

In a pan, combine the marinade ingredients. Add the chicken thighs, cover, and set aside to marinate for about 20 minutes.

Heat 2 tablespoons of the oil in a wok over high heat. Add the green onions and cook for about 30 seconds. Lift the chicken from the marinade, and stir-fry until it begins to brown, 2 or 3 minutes. Add the oyster sauce along with about ½ teaspoon sugar and 6 tablespoons of the chicken broth. Cover, reduce the heat to medium, and cook until the chicken is done, 10 to 15 minutes. Remove to a warmed bowl and set aside.

While the chicken is cooking, place the dried mushrooms in water to cover in a 2-cup glass measure and microwave for about 4 minutes. Alternatively, heat the mushrooms in boiling water on the stove top until they're softened. Drain. Discard the stems, then chop the mushroom and mix with the fresh chopped cremini mushrooms. Set aside.

Reheat the wok and add 1 tablespoon of oil. Add the broccoli and stir-fry until it begins to brown, 2 or 3 minutes. Toss in about 2 tablespoons chicken broth. Cover and cook for 2 to 3 minutes, or until the broccoli is crisp-tender, but still bright green. Season to taste with about 1 teaspoon salt and ½ teaspoon sugar. Toss, then lift out to the warmed bowl. Cover and set aside.

Reheat the wok over high heat and add an additional tablespoon of oil, swirling the pan to coat it. Stir-fry the carrots and sugar snaps just until the surfaces are seared, 2 to 3 minutes.

Kim Chee

Stir-Fried
Chicken Thighs
with Sugar Snaps,
Shiitakes, Carrots,
and Broccoli

Fluffy White Rice

Green Tea

Assorted
Fresh Fruits

Add about ¼ cup broth, and lower the heat to medium. Cover and cook until tender, about 7 to 10 minutes. Season to taste with salt, and stir-fry over high heat until the broth evaporates. Add 1 teaspoon sugar and stir-fry a moment, then remove to the warmed bowl.

Add the green onions and mixed mushrooms to the hot wok. Stir-fry over high heat for about 2 minutes, adding about 1 tablespoon oyster sauce and ½ teaspoon sugar. Return the chicken to the pan and cook over high heat for 2 minutes. Place the chicken in the center of a large warmed platter, cover, and set it aside.

Reheat the carrots, peas, and broccoli in the hot wok for a couple of minutes, then make a ring of vegetables around the chicken. Serve at once with the rice.

How to use a wok:

Practice, practice, practice are the watchwords here. The wok is used by preheating it *dry* over very high heat, adding and heating the oil, then seasoning the pan by adding green onions (scallions) and/or garlic or red chile flakes, and finally adjusting the heat as the recipe dictates to complete the cooking. One trick we learned in keeping the pan well seasoned was to add sugar and salt directly onto the food and not onto the hot pan surface, where it may stick and burn. See page 13 for more about stir-frying.

**A Vouvray
with its herbal note
will nicely complement
the vegetables in this dish.**

Chicken-Walnut Stir-Fry

Chinese cooks have long known the value of one-dish dinners made in a wok. But don't fret if you don't own a wok. Most Asian markets sell great woks for under $15, or, in a pinch, any large skillet will do. Just preheat it well, don't overcrowd the pan, cook the food in sequence, adding cooked foods to a warmed bowl as you go, and you'll be pleased with the results.

PREPARATION TIME: 15 MINUTES   MAKES 6 SERVINGS
COOKING TIME: 15 MINUTES

All the Trimmings

Plate service works well for this dish. Warm the plates in the oven or microwave, then scoop out the servings at the stove and transfer them to a table that's been preset with crudités. Use a rice cooker to make a pot of rice, if you wish, and it's dinner in no time.

Don't try making stir-fry ahead, but do know you may reheat leftovers in the microwave and serve them for lunch the next day.

1 CUP WALNUT HALVES

1 TABLESPOON SOY SAUCE

2 TABLESPOONS FISH SAUCE (NAM PLA)

3 TABLESPOONS CORNSTARCH

$1/2$ TEASPOON KOSHER SALT

1 TABLESPOON SUGAR

$1^{1}/_{2}$ POUNDS CHICKEN TENDERS (BONED AND SKINNED BREAST MEAT STRIPS)

$1/4$ CUP PEANUT OIL

2 CLOVES GARLIC, CHOPPED

$1/2$ TEASPOON RED PEPPER FLAKES (OR TO TASTE)

1 HEAD NAPA CABBAGE, WASHED, CUT CROSSWISE INTO $1/8$-INCH-THICK SLICES, AND SPUN DRY

8 STALKS CELERY, CUT INTO $1/8$-INCH-THICK SLICES ON THE DIAGONAL

1 LARGE RED ONION, QUARTERED AND SEPARATED INTO SEGMENTS

1 POUND SNOW PEAS OR SUGAR SNAPS, TRIMMED

1 (8-OUNCE) CAN WATER CHESTNUTS, DRAINED

$1/2$ CUP CHICKEN BROTH

3 CUPS STEAMED RICE

Cover the walnuts with water in a 2-cup glass measure and cook them in the microwave for 4 minutes on high (100% power). (Alternative: Boil on the stovetop for 3 minutes.) Drain and set the nuts aside.

In a glass pie plate, combine the soy and fish sauces, cornstarch, salt, and sugar, and stir well. Add the chicken tenders and rub the marinade into the meat. Cover with plastic wrap and set aside.

Heat a large wok or skillet over medium-high heat, then add 2 tablespoons of the oil. Heat, then add the garlic and red pepper flakes, and toss for 15 seconds. Add the cabbage, celery, onion, and snow peas, and stir-fry until they're crisp-tender, about 3 minutes. Remove the vegetables to a warm bowl and set aside.

How to cook perfect rice:

Making rice isn't rocket science, but it's made even simpler if you have a rice cooker, and if you learn one Asian cooking trick, whether you're cooking 1 cup of rice to feed 4 people, or making an enormous commercial rice cooker-full. Just pour white rice into a pan or rice cooker. Place your forefinger on top of the rice and add water until it comes up to your first knuckle. Throw in a little salt, cover, and heat to a boil. Turn the heat down to "simmer." Cook for 15 to 20 minutes, or until all the water is absorbed. If you use a rice cooker, the first-knuckle method is sure-fire. Of course, the machine does the thinking and will hold the rice at the perfect serving temperature until the rest of the dinner is done.

How to stir-fry: See page 13.

Pour in 1 tablespoon more of the oil and add the walnuts. Sauté them until they're lightly browned, about 2 minutes, then remove to the bowl. Add the water chestnuts and sauté for 1 to 2 minutes more. Transfer to the bowl.

Heat the remaining tablespoon of oil in the wok until very hot. Lift the chicken from the marinade and add it to the pan, reserving the marinade. Stir-fry the chicken until it's cooked through, 3 to 4 minutes. Add the chicken broth and marinade, and cook until they're bubbling and transparent, about 2 minutes. Return the vegetables to the wok, toss, and heat through. Serve over steamed rice.

A dry or semi-dry Riesling from the Mosel region of Germany is always a great complement to Asian food. Look for a wine with an alcohol content below 13 percent. We also love to serve a New York State Finger Lakes dry or semi-dry Riesling from the Herman J. Weimer Winery. The fruity, slightly sweet flavor of Riesling complements a spicy cuisine.

Crudités

Chicken-Walnut
Stir-Fry

Steamed
White Rice

Fortune
Cookies

Green
Tea

Japanese Eggplant, Bell Pepper, and Lamb Stir-Fry

Purple Japanese eggplant, green bell pepper, and lamb make a beautiful dish. You'll recognize the Japanese eggplants—they're the long, skinny ones.

PREPARATION TIME: 15 MINUTES
COOKING TIME: 12 MINUTES

MAKES 4 SERVINGS

All the Trimmings

This is a family-style dinner, to be sure. Pass the dumplings, followed by the dipping sauce, to be served on little bread plates. Serve the eggplant over rice in the middle of the table with a cover over the dish to keep it warm. Let everyone help themselves. In the Chinese tradition of togetherness at a meal, this is a great way to entertain.

1 POUND LAMB SHOULDER CHOPS, CUT INTO JULIENNE STRIPS

2 TABLESPOONS CORNSTARCH

3 TABLESPOONS PEANUT OIL

6 SMALL JAPANESE EGGPLANT, CUT INTO JULIENNE STRIPS

2 LARGE GREEN BELL PEPPERS, SEEDED AND CUT INTO JULIENNE STRIPS

1 (1-INCH) PIECE FRESH GINGER, GRATED, OR 2 TABLESPOONS CHOPPED FRESH GINGER

3 CLOVES GARLIC, CHOPPED

2 TEASPOONS CORNSTARCH DISSOLVED IN 1 1/2 TEASPOONS COLD WATER

1/2 CUP WATER

1 TEASPOON SUGAR

1 TABLESPOON SOY SAUCE

1 TABLESPOON SHERRY

3 CUPS COOKED WHITE RICE

Preheat dry wok for about 2 minutes over medium-high heat. Meanwhile, toss the lamb in cornstarch. Add the peanut oil to the wok and heat for 1 minute, or until the oil just begins to smoke. Toss in the lamb and sear to brown for about 3 minutes. Remove the lamb to a plate. Add the eggplant, bell peppers, ginger, and garlic. Sauté for 2 to 3 minutes or until just brown. Add the dissolved cornstarch, water, sugar, and sherry. Return the meat and any juices that have collected on the plate to the pan. Cook just until the sauce thickens and clears, about 2 to 3 minutes. Serve immediately over rice.

How not to make a cake:

If you haven't visited a Chinese bakery before, locate one and get yourself there. Chinese cakes and pastries are the lightest yellow sponge cakes you have ever tasted. You have a choice of butter cream or whipped cream icing with great fruit fillings. We like the whipped cream, but both are sublime. With the large influx of Chinese immigrants, many communities have a Chinese bakery. Just find one. You may never make a cake at home again.

The earthy, yet fruity taste of a Petite Sirah from the Languedoc region of France will complement this dish by playing on the earthy flavors of the lamb and eggplant.

Chinese
Dumplings
(page 107)

Japanese Eggplant,
Bell Pepper,
and
Lamb Stir-Fry

Steamed
White Rice

Chinese
Pastries

Chinese Sweet and Sour Pork with Eggplant

Serve this dish with or without a bed of rice. The punched-up flavors can be adjusted to your palate by adding or taking away red pepper flakes. We like to hit the hot stuff, so every bite gives us not only the sweet and sour taste, but a hot, salty, bitter one as well.

PREPARATION TIME: 15 MINUTES   MAKES 6 SERVINGS
COOKING TIME: 30–35 MINUTES

All the Trimmings

Serve this hot and spicy dish right from the wok, if you wish, along with a steaming mound of rice. To keep the Asian theme, serve the sweet and sour pork in rice dishes or wide-rimmed soup bowls. Get out the chopsticks if you have them. Don't forget to throw a silk scarf over the lamp shade and light the candles. Float flowers in water in a shallow dish as a centerpiece and play soft string music in the background.

Make this dish at your leisure, but don't add the cilantro and sesame seeds until serving time. Cover and refrigerate the dish, then reheat to boiling on the stovetop, sprinkle with the garnishes, and serve. This will keep for 2 to 3 days in the refrigerator.

1/2 CUP PEANUT OIL

1 MEDIUM EGGPLANT (ABOUT 1 1/2 POUNDS), CUT INTO BITE-SIZE CHUNKS

1 1/2 POUNDS BONELESS PORK LOIN, CUT INTO BITE-SIZE CHUNKS

1 TEASPOON KOSHER SALT

1/2 TEASPOON CRACKED PEPPERCORNS

1/2 TEASPOON CAYENNE

1 MEDIUM YELLOW ONION, FINELY CHOPPED

1/2 TEASPOON RED PEPPER FLAKES, OR TO TASTE

6 CLOVES GARLIC, SMASHED

2 TABLESPOONS TOMATO PASTE

1 CUP CHICKEN BROTH

1/3 CUP RED WINE VINEGAR

1 TABLESPOON SOY SAUCE

3 TABLESPOONS BROWN SUGAR

2 TABLESPOONS TOASTED SESAME SEEDS

1 CUP LOOSELY PACKED CILANTRO LEAVES

Heat 2 tablespoons of the oil in a wok or large skillet over high heat, and brown the eggplant in batches, one layer deep, for about 1 minute per side, stirring. Transfer the browned eggplant to a bowl as it cooks, and add more oil to the pan as needed.

Season the pork pieces with the salt and peppers. Add another 2 tablespoons of oil to the pan and brown the pork pieces in batches, stirring to brown all sides, for about 2 minutes. Transfer each batch to the bowl as it browns.

Add 2 tablespoons or so of oil to the pan and brown the onion, stirring until it's fragrant and golden, about 5 minutes. Add the red pepper flakes and cook a minute or so. Lower the heat to medium and add the garlic. Cook for 1 minute, then stir in the tomato paste. Cook for 2 minutes, stirring, then pour in the chicken broth, vinegar, soy sauce, and brown sugar. Cook for

How to make cucumber ribbons:

You can create an instant Asian pickle by making cucumber ribbons with a potato peeler, then placing the ribbons in a shallow bowl with some rice wine vinegar, sugar, red pepper flakes, and heaps of ice cubes. Let this sit until you are ready to serve. Lift the ribbons from the liquid with a slotted spoon and place them on a shallow plate garnished with cilantro. Too easy.

2 minutes, stirring, then return the eggplant and pork to the pan along with all the pan juices. Stir to mix thoroughly. Cover and cook over medium heat until the meat and vegetables are cooked through and tender, about 15 to 20 minutes. Taste and adjust the seasonings.

Toss with sesame seeds and cilantro leaves and serve on a wide, shallow platter.

Hot Dried
Wasabi Peas
and Mixed
Japanese Crackers

Chinese Sweet and Sour
Pork with Eggplant

Steamed Rice

Cucumber Ribbons
in Rice Wine Vinegar,
Sugar, and
Red Pepper Flakes

Chopped Mango over
Pineapple Sherbet

Hot Tea

**A Petite Sirah
from the Napa Valley
will stand up to this classic
Chinese-American dish.
Only recently have vintners in
Napa Valley begun to grow this grape.
They have met with much success.**

Stir-Fried Sirloin and Bitter Greens

Bitter flavors have been underappreciated by Americans until recently. This recipe does the most with the strong underpinnings that bitter greens give the dish. The addition of sweet-sour balsamic vinegar and the rich taste of beef, along with caramelized sweet onions and peppers, makes for a powerful flavor statement. Dishes like this one—with a balance of sweet, sour, bitter, hot, and rich—make the most satisfying meals. And think about it—all done in one pan in an hour, and that includes a half hour for marinating.

PREPARATION TIME: 15 MINUTES   COOKING TIME: 10 MINUTES

MARINATING TIME: 30 MINUTES   MAKES 6 SERVINGS

All the Trimmings

Preset the table with salads on the side, a vase of fresh flowers, and candles everywhere. A saucer next to each place with a little extra-virgin olive oil and a drop of balsamic vinegar will provide the perfect dip for the hot country bread. When it's time for dessert, serve the chocolate cake wedges on a slab of marble with scoops of gelato and let your guests serve themselves. You can pick up a square of marble from a tile store, glue some cork feet on it so it won't scar your table, and you've got yourself a perfect dessert server. Ice cream won't melt on it too fast. And the cakes, tarts, or pies you buy from the bakery will look marvelous. Perhaps most importantly, your guests will be able to decide just what and how much dessert they want.

This is a make-and-eat meal. However, leftovers, covered and refrigerated, may be reheated on the stovetop and enjoyed for lunch the next day.

MARINADE:

- ¼ cup extra-virgin olive oil
- 3 tablespoons balsamic vinegar
- 4 cloves garlic, crushed
- 1 teaspoon kosher salt
- ½ teaspoon dried thyme
- ½ teaspoon cracked peppercorns

- 1½ POUNDS TOP SIRLOIN OR FLANK STEAK, CUT ¾ INCH THICK
- 4 TABLESPOONS PEANUT OIL
- 1 MEDIUM RED ONION, THINLY SLICED
- ½ CUP DRAINED ROASTED RED PEPPER STRIPS FROM A JAR
- 4 CUPS BROCCOLI RABE, BEET GREENS, SPINACH, OR OTHER BITTER GREENS
- ¼ CUP BALSAMIC VINEGAR

In a medium glass bowl, combine the marinade ingredients.

Trim and discard the fat from the steak. Cut the steak in half, lengthwise, then into 3-×-⅛-inch strips. Toss the beef with the marinade, cover, and set it aside for 30 minutes or so. Lift out the beef and reserve the marinade.

Preheat a large heavy skillet over medium-high heat, film with peanut oil, and cook the beef in batches, stir-frying for 1 minute, or until the outside surfaces are no longer pink. Transfer the meat to a warmed platter as it cooks. Add some of the reserved marinade to the pan, then add the onion and red pepper strips. Stir-fry over high heat until glistening and golden, about 2 minutes. Remove to the warmed platter, cover, and set aside.

How to stir-fry:

Stir-frying is one of the most ancient methods known for getting the most flavor out of meat and vegetables in a hurry. We were fortunate enough to have had a lesson from Lorraine Leong, who learned how to cook from her mother, Renée Leong. Meals in the Leong family have always been the most important part of the day, with 10 to 12 family members present on a regular basis. Today Lorraine's family carries on the multigenerational tradition as her 2 sons, Eric and Keith, learn to cook from their grandmother.

Start with a lean, tender piece of meat cut into uniform strips, about ⅛ inch thick and no more than 3 inches long. Infuse the meat with a marinade if you wish, then quickly cook it in a very hot pan just until the pink color has vanished. Scoop the meat out onto a warm platter, cover, and reserve while you cook the next batch.

The main difficulty with stir-frying on home stoves is that they don't get hot enough. If you dump all the meat into the pan—whether you've preheated it or not—you're likely to cool the skillet too much, and it won't return to the proper temperature before all the good flavor is boiled out of the meat, leaving you with nothing more than thin, gray, tasteless strips. Be bold. Crank the heat up as high as it will go. Put the food in the pan in small batches. Stand there and watch it, and transfer the food to a warm platter the instant it's cooked to perfection—usually a minute or less.

Turn the heat to high and wipe the skillet with a little more oil. Quickly stir-fry the bitter greens, just until wilted, about 2 to 3 minutes. Add vinegar and toss. Return the steak, peppers, and onion to the skillet and heat without stirring a minute or so. Transfer the mixture to the warmed platter, taking care to slide it out onto the platter with the greens on the bottom and the steak and vegetables on top. Serve hot.

Try a Malbec from Argentina.
The inky dark color and herbal note
of the Argentinean wine will work well
with the bitter greens and beef flavors
of this dish.

Fresh Figs,
Red Pepper Flakes,
and Lemon Zest
with
Freshly Grated
Parmigiano-Reggiano
Cheese

Stir-Fried Sirloin and
Bitter Greens

Hot Italian Country
Bread with Olives

Flourless
Chocolate Cake
and Gelato

Espresso

Beef and Tomato Stir-Fry with Whiskey and Black Bean Sauce

A Renée Leong classic, you can make this almost as fast as you can say the name, once you have the meat and vegetables cut. Remember, if the meat you are using is about half-frozen, it's easier to make perfect cuts to yield rectangles about the size of old-fashioned dominoes. It's worth a trip to an Asian market for a package of dried salted black beans, but if you can't find them, you'll find Chinese-style black bean garlic sauce in any grocery store. This makes a fair substitution although there's nothing like beginning with the real McCoy. Salted black beans are a staple in good Cantonese cooking and contribute to the delicate, subtle flavor you'll get from the dish.

PREPARATION TIME: 15 MINUTES   COOKING TIME: 10 MINUTES

MARINATING TIME: 20 MINUTES   MAKES 6 SERVINGS

All the Trimmings

When Lorraine Leong came to teach us the traditional Cantonese dishes that her 81-year-old mother still cooks for their large extended family in Brooklyn, she explained that Chinese family meals are served with all the dishes presented at once. A rice cooker is in constant use at Lorraine's house. And dessert is simply fresh fruit. You can follow suit. Set the table with nothing more than plates and forks or chopsticks, and don't forget to serve the rice. We like to make a ring of rice on a platter, then pour the stir-fry in the middle.

Like most stir-fried Cantonese food, this dish is meant to be made and eaten, but believe us, the leftovers taste great the next day. Cover and refrigerate, then reheat on the stovetop.

MARINADE:

    2 teaspoons kosher salt

    1 tablespoon soy sauce

    1 teaspoon whiskey

    1 teaspoon cornstarch

    2 teaspoons peanut oil

1 POUND LEAN FLANK STEAK, CUT INTO THIN SLICES ACROSS THE GRAIN

1 TABLESPOON DRIED SALTED BLACK BEANS, OR 2 TABLESPOONS CHINESE-STYLE BLACK BEAN GARLIC SAUCE

2 CLOVES GARLIC, CRUSHED

3 TABLESPOONS WATER

2 TABLESPOONS PLUS 1 TEASPOON PEANUT OIL

1 GREEN ONION WITH TOP, MINCED

6 MEDIUM PLUM TOMATOES (ABOUT 1½ POUNDS), CORED AND QUARTERED

1½ TEASPOONS SUGAR

½ CUP CHICKEN BROTH

1 TABLESPOON OYSTER SAUCE

4 CUPS COOKED WHITE RICE

In a medium bowl, combine the marinade ingredients. Add the flank steak slices and rub the mixture into the meat with your fingers. Cover, and set aside to marinate for about 20 minutes.

Meanwhile, in a bowl mash the black beans and garlic together, stir into the water, and set aside. If you're using black bean sauce, skip the water and the garlic.

How to cook meat the Chinese way:

Choose good-quality flank steak that is inherently tender. If you half-freeze it, you'll find the cutting is easier. Using a Chinese cleaver or French chef's knife, hold the meat firmly on the chopping block and slice straight down, across the grain, to break up the fibers and make the meat more tender when it's cooked. If you're learning to use a cleaver, protect your fingertips. Hold the cleaver with your index finger over the far side of the top of the cleaver and your thumb on the side nearest you to guide the cutting edge. Hold the meat with your other hand, turning your fingers under for safety. Let your knuckles be your guide.

Heat a wok over medium-high heat and add 2 tablespoons of the oil. Add the green onion and stir-fry for about 30 seconds. Add the black bean garlic sauce and stir-fry for about 15 seconds. Add the meat and cook, stirring, until it begins to lose its pink color, about 2 to 3 minutes. Transfer the meat to a bowl and set it aside.

Add an additional teaspoon of oil to the wok and reheat, then add the tomatoes. Stir-fry a minute or 2, just until they begin to lose their shape, sprinkling them with the sugar to hasten the browning. Add the broth, cover, and continue cooking until the tomatoes are thickened, about 2 minutes. Return the meat to the pan and add the oyster sauce. Stir-fry for 1 minute more, then serve with the rice.

NOTE: Shrimp dip is available at the fish counter of quality supermarkets

**A subtle French
or California Merlot
with earthy flavors
will best complement
this subtly flavored beef dish.**

Sesame
Crackers
and Shrimp Dip
(see Note)

Beef and Tomato
Stir-Fry with Whiskey
and
Black Bean Sauce

Fluffy
White Rice

Fresh Fruit
Compote

Thai Curried Coconut Salmon and Spinach Stir-Fry with Basil

The flavor of curry powders varies from place to place even though they begin with a blend of spices, including pepper, cinnamon, cloves, coriander, cumin, ginger, mace, and turmeric. But every curry maker adds particular spices. Choose Madras curry powder and you'll get a hotter, more pungent dish. Bombay curry is notably sweeter. Buy Chinese curry powder for a hotter, more peppery flavor. Thai curry paste is the hottest. Get your curry powder from the supermarket and you'll definitely need to kick it up with a hefty dose of cayenne. Fry the curry in oil or butter first to release the explosion of taste that drives the dish.

PREPARATION TIME: 10 MINUTES   MAKES 8 SERVINGS
COOKING TIME: 15 MINUTES

All the Trimmings

Serve the hot dried wasabi peas in the living room with a big glass of Chardonnay (non-oaked, of course). The rest of the meal is best served family style. The sliced tomatoes should be fanned out on a platter, and passed. The coconut salmon should be served over the spinach and passed as well. Serve the steamed rice in a big covered bowl. Bright orange mango slices with lime juice and wedges of lime can be waiting in the refrigerator on individual plates. Enjoy!

Make this dish as much as 1 day in advance, cover, and refrigerate, then reheat it over medium heat about 10 minutes, or in a microwave to just under the boil, about 2 minutes.

4 TABLESPOONS PEANUT OIL

4 CLOVES GARLIC, SMASHED

1 MEDIUM YELLOW ONION, THINLY SLICED

2 TABLESPOONS SESAME SEEDS

1 BUNCH FRESH SPINACH LEAVES, THOROUGHLY WASHED, DRAINED, AND STEMMED, OR 1 (16-OUNCE) PACKAGE FROZEN

4 SPRIGS FRESH BASIL LEAVES

3 TABLESPOONS CURRY POWDER

1/2 TEASPOON CAYENNE, OR TO TASTE

1/2 TEASPOON KOSHER SALT

2 POUNDS SALMON FILLETS, CUT INTO LARGE CHUNKS

1 (13 1/2-OUNCE) CAN UNSWEETENED COCONUT MILK

In a wok, a large skillet, or a sauté pan over high heat, heat 2 tablespoons of the oil, tilting the pan to coat the surface. Stir-fry the garlic, onion, and sesame seeds for 30 seconds, then add the spinach and basil and stir-fry until the spinach is bright green and glistening, about 2 minutes. Transfer the mixture to a warm bowl, cover, and reserve.

In a bowl, combine the curry, cayenne, and salt. Dry the salmon pieces with a paper towel, then massage the spices into the salmon, coating all sides. Add the remaining 2 tablespoons of oil to the pan and heat over high heat, tilting the pan to coat the bottom. Add the salmon and stir-fry until all the surfaces are crisp golden, 3 to 4 minutes. Pour the coconut milk into the wok and reduce the heat to medium. Boil gently until the salmon is cooked through, 3 to 5 minutes. Pour the salmon mixture over the spinach and serve at once.

Hot
Dried
Wasabi Peas
and
Rice Cracker Snacks

Sliced Tomatoes
with Sesame Oil
and Rice Vinegar

Thai Curried Coconut
Salmon and Spinach
Stir-Fry with Basil

Steamed Rice

Mango Slices with
Lime
Wedges

Try a non-oaked
Chardonnay from
the David Wynn
Winery in South Africa.
The tropical fruit note
to this South African
Chardonnay will pick
up the coconut flavor.
You could also try our
old standby—Riesling.

STYLISH ONE-DISH DINNERS

How to get the most out of salmon fillets:

First, buy top-quality fillets cut from the thick end (not the tail) of the fish. Pat the fillets dry with paper towels and cut them into uniform pieces so you can judge the cooking time precisely. Season the salmon carefully, rubbing in the spices. Let the fish sit for about 15 minutes to allow the seasonings to permeate the flesh of the fish. Thoroughly preheat the wok, add the oil, then sear the fish fillets. Within a minute or so, the flavorings will brown beautifully and adhere perfectly.

To change the taste, vary the cooking oil. Instead of peanut oil, choose canola or olive oil. Add a few drops of sesame oil, or choose a hot chili oil accent. Soon you'll make this method your own.

Think of stir-frying as the Asian answer to sauté cookery. The principle remains the same. Cooking in a small amount of oil over dry heat seals the surfaces of the food, caramelizes it, and develops good flavors. The heat should be hot enough to cook the food thoroughly, but not burn it. You may have to adjust the heat as you add different ingredients. Most home ranges don't even begin to get as hot as restaurant ranges. Unless you have a commercial range, you probably can't get your stove too hot. Go for it.

This cooking method demands the complete attention of the cook—but only for a few moments. Using a wok or a large sauté pan with curved sides, preheat the pan dry over high heat, then add a small amount of fat. Peanut oil is ideal because it has a high burning point and will withstand intense heat without breaking down. Tilt the pan to coat all sides, and just as the fat begins to smoke, add the foods to be stir-fried.

The curry powder used in this dish develops its full flavor by being started with hot fat. Most Indian and other Asian cooks begin by frying spices in clarified butter (ghee) to get the most flavor from them. Make sure the foods are cut into uniform pieces and are as dry as possible to prevent steaming and splattering. Place the food in the pan in a single layer and cook and toss to develop the correct color. Use a spatula or tongs to turn the food without piercing it. With some practice, you can learn to toss the food in a sauté pan as chefs do without getting most of it on the stove or the floor. But if you are tossing ingredients, try to keep the pan directly on the heat as much as possible so it doesn't cool off too much. Many stir-fried or sautéed dishes have a sauce that's made right in the pan using the principle of reduction, and because of the high heat, many dishes are cooked in stages, using one pan, but stir-frying and transferring the various ingredients to a warmed bowl while you cook the next batch, so that all the ingredients cook evenly and no one food is overcooked.

Stir-Fried Shrimp and Onions in a Catsup Sauce

Sure this sounds funny, but I'll bet you've eaten a catsup sauce in Chinese restaurants more than once without knowing it. What you get by using this simple seasoning is an intense rosy-pink-colored shrimp and a golden-rose-colored onion ring mixture with a perfumed, spicy flavor that leaves you begging for more. Think of it as low-brow fusion cooking. It is, no doubt, what Chinese cooks discovered when they got to America: Our own native condiment goes well with everything.

PREPARATION TIME: 10 MINUTES   MAKES 3 TO 4 SERVINGS
COOKING TIME: 15 MINUTES

All the Trimmings

This dish, with the rosy shrimp surround by lichees and pineapple, should be brought to the table on a platter and passed. The traditional Chinese way to serve rice is in individual bowls. Guests then spoon the shrimp, lichees, and pineapples over the rice.

Meant to be made and eaten at once, this dish can, nevertheless, be covered and refrigerated, then reheated the next day on the stovetop or for a moment in the microwave. Who are we kidding? You'll eat all of it and more on the first shot.

1½ POUNDS LARGE RAW SHRIMP, SHELLED AND DEVEINED

2 TEASPOONS SUGAR

1 TEASPOON WHISKEY

4 MEDIUM YELLOW ONIONS (ABOUT 1½ POUNDS), CUT INTO RINGS

2 TABLESPOONS PEANUT OIL

5 TABLESPOONS CHICKEN BROTH

6 TABLESPOONS CATSUP

2 GREEN ONIONS WITH TOPS, MINCED

CANNED LICHEES, FOR GARNISH

CANNED PINEAPPLE CHUNKS, FOR GARNISH

4 CUPS COOKED WHITE RICE

In a small bowl, combine the shrimp with a teaspoon of sugar and the whiskey. Cover and set it aside while you prepare the onions.

Heat a wok over high heat, then add about 1 tablespoon of the oil. Swirl to coat the pan thoroughly. Stir-fry the onion rings for about 2 minutes, then add ¼ cup of the broth. Cover and cook until the onions begin to brown, about 3 minutes. Add ¼ cup of the catsup and the remaining teaspoon of sugar, stirring to coat the onions. Cook for about 2 minutes more, then remove to a warmed platter and reserve.

Reheat the wok, adding the remaining tablespoon of oil. Add 1 tablespoon of the green onions and stir-fry for about 2 minutes. Add the shrimp and stir-fry until the color begins to change from translucent bluish-white to a pink opaque color, about 2 to 3

How to make cold marinated bean sprouts:

Pick up about 2 cups fresh mung bean sprouts at the market the day you plan to make this dinner. Rinse them under cold running water and drain, then toss them with ½ teaspoon red chili flakes, 3 tablespoons rice wine vinegar, and 2 tablespoons soy sauce. Finish with a tablespoon of fresh-chopped cilantro and ½ teaspoon chopped garlic. Cover and refrigerate until serving time.

minutes. Add the remaining 2 tablespoons of catsup and the remaining teaspoon of broth and cook for about 2 minutes more. Mound the shrimp over the onion and top with the remaining green onions. Alternate rings of lichee and pineapple around the shrimp. Serve at once with hot rice.

The rich flavor of the shrimp will be complemented by the rich flavor of a non-oaked Chardonnay from California, but be sure to ask for a non-oaked bottle. Oaked Chardonnays are okay to drink before dinner, but a heavily oaked wine will overwhelm most food.

Cold
Marinated
Bean Sprouts

Stir-Fried
Shrimp and Onions
in a
Catsup Sauce

Fluffy White Rice

Green Tea

Ice Cream
and
Cookies

Skillet Sautés

Blueberry Chicken

We don't know about you, but we have been served way too many boring chicken breasts. Zip that chicken up with berries and cream and, hey, it tastes great. Can't find blueberries? Try raspberries or blackberries. The main idea here is to lift the chicken into flight with fat and fruit.

All the Trimmings

Serve the fennel and celery in the living room without any dressing. The crunchy vegetables will set up the palate rather nicely for the upcoming rich entrée. Buy polenta ready-made from a tube. Just slice and sauté in olive oil and butter just before serving. The blueberry chicken and polenta will be enough for the plate. Pass a basket of good bread and enjoy. Lemon sorbet is a charming ending to this rather rich meal. The tartness will serve as a foil for the creamy entrée.

PREPARATION TIME: 10 MINUTES
COOKING TIME: 20 MINUTES

MAKES 4 SERVINGS

2 TABLESPOONS BUTTER

2 TABLESPOONS PEANUT OIL

4 BONELESS, SKINLESS CHICKEN BREASTS, SPLIT AND POUNDED OUT TO $1/2$-INCH-THICK CUTLETS

$1/4$ TO $1/2$ TEASPOON EACH SALT AND FRESHLY GROUND BLACK PEPPER

3 SHALLOTS, FINELY CHOPPED

$1/4$ CUP BLUEBERRY VINEGAR

$3/4$ CUP CHICKEN BROTH

$1/2$ CUP WHIPPING CREAM

$1/2$ SMALL TOMATO, FINELY MINCED

$1/2$ CUP FRESH BLUEBERRIES

In a 12-inch skillet over medium-high heat, heat the butter and oil until the butter foams, about 1 minute. Sprinkle salt and pepper on the chicken. Add the pounded-out seasoned chicken breasts, and brown them lightly on both sides, about 2 minutes per side. The chicken will finish cooking in the sauce. Remove the breasts from the pan, add the shallots, and cook until they're translucent, about 3 minutes. Add the vinegar and cook for about 2 minutes. The vinegar will deglaze the pan and much of the vinegar will boil off. Add the broth, whipping cream, and tomato, and return the chicken breasts to the pan. Cook for 5 to 10 minutes uncovered, until the chicken is cooked through. Add the blueberries and cook for 1 minute. Serve at once.

How to choose and use varieties of vinegar:

If you haven't yet discovered how wonderful it is to have several types of interesting vinegars around, you must stock up. It is much less expensive to stock a diverse set of high-quality vinegars than to buy ready-made vinaigrette. The other advantage is that for recipes like the blueberry chicken, you can substitute other interesting vinegars and different fruits and come up with original and wonderful flavor combinations. Try sherry wine vinegar and strawberries, or balsamic and prunes. As far as having a choice of vinegars for salads, once you have mastered the simple art of vinaigrette, you will drastically cut down on your grocery bill. (See page 25 for a basic vinaigrette.) We freely admit we do keep a bottle or two of Annie's Salad Dressing in the refrigerator for emergencies. It is, after all, great.

This rich dish is complemented
by a California Merlot.
The black fruit flavor will
pick up the black fruit flavor of the
blueberries and marry well with this dish.

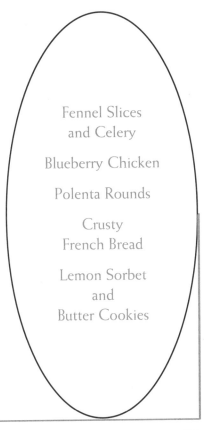

Fennel Slices
and Celery

Blueberry Chicken

Polenta Rounds

Crusty
French Bread

Lemon Sorbet
and
Butter Cookies

Berkeley Panned Chicken
with Polenta, Peppers, and Corn

Alice Waters served a version of this luscious panned chicken breast to us, cooked California style—under a weight—at Chez Panisse. This quick cooking method yields a brightly flavored, golden on the outside, tender on the inside dish that becomes perfect when served alongside a wheel of polenta, sautéed red pepper strips, and corn kernels. The flavors are kicked up with a touch of extra-virgin olive oil drizzled on at the very end. Adding flavorful fat just before serving is an old restaurant trick, and one worth emulating at home.

PREPARATION TIME: 15 MINUTES   MAKES 4 SERVINGS

COOKING TIME: 10 MINUTES

All the Trimmings

Plate service works well for this menu. Set the table first, presetting the salad by lining salad plates with mixed baby greens, topping them with slices of dripping sweet pears sprinkled with gorgonzola, hazelnuts, and a bracing vinaigrette. Grind some black pepper over all and you're ready to roll. Light the candles, start the music. Let the dinner begin.

Keep the plates hot in the oven set at 200°F., so that when it comes time to eat you can whisk the food from the skillet onto warmed plates and everything will be hot.

Although this restaurant method is meant to be made and eaten at once, we find that the leftovers are quite lovely reheated just to sizzling on the stovetop the next day. If you'd like to get a jump on the preparation, pound out the chicken the morning of your dinner, and store it in the refrigerator between sheets of wax paper.

4 (4-OUNCE) BONELESS, SKINLESS CHICKEN BREASTS

1/4 CUP EXTRA-VIRGIN OLIVE OIL

SALT AND FRESHLY GROUND BLACK PEPPER

1 TABLESPOON CHOPPED FRESH ROSEMARY, PLUS 4 SPRIGS FOR GARNISH

1 CUP CORN KERNELS, CUT FROM THE COB OR FROZEN

1 RED BELL PEPPER, SEEDED AND CUT INTO STRIPS

8 (1/2-INCH-THICK) SLICES COOKED POLENTA ROUNDS

Dry the chicken breasts with paper towels so they won't steam in the skillet. On a sheet of wax paper or plastic wrap, spread 1 tablespoon of the olive oil, then lay out the chicken breasts. Season them generously with salt and pepper and sprinkle with 1 tablespoon of the chopped rosemary and a sprinkling of olive oil. Fold the paper over the chicken, and pound the breasts to a uniform 1/2-inch thickness with a mallet or the bottom of a heavy glass.

Preheat 2 skillets—one iron-clad 12-inch and one heavy cast-iron 10-inch—over medium-high heat. When the skillets are so hot that water flicked onto the surface jumps off, coat the larger skillet with olive oil. Lift the chicken breasts off the paper and place them in the larger skillet. Use the smaller heavy skillet as a weight on top of the chicken breasts, pressing the bottom of the

How to prepare panned meats:

"Panned" meats are done in restaurants using a weight that has been preheated on the stovetop. The procedure works well to quickly sear and seal tender cuts of meat that have been pounded to a uniform thickness. The resulting flavors are caramelized, crisp, and delicious. It's an efficient way to prepare meats in a hurry.

It's important to completely preheat both the skillet and the weight. For home use, we suggest using 2 heavy cast-iron skillets, one that fits inside the other. Prepare the meat by blotting up any moisture so that the meat won't steam, then pounding and seasoning it. Preheat the skillets over high heat, then coat the larger skillet with oil. Add the meat, cover immediately with the smaller skillet, and cook without moving the meat for a couple of minutes, until the meat is well seared and golden on the bottom. Turn once and cook the second side.

You can cook chops, steaks, or chicken this way. Just begin with an inherently tender piece of meat, and prepare to stand and watch it, because it's cooked almost before you know it. And that's the beauty of it.

heated skillet onto the meat. Cook until the chicken is golden on the bottom, 2 to 3 minutes, then turn the breasts, replace the weight, and continue to cook until the second side is golden and the meat is cooked through and opaque, no more than a minute or two. Remove the chicken to a warmed plate, cover and reserve it.

Add a little more oil to the larger skillet over medium-high heat and add the corn kernels, red pepper, and polenta rounds. Cook and stir until everything is beginning to brown, about 5 minutes, turning the polenta slices once with a spatula.

To serve, arrange 2 slices of polenta on a plate, drizzle each serving with a little olive oil, then add a chicken breast, corn, and red pepper slices. Garnish each plate with a sprig of rosemary and serve at once.

NOTE: Three-citrus vinaigrette is simply the juice of a lemon, a lime, and an orange whisked with 1 teaspoon rice wine vinegar, 1/4 cup extra virgin olive oil, then seasoned with kosher salt and freshly milled black pepper to taste.

**Try an Italian wine from the
Sicilian Malvasian grape. Bianca Ca del Sol
from Santa Cruz, California, also makes a good choice.
This unusual fruity white wine will complement the
chicken, red pepper, and corn.**

Ripe Pears
on a Bed of Greens
with Gorgonzola,
Hazelnuts, and
Three-Citrus Vinaigrette
(See Note)

Berkeley Panned Chicken
with Polenta, Peppers,
and Corn

Ciabatta Bread and
Sweet Butter

Chocolate Ice Cream
and Butter Cookies

Espresso

Cinnamon Lamb Sauté

Cinnamon, lamb, and tomatoes create a wonderful Middle Eastern flavor combination.
Served with couscous, this is a real knockout for company.

All the Trimmings

Serve the babaganoush and pita in the living room. The cinnamon lamb is best served on a platter with a ring of couscous around it. Pass the lamb dish. The aroma will make your guests get that funny, far-away look in their eyes. And that's before dinner. The romaine salad with lemon vinaigrette is a natural foil to the cinnamon flavor. Ending with a citrussy strawberry dish will knock your guests out. And that's after dinner.

¼ CUP OLIVE OIL

4 LARGE LAMB SHOULDER CHOPS, BONED AND CUT INTO BITE-SIZE PIECES

3 YELLOW ONIONS, COARSELY CHOPPED

4 CLOVES GARLIC, FINELY CHOPPED

1 TEASPOON GROUND CINNAMON

1 (28-OUNCE) CAN COARSELY CHOPPED TOMATOES WITH THEIR JUICE

SALT AND FRESHLY GROUND BLACK PEPPER TO TASTE

Preheat a 10-inch skillet for 1 minute. Add the olive oil and cook for 1 minute. Over medium-high heat, add the lamb and brown them on all sides for 5 minutes. The lamb does not need to cook through, as it will finish cooking in the sauce. Once it is browned, remove the meat from the pan. Add the onions to the pan and cook for 5 minutes, until they become translucent. Add the garlic and cinnamon and cook for 1 minute more. To deglaze the pan, add the tomatoes and their juice, scraping up all the browned bits from the bottom. Return the lamb to the pan and cook uncovered for 30 minutes over low heat. Serve over rice couscous.

How to prepare strawberries Romanoff:

To make strawberries Romanoff, halve the strawberries and marinate them for as long as possible, or overnight, in orange juice and an orange liqueur such as Curaçao, Grand Marnier, or Triple Sec. Serve with fresh whipped cream.

**Try a Madiran
from the Languedoc region of France.
The tannic quality of this wine will
complement the earthy lamb and cinnamon.**

Babaganoush
and Pita Bread

Cinnamon Lamb
Sauté

Couscous

Romaine Lettuce Salad
with
Lemon Vinaigrette

Strawberries
Romanoff

Spanish Steak
with Sautéed Peppers and Walnuts

When June Cleaver made this dish, she started with a chuck roast and cooked it all afternoon until Ward and Wally and the Beave got home. You? You've got it made in half an hour, thanks to sirloin.

PREPARATION TIME: 15 MINUTES   MAKES 6 SERVINGS
COOKING TIME: 15 MINUTES

All the Trimmings

Preset the table with tomatoes, radishes, celery, and eggs. Place wide-rimmed soup bowls over the dinner plates. Arrange the sirloin and peppers on a flat platter in the middle of the table and let people serve themselves. Pass the hot bread along with sweet butter. Then, once dinner is done, remove the bowls and let the dinner plates serve as a home for dessert. Pass the flan, cut into wedges, along with a bowl of fruit.

Although this dish is meant to be made and eaten right away, we find that the leftovers make a terrific lunch. Cover and refrigerate any leftovers, then serve them at room temperature over a bed of baby greens.

1½ POUNDS BONELESS BEEF TOP SIRLOIN, CUT ¾ INCH THICK

6 CLOVES GARLIC, SMASHED

½ TEASPOON CRACKED PEPPER

2 TABLESPOONS EXTRA-VIRGIN OLIVE OIL

1 TEASPOON KOSHER SALT, OR TO TASTE

3 BELL PEPPERS (GREEN, RED, AND YELLOW), SEEDED AND CUT INTO THIN STRIPS

1 LARGE PURPLE ONION, THINLY SLICED

½ CUP WALNUT PIECES

½ TEASPOON CHILI POWDER

½ CUP SOUR CREAM

Trim any fat from the steak and cut it into 6 pieces. Rub the garlic and cracked pepper into the meat using the heel of your hand to really infuse the meat with the flavor. Preheat a large heavy skillet with 1 teaspoon of the olive oil, then cook the beef in the skillet for 8 to 10 minutes, for rare or medium doneness, turning it only once. Remove it to a warm platter, season with ½ teaspoon of the kosher salt, cover, and reserve.

In the same skillet, heat the remaining oil over medium-high heat, then add the peppers, onion, and walnuts. Cook and stir until the peppers begin to brown and the onions turn golden, 3 to 4 minutes, sprinkling the vegetables with the remaining salt and then the chili powder during the last 2 minutes. Once the vegetables are limp and glistening, spoon them into the middle of a serving platter, arranging the steaks on top. Top each steak with a dollop of sour cream and serve.

How to sauté meat:

Sautéing is a quick-cooking method best suited to tender cuts of meat. Use a high temperature, keep an eye on the meat so you don't overcook it, use tongs instead of a fork to turn it so that you don't puncture the meat and allow the juices to leak out, and before you know it you'll have a mouthwatering piece of meat.

Among the cuts that work well for sautéing are the top loin or New York strip steak, the tenderloin or fillet, or the T-bone or porterhouse. You can also use this high heat method with top round, rib eye, top sirloin, or ground beef. The idea is to sear the surfaces so that you get a great caramelized flavor and a tender, rare, flavorful middle.

The difference between sautéing and pan-broiling is that you add a little fat to the pan when you sauté, whereas pan-broiling is done in a dry skillet. Pan-broiling also depends upon a well preheated heavy skillet to seal the surfaces of the meat.

Another important feature of this cooking method is that you shouldn't be moving the meat around once you've put it in the preheated pan. Leave it alone, watch it, and only turn it ONCE. You can tell it's ready to turn by looking at the top of it. If a little blood is beginning to pool on the uncooked surface, it means it's getting there. Touch the meat. If it's soft, it means it's still quite rare. If the meat feels like the palm of your hand, it's medium, and if it feels like the end of your nose, it's cooked well done. In other words, you've probably overcooked it.

This kind of cooking demands attention, but not for long. Just be sure you've done everything else first. You've set the table. You've poured the wine. Now you can concentrate on turning out a perfect piece of meat.

Thick
Beefsteak
Tomato Slices,
Whole Radishes,
Celery Stalks,
and
Hard-Cooked Eggs

Spanish Steak with
Sautéed Peppers
and Walnuts

Hot Olive Bread
and Sweet Butter

Flan

Espresso

**The tannins in a
Madiran from the Languedoc
region of France will complement
the steak and the bitter flavor of the walnuts.**

Grouper Veracruz

Almost anyone who's ever lived in Texas has vacationed in Veracruz, Mexico, or knows somebody who did. Restaurants down there hand out some version of this recipe to anybody who asks. We like it because it can all be made in a skillet, the flavors are bright and beautiful, and we can serve it unadorned. About the only real requirement is a tall, frosty margarita on the side.

All the Trimmings

Warm breezes, candle smoke, and the smell of fresh flowers define a Mexican dining experience. The candles and the flowers you can manage pretty easily. The warm breezes? Depends on where you are. Who knows? You might have to stand in front of the oven and fan hot air out with a pot holder. The main thing is to pretend you're in the tropics, whatever it takes. Preset the table with orange slices and jicama cut into matchstick julienne and dusted with chili powder. It makes the meal go more smoothly to get this part of the table setting done ahead of time.

Start the marinade at your leisure, but once you get this Mexican seacoast menu made, serve it forth. Store leftovers covered in the refrigerator and reheat them on the stovetop in a skillet just until sizzling.

6 (6-OUNCE) GROUPER, SNAPPER, OR BASS FILLETS

½ TEASPOON KOSHER SALT

4 CLOVES GARLIC, SMASHED

JUICE AND ZEST OF 2 LIMES

2 TABLESPOONS EXTRA-VIRGIN OLIVE OIL

1 LARGE YELLOW ONION, THINLY SLICED

3 CUPS CHOPPED TOMATOES, FRESH OR FROM A 28-OUNCE CAN WITH JUICE

½ CUP CHOPPED GREEN OLIVES

1 LARGE JALAPEÑO PEPPER, SEEDED AND MINCED

¼ TEASPOON DRIED OREGANO

¼ TEASPOON DRIED THYME

2 BAY LEAVES

¼ TEASPOON SUGAR

2 TABLESPOONS BUTTER

1 TABLESPOON CAPERS

1 CUP LOOSELY PACKED CILANTRO LEAVES

Place the fish fillets in a single layer in a shallow glass dish. Sprinkle with the salt and rub the garlic into the flesh of the fish. Add the lime juice and zest and turn to coat the fillets on all sides. Cover and refrigerate for 1 to 2 hours.

About a half hour before you are ready to serve, heat the olive oil in a large skillet over medium heat and gently sauté the onion until golden, about 5 minutes. Add the tomatoes, olives, jalapeño, oregano, thyme, bay leaves, and sugar. Simmer, uncovered, for about 10 minutes, stirring from time to time. Stir in the capers. Pour this sauce into a bowl and reserve it on the back of the stove.

How to prepare Mexican roasting ears:

Mexican-style roasting ears are easily made. Soak whole roasting ears of corn in their shucks in water then throw them on the grill—gas or charcoal—and let them roast until the steam rises and the shucks look black. Whack off the ends, peel off the shucks and silks, then roll the hot corn in a mixture of butter and lime juice. Add a little kosher salt and chili powder and pass 'em quick. If you don't have a grill, just do the same thing in the microwave. Throw the whole ears of corn *in the shucks* into the microwave without soaking and cook 4 minutes per ear at HIGH. Too easy.

Heat the butter in the skillet over high heat until it foams, then add the fish fillets and sauté until golden on both sides, turning only once, no more than 5 minutes total. Pour the sauce back into the skillet, reheat to boiling, then sprinkle capers and cilantro over all and serve at once on warmed dinner plates.

Try a white Spanish Albariño or a Portuguese vinno verde. These slightly acidic dry white wines will complement the subtle flavors of the fish and the acidic flavors of the tomatoes and olives.

Sliced
Oranges and
Jicama Dusted with
Chili Powder

Grouper Veracruz

Mexican Roasting Ears

Rice and Refried Beans
(page 45)

Hot Flour Tortillas,
Sweet Butter, and
Apricot Preserves

Hot Fudge Sundaes
and Butter Cookies

Coffee

Martini Scallops on a Bed of Spinach

Scallops soaked in gin and vermouth, then stir-fried and served over a bed of orange-spiked spinach: It's dinner in one pan made in less than half an hour; a dinner Dashiell Hammett's Nick and Nora would have adored.

PREPARATION TIME: 15 MINUTES   MAKES 4 SERVINGS
COOKING TIME: 15–20 MINUTES

All the Trimmings

Keep the setting spare for this Asian-inspired one-dish dinner. Preheat the plates in the oven. Preset the celery and black and green olive salad at the table. How about a single potted Dendrobium orchid for a centerpiece? Good move. Now you'll have an orchid to enjoy for months.

Get out the chopsticks if you have them, and don't forget to end the meal with American-style cookies. This light dinner can take a rich chocolate chip cookie. It makes the perfect finish.

Although this dish is meant to be chopped, cooked, and eaten at once, you'll be hoping for leftovers. Store, covered in the refrigerator, then zap in the microwave just until hot, no more than 1 minute, or on the stovetop in under 5.

20 LARGE SEA SCALLOPS (ABOUT 1½ POUNDS)	2 BUNCHES FRESH SPINACH (ABOUT 1½ POUNDS)
1 KNOB GINGER, 1 × 2 INCHES	4 TABLESPOONS BUTTER
4 CLOVES GARLIC, MINCED	JUICE OF 1 ORANGE
2 GREEN ONIONS WITH TOPS, CUT INTO FINE RINGS	1 TEASPOON ORANGE ZEST
½ CUP GIN	½ TEASPOON KOSHER SALT
¼ CUP EXTRA-DRY VERMOUTH	FRESHLY GROUND BLACK PEPPER TO TASTE

Place the scallops in a large flat dish. Scrub the ginger (don't peel) and cut it in half. Place it flat side down and, using a rocking motion with a chef's knife, shave it into fine shreds. Place half the ginger on the scallops. Reserve the remaining ginger shreds in a small bowl.

Place half the minced garlic and half the green onions on the scallops and add the remaining half of each to the reserved ginger.

Pour the gin and vermouth over the scallop mixture and turn the scallops to coat completely. Cover and refrigerate.

Plunge the spinach into a big bowl of ice water and let it stand for a few moments so the sand will fall to the bottom. Lift the spinach from the water and shake it dry. Stack the spinach leaves on the cutting board—like a big cigar, rolling the leaves tight, and using a rocking motion, cut the spinach leaves into fine shreds (chiffonade), discarding the stems. Twist in a paper towel to dry.

Over high heat, heat a 12-inch skillet, then add half the butter. Sauté the garlic, ginger, green onion mixture for a few moments, then add the orange juice and zest and bring it to a vigorous boil. Add the salt and pepper and the spinach, and toss to stir-fry until the spinach wilts and most of the liquid evaporates (only takes a couple of minutes). Mound the spinach on 4 warmed dinner plates.

Lift the scallops from the marinade. Add the remaining butter to the pan and heat it to foaming, then sear the scallops just until brown around the edges, about 2 minutes on each side. Arrange the scallops on the spinach.

Pour the reserved marinade into the skillet and heat it to boiling over maximum heat. Boil down to about 4 tablespoons, then spoon a tablespoon of sauce over each portion of scallops and serve at once.

Hot Peanuts,
Asian Mixed Peas,
and Crackers

Martini Scallops
on a Bed of Spinach

Baguette of Hot Bread
with Sweet Butter

Celery and Black and
Green Olive Salad in a
Vinaigrette

Chocolate Chip
Cookies

Try a Vouvray.
The dry herbal quality of this
French wine will complement the
dry flavors of the scallops and vermouth.

Mustard Salmon
with Buttered Egg Noodles

Salmon is a wonderfully rich meat that is nicely complemented by this rich mustard sauce, which also looks beautiful against the pink salmon flesh.

PREPARATION TIME: 20 MINUTES
COOKING TIME: 25 MINUTES

MAKES 6 SERVINGS

All the Trimmings

Sugar snap peas are great raw or just blanched and chilled and served with a bowl of curried mustard. The bright yellow curry against the bright green peas just says summer. Serve the mustard salmon on a large platter on top of the noodles. Pass the tomatoes, which will fit nicely on the dinner plates next to the main course. The bread will soak up the tomato liquor and the vinegar as well as the mustard sauce. Buy a beautiful chocolate mousse cake at a good bakery. What an easy and beautiful dinner.

2 POUNDS SALMON FILLETS

1 CUP DIJON-STYLE MUSTARD (PREFERABLY WHOLE GRAIN)

1 TABLESPOON VEGETABLE OIL

2 TABLESPOONS BUTTER

1 LARGE YELLOW ONION, OR 2 MEDIUM ONIONS, COARSELY CHOPPED

1 TABLESPOON FLOUR

1 BOTTLE DRY WHITE WINE

SEVERAL BUNCHES OF FRESH THYME OR 1 TEASPOON DRIED

1 BAY LEAF

1/2 TEASPOON SALT

FRESHLY GROUND BLACK PEPPER TO TASTE

COARSELY CHOPPED FRESH PARSLEY

1 POUND DRIED EGG NOODLES COOKED ACCORDING TO PACKAGE DIRECTIONS

Carefully spread the salmon fillets with 1/2 cup of the mustard until they are thoroughly coated.

Heat the oil and 1 tablespoon butter in a 12-inch skillet or a Dutch oven over high heat. Brown the salmon fillets, skin side down, for 3 minutes, then turn and brown the other side for 3 minutes more. Be careful not to crowd the fillets in the pan. The salmon will finish cooking in the sauce.

Remove the fillets from the pan as they are cooked and set them aside on a plate. Add the onions and cook for 5 minutes, or until the onions are translucent. Add the flour and cook for 1 to 2 minutes more. Deglaze the pan with half the bottle of wine, scraping the bottom to loosen all the brown bits. Add the remaining 1/2 cup of mustard and half bottle of wine, the thyme, bay leaf, and salt and pepper. Return the salmon to the pot and simmer uncovered on very low heat for 10 minutes. Taste and adjust the salt and pepper if needed. Serve salmon over egg noodles, topped with coarsely chopped fresh parsley.

How to prepare egg noodles:

Buttered egg noodles are best if made and served immediately. Bring a pot of water with 3 tablespoons of salt to a boil. Add the noodles, stirring very well at first. Cook al dente, or to desired doneness. Remove and reserve 1 cup of the cooking liquid. Drain the noodles, but do not rinse them. Return the hot noodles to the pot and stir in 1 tablespoon butter. If the noodles start to stick together, add some of the reserved cooking liquid, as needed.

Sugar
Snap Peas
with
Curried Mayonnaise

Mustard Salmon
with
Buttered Egg Noodles

Sliced Beefsteak Tomatoes
with Basil and
Red Wine Vinegar

French Baguette

Chocolate
Mousse Cake

Try a rich, buttery, non-oaked
French or California Chardonnay
to complement this rich dish. Alternatively,
an Oregon Pinot Noir will pick up the earthy flavor
of the mustard and complement the fish nicely.

Lamb and Mint Paella

Though its seafood cousin is what most people think of when they imagine paella, in fact, seafood is a rather new addition. The word *paella* derives from the Latin word *patella*, which means "pan." Though there are thousands of paella recipes, the dish was originated by Spanish sheepherders, who probably didn't have access to fresh shellfish easily, and is the signature dish of Spain. This version is reminiscent of earlier paellas. However, we are grateful for frozen peas and beans. And although the original dish was no doubt scented with wild mint and might have had a snail or two thrown in, we believe sheepherders would approve of the convenience of supermarket supplies.

All the Trimmings

Paella is best served directly from the pan in which it was cooked. The drama of a sizzling pan of paella on the table will impress even the most sophisticated guest.

PREPARATION TIME: 20 MINUTES
COOKING TIME: 50 MINUTES

MAKES 6 SERVINGS

This can be made one day in advance, covered, and refrigerated. Reheat on the stovetop until bubbling, about 3 to 4 minutes.

½ CUP EXTRA-VIRGIN OLIVE OIL

2 POUNDS CUBED LAMB STEW MEAT

1 LARGE ONION, CHOPPED

3 CLOVES GARLIC, THINLY SLICED

2 STALKS CELERY, CHOPPED

2 CUPS MEDIUM-GRAIN (ARBORIO-TYPE) RICE

1 PINT CREMINI (BROWN) MUSHROOMS

2 (16-OUNCE) CANS BEEF BROTH

3 CARROTS, CUT INTO MATCHSTICK JULIENNE

1 CUP FROZEN AND THAWED, OR CANNED AND DRAINED ARTICHOKE HEARTS

1 (28-OUNCE) CAN TOMATOES WITH THEIR JUICE

½ CUP FROZEN GREEN BEANS

½ CUP FROZEN PEAS

1 CUP COARSELY CHOPPED FRESH MINT (RESERVE 9 OF THE NICEST WHOLE MINT LEAVES FOR GARNISH)

How to cook rice the Mediterranean way:

For best results, choose an imported Italian or Spanish medium-grain rice such as an Arborio. By browning the rice in the oil after you have browned the other ingredients, the rice is infused with the other flavors, improving the overall taste of the dish. This principle is true for paella, risotto, and Spanish rice.

In a 12-inch skillet or paella pan, heat the olive oil and sauté the lamb, onion, garlic, and celery for about 5 minutes, until the onion is translucent. Add the rice and cook for 1 minute. Add the mushrooms, beef broth, carrots, artichoke hearts, and tomatoes with their juice. Cook, covered, for 45 minutes. Five minutes before serving, add the green beans, peas, and mint. Serve hot, in wide-rimmed soup bowls. Garnish each bowl with 3 mint leaves.

Goat Cheese
Disks,
Crackers,
and Grapes

Lamb and Mint
Paella

Crusty
Country Bread

Sliced Strawberries
with Pepper
and
Grand
Marnier

Try a red wine from the Rioja region of Spain. These delicious and earthy dry red wines made from a blend of Spanish grape varietals will complement the earthy flavor of the lamb.

Seafood Paella
with Artichoke Hearts

Seafood paella has become an international favorite. This version comes from Seville.

PREPARATION TIME: 10 MINUTES   MAKES 6 SERVINGS
COOKING TIME: 50 MINUTES

All the Trimmings

Serve the cauliflower and carrots to your guests as they are waiting for the paella. You would not want them to fill up on the appetizer before this sumptuous main course. We love the drama of serving straight from the pan the paella is cooked in. Of course, you can also serve the paella from a platter, but this is communal food. Your guests will no doubt have seconds, maybe even thirds. Buy the flan. Boxes of flan mix are available in the Latin sections of many grocery stores, and custard may be available in the deli section of your grocery store.

The first 8 ingredients may be sautéed and stored in the refrigerator the day before, though you will have to allow 10 minutes more of cooking time the next day.

¼ CUP EXTRA-VIRGIN
    OLIVE OIL

6 CHICKEN THIGHS

½ POUND CHORIZO SAUSAGE,
    REMOVED FROM THE CASINGS
    AND CRUMBLED

1 LARGE YELLOW ONION,
    COARSELY CHOPPED

2 CLOVES GARLIC, CHOPPED

1 YELLOW HUNGARIAN
    WAX PEPPER,
    SEEDED AND CHOPPED

2 TABLESPOONS PAPRIKA

½ TEASPOON SAFFRON THREADS,
    CRUSHED

1 (13-OUNCE) CAN
    CHICKEN BROTH

1 (6-OUNCE) BOTTLE CLAM BROTH

1½ CUPS LONG-GRAIN RICE

¾ CUP WATER

1 LARGE RIPE TOMATO, CHOPPED

12 LARGE SHRIMP,
    SHELLED AND DEVEINED

12 CLAMS, TIGHTLY SHUT

12 MUSSELS,
    IN THEIR SHELLS

1 POUND SEA BASS
    OR OTHER OCEAN
    WHITE FISH FILLETS

½ CUP FROZEN GREEN PEAS

½ POUND FROZEN AND THAWED
    ARTICHOKE HEARTS,
    OR 1 SMALL JAR, DRAINED

FRESHLY GROUND
    BLACK PEPPER TO TASTE

½ CUP COARSELY CHOPPED
    FRESH FLAT-LEAF PARSLEY

In a paella pan or large Dutch oven over medium-high heat, heat the oil and sauté the chicken thighs for 2 to 3 minutes on each side to brown. Remove the chicken from the pan and set it aside. The thighs will finish cooking in the broth. In the same pan, sauté the chorizo, onion, garlic, Hungarian wax pepper, and paprika until the onion is translucent, about 5 minutes. Remove the vegetables from the pan. Add the saffron threads, chicken broth, clam broth, water, rice, and tomato, and stir to combine. Add the sautéed

How to make sangria:

Mix together sliced oranges, green apples, a can of crushed pineapple—juice and all—strawberries, and any other fruit; a splash of orange juice; and a big bottle of dry red wine. Cover and set aside at room temperature for an hour. Chill, then add more wine and at least a cup of brandy and serve. Sangria can best be kept cold by putting ice into a jar and floating it in the punch bowl or pitcher. This prevents the sangria from being watered down by the melting ice.

How to choose mollusks:

When buying clams, always look for those that are tightly shut. These are the ones that are freshest—still alive, in fact. If the clam doesn't open up after 15 minutes of cooking, throw it away. Mussels, on the other hand, might be a little open, but should close when you touch them. If the mussels don't open up wide after being cooked, they too should be discarded.

ingredients, cover, and cook on medium-low heat for 20 minutes, or until the chicken is cooked through. Add the shrimp, clams, mussels, sea bass, peas, artichoke hearts, and black pepper. Cover and cook for 10 minutes more, or until the clams and mussels open up. Serve on a platter with the parsley sprinkled on top.

Fresh
Cauliflower
and Carrots
with
Sour Cream Dip

Seafood Paella
with
Artichoke Hearts

Crusty Bread

Flan

We recommend a Sangria
made from a dry Spanish
red wine with this meal. Make
up the base of the Sangria the day
before and add the final bottle of wine
at serving time. Be sure to eat the fruit, but
watch out—the alcohol can sneak up on you!

Turkey and Cranberry Couscous

Think of this as turkey inside out. It's a main-dish dressing you make in the pan in 5 minutes, then add turkey for a meal-in-one. Whether you are using yesterday's leftover turkey or smoked turkey from the deli, you'll get the flavors of Thanksgiving all in one pan in only 15 minutes. It's colorful, it's flavorful, it's home.

PREPARATION TIME: 10 MINUTES   MAKES 6 SERVINGS
COOKING TIME: 5 MINUTES

All the Trimmings

So you want to invite friends over during the long holiday weekend, but you don't want to go full bore for a Thanksgiving dinner. Spread the table with autumn leaves, mini pumpkins, and nuts. Light the candles. Serve the couscous on a large platter. Plate the soup in the kitchen and preset it. Heat the rolls. Haul out the condiments. Now, you can say Happy Thanksgiving to yourself.

"Preset" is one of those restaurant terms that means you put the food on the table before the diners sit down. A preset course has a calming effect on people. Seeing the food laid out lets them know you thought about them and are prepared.

Make this the day before, cover, and refrigerate it until serving time. Reheat it on the stovetop to warm it.

2 CUPS CHICKEN BROTH

1 (10-OUNCE) PACKAGE COUSCOUS

1/2 CUP DRIED CRANBERRIES

2 STALKS CELERY WITH LEAVES, FINELY CHOPPED

1/2 CUP PECAN PIECES

1 CUP COOKED TURKEY MEAT, CUT INTO BITE-SIZE CHUNKS

2 GREEN ONIONS WITH TOPS, MINCED

1 LARGE BRAEBURN APPLE (OR OTHER CRISP, SWEET VARIETY), CORED AND CHOPPED

DRESSING:

1/4 cup extra-virgin olive oil

3 tablespoons sherry vinegar

2 teaspoons Dijon-style mustard

1 teaspoon sugar

1/2 teaspoon dried thyme

1/2 teaspoon black pepper

1/2 teaspoon kosher salt

In a 10-inch skillet, heat the broth to boiling, then sprinkle in the couscous and add the cranberries. Cover and let stand for 5 minutes off the heat.

Meanwhile, in a bowl, combine the celery, pecans, turkey, onions, and apple.

In a jar, combine the dressing ingredients, cover, and shake to mix.

Fluff the couscous with a fork and add the turkey mixture. Toss to mix, then sprinkle with the dressing. Serve warm or at room temperature.

How to prepare Ad Lib Pumpkin Soup:

You can make ad lib soups as easy as pie. For example, pumpkin soup can be made by turning the can opener on a couple of cans, one of chicken broth and the other of pumpkin puree. Cut up a few pieces of bacon and sauté the bacon in olive oil with onion and garlic. Pour in the chicken broth to deglaze the pan. Add the pumpkin puree and more broth or water as needed to achieve the texture you prefer. Heat to a simmer, whisk in sour cream to taste, season with chives, salt, and peppers—red, black, and white—and plate it. Add a swirl of sour cream the way restaurants do. People will swear you killed yourself. Let 'em think it.

If you are
making this dish
between the months of
October and December,
try a Beaujolais Nouveau.
After January, Beaujolais Nouveau
is not supposed to be sold, as
it is a green wine, meant to be drunk
soon after bottling. The fruity flavor of
this wine will complement the fruity
flavor of the cranberry. If you are making
the dish between January and September, try an
Oregon Pinot Noir or a good French Burgundy.
These light red wines will also complement the red
fruit of the cranberry and the subtle flavors of the turkey.

Ad Lib
Pumpkin Soup

Turkey and
Cranberry Couscous

Black Olives,
Celery Sticks,
Cranberry Dressing

Hot Rolls
and Sweet Butter

Mincemeat Pie
and
Whipped Cream

Dave's Yankee Dirty Rice

Though very different from traditional Cajun dirty rice seasoned with thyme, garlic, cayenne, livers, gizzards, and other yummies, this Yankee version developed by David Murray, Katherine's father-in-law, who uses cumin as the main seasoning, is an interesting twist on the original recipe. Dave's Yankee dirty rice is always being requested at parties in Dutchess County, New York, and we can see why.

PREPARATION TIME: 10 MINUTES
COOKING TIME: 35 MINUTES

MAKES 4 SERVINGS

All the Trimmings

One of the problems with rice-based main dishes is their shapelessness. We have two suggestions. For center-of-the-table family-style service, press the rice into a Bundt cake mold just after removing it from the heat. Let it sit for a couple of minutes. Just before serving, flip the rice onto a plate. It will not keep the perfect shape, but it will have some shape. If you do not have a Bundt pan, try using a large bowl, giving the rice a domed look. Surround the rice with the tomatoes. If you wish to have table service, press the rice into individual cereal bowls and give each person his or her own dome of rice. Serve the tomatoes fanned out next to the rice. Of course, buy the cake, and just before you're ready to serve, whip the cream. The whipped cream in a can just never cuts it!

2 TABLESPOONS OLIVE OIL

1 POUND BULK SAUSAGE, BROKEN UP

1 LARGE YELLOW ONION, CHOPPED

1 LARGE GREEN BELL PEPPER, SEEDED AND CHOPPED

1 LARGE RED BELL PEPPER, SEEDED AND CHOPPED

2 STALKS CELERY, CHOPPED

2 CLOVES GARLIC, FINELY CHOPPED

1 TABLESPOON GROUND CUMIN

1/2 TEASPOON DRIED OREGANO

1 TEASPOON SALT

FRESHLY GROUND BLACK PEPPER TO TASTE

1 (15-OUNCE) CAN CHICKEN BROTH

1/2 CUP WATER

1 CUP WHITE LONG-GRAIN RICE

Preheat a Dutch oven over medium-high heat for 1 minute. Add the olive oil and heat for 30 seconds, then add the broken-up sausage. Sauté the meat for about 5 minutes, or until it begins to brown. Drain off the excess fat and add the onion, peppers, celery, garlic, cumin, oregano, salt, and pepper. Cook for 5 minutes more until the vegetables become limp. Reduce the heat to medium and deglaze the pan by adding the chicken broth and water, scraping up the brown bits from the bottom. Stir in the rice, cover over low heat, and cook for 20 to 25 minutes or until the liquid is absorbed.

What is PickaPepper sauce?

One of a number of tomato-tamarind-mango-based chili sauces made in the Jamaican Caribbean, it's a close cousin to A.1. steak sauce and Lea & Perrins Worcestershire Sauce. You can use these sauces interchangeably. Worcestershire sauce was actually invented during the reign of Queen Victoria by a couple of chemists named (guess what?) Lea and Perrins. Their sauce uses tamarind, sugar, molasses, and anchovies in its secret recipe. Because it has a special affinity for cheese, it will make a brick of ordinary cream cheese stand at attention and salute. All you do is pour it over a brick of cheese and serve with crackers.

**Try a good selection
of beers with this meal.**

Cream Cheese
with
PickaPepper Sauce
and Crackers

Dave's Yankee Dirty Rice

Sliced Tomatoes
with Salt, Pepper,
and Balsamic Vinegar

Bread and Butter

Lemon Pound Cake
with Fresh
Whipped Cream
and Fruit

Quesadillas Primavera

Golden-brown vegetable and cheese-filled quesadillas make the best use of spring garden produce for a quick lunch. Quesadillas are the Mexican sandwich. Quick to make in a skillet, easy to eat, they are welcomed by children as well as adults. Don't be put off by the long list of ingredients. They are mostly just vegetables you'll toss into the skillet.

All the Trimmings

Impromptu cooking calls for impromptu decorations. Turn up the salsa music. Plunk a cactus plant in the middle of the table. Drag out those funny curios you couldn't live without on your last vacation down south. Blow the dust off and put them on the table. Preset the table with the cheeses and fruits, then compose on the dinner plates the quesadilla wedges, guacamole, beans, and salsa. Pour the chips into a basket. Put the beers in an ice bucket nearby. It's a party.

Don't even consider making these ahead. Make 'em and eat 'em as fast as you can.

1/2 CUP EXTRA-VIRGIN OLIVE OIL

8 CLOVES GARLIC, MINCED

2 GREEN ONIONS WITH TOPS, CHOPPED

1 TABLESPOON CHOPPED FRESH CHIVES

1/2 TEASPOON KOSHER SALT

1/4 TEASPOON CAYENNE

FRESHLY GROUND BLACK PEPPER TO TASTE

2 PORTOBELLO MUSHROOMS, THINLY SLICED

1/2 CUP SNOW PEAS

4 LARGE FLOUR TORTILLAS

1/2 CUP CRUMBLED MEXICAN WHITE CHEESE

3 TABLESPOONS CHOPPED FRESH CILANTRO

2 TABLESPOONS CHOPPED FRESH FLAT-LEAF PARSLEY

2 CUPS MIXED BABY LETTUCES

2 TABLESPOONS SOUR CREAM

SALSA

BLACK OLIVES OR FRESH JALAPEÑOS, FOR GARNISH

Heat a large non-stick sauté pan and lightly coat it with a tablespoon of oil. Add the garlic, green onions, and chives. Season with salt, cayenne, and black pepper. Cook until the garlic and green onions are beginning to brown, 3 to 5 minutes. Add the mushrooms along with a tablespoon of the oil and cook them along with the other vegetables, 3 to 4 minutes. Add the snow peas during the last minute or so of cooking. Remove the vegetables from the pan and reserve them in a warm, covered bowl.

Preheat the pan again and lightly coat it with another tablespoon of oil. Place a tortilla in the pan so it lies flat. Add 2 tablespoons of the crumbled cheese to cover half the tortilla completely, and top it with a quarter of the sautéed vegetables. Fold the other tortilla half over the vegetables and cheese. Use a spatula to press down. Turn the tortilla once after the bottom has

How to prepare refried beans:

We love those canned beans. Buy frijoles refritos in a can and all you have to do is heat them in the microwave. Can't find refried beans? Open a can of black or pinto beans, rinse and drain them, then heat oil or lard in a skillet and add the beans. Mash them with a potato masher as they heat. See? You just made refried beans the way Mexican cooks do. Except they probably started with dried beans. Want to begin there? Rinse the beans, then cover them by at least 1 inch with barely salted water. Heat to a gentle boil and cook, adding more water as needed until the beans are tender. Toss in an onion and some garlic, perhaps a strip or two of bacon. Now you've made a pot of beans. You don't need to soak the beans unless you live 3,000 feet or more above sea level. Allow from 1 to 3 hours for the beans to cook.

browned, about 2 to 3 minutes. Once the second side is browned, after a minute or so, remove the tortilla from the pan and cut into 2 pie-shaped wedges. Oil the pan again with about a teaspoon of oil and repeat until you have used all 4 tortillas, all the cheese, and all the vegetables.

To serve, put 2 wedges on a plate and garnish with fresh baby lettuces, a jot of sour cream, and a spoonful of salsa. Add a black olive or a fresh jalapeño for garnish.

**We love beer
with Mexican-influenced dishes,
and this quesadilla is no exception.**

Guacamole
and
Fresh Tomato Salsa
with
Hot Tortilla Chips

Quesadillas Primavera

Refried Beans

Assorted Tropical Fruits:
Papaya, Guava,
Mango, Pineapple

Mexican White
Cheeses

Pan Dulce
(Mexican Bread
Pastries)

Basically Braised

Braised Bok Choy and Chicken in a Ginger Sauce

If you've never made Chinese food and want to have a successful first venture, this is a good recipe to begin with. You don't need a wok. One big soup pot will do. You don't need much skill, either, just fresh ingredients, a Chinese cleaver to whack the chicken thighs into pieces, and the patience to cut up ginger into matchstick julienne. The resultant dish is gorgeous, good for you, and a winner to serve to company.

PREPARATION TIME: 15 MINUTES   MAKES 6 SERVINGS
COOKING TIME: 25–30 MINUTES

All the Trimmings

Because this chicken dish is so good looking, you should serve it in a way that plays up its best features. Choose a flat platter and lay the bok choy on the platter in an alternating pattern: white bulb end beside leafy tip. You'll get a striped green and white look for the base. Then top it with the cooked chicken and sauce. Place the platter in the middle of the table and let your guests help themselves. Chopsticks are great if you have them.

This is meant to be made and eaten at once, but you can cover and refrigerate the leftovers, then reheat them on the stovetop or in the microwave to just under the boil for lunch the next day. All you'll miss is eating it standing over the kitchen sink from a white cardboard box.

6 LARGE CHICKEN THIGHS, WHACKED INTO 3 PIECES EACH WITH A CHINESE CLEAVER

1½ TEASPOONS KOSHER SALT, OR TO TASTE

1 (½-×-1-INCH) PIECE GINGERROOT, CUT INTO MATCHSTICK JULIENNE

4 GREEN ONIONS WITH TOPS, CUT INTO MATCHSTICK JULIENNE

1 HEAD BOK CHOY, WASHED, RINSED, AND EACH LEAF CUT LENGTHWISE INTO 2 PIECES

1 TABLESPOON CORNSTARCH DISSOLVED IN 2 TABLESPOONS WATER

1 TEASPOON GROUND GINGER

Salt the chicken meat and set it aside while you bring a large stockpot of water to a boil. Add the chicken to the boiling water, then add half the fresh ginger and half the green onions. Reduce the heat to a simmer and poach the chicken until it's cooked

How to poach chicken the Chinese way:

Simmering the chicken in perfumed water until it is just tender but not overcooked is central to the Chinese cooking technique. It takes only a few moments, and by leaving the chicken on the bone, then cutting the bones so you can have the benefit of that flavor in the poaching liquid, you'll get a delicate flavor that will make you love chicken again.

through and tender, 15 to 18 minutes. Lift out the cooked chicken and drain it, then transfer it to a warmed dish and set it aside.

Bring the chicken cooking liquid to a good, rolling boil and add the bok choy. Cook, uncovered, just until tender, 10 to 15 minutes. Lift the bok choy from the broth, drain, and arrange it on a large, flat tray, alternating stem with leaf ends so that you get a white-green alternation in color. Mound the cooked chicken in the middle. Cover and reserve.

To make the sauce, pour off all but 1 cup of the cooking broth. (Save it for soup. It's too good to waste. Store it in the freezer in 2-cup portions.) Add the remaining fresh ginger and green onions to the remaining broth and bring it to a boil. Stir in the cornstarch mixture, salt to taste, and the ground ginger. Cook and stir until you have a shiny, clear, aromatic sauce, about 2 to 3 minutes. Pour the sauce over the chicken and serve at once.

A dry or semi-dry Riesling with fruity and slightly sweet flavors from the Mosel region of Germany is always a great complement to ginger and chicken. Look for a wine with an alcohol content below 13 percent. Our all-time favorite Rieslings are the New York State Finger Lakes dry and semi-dry vintages from the Hermann J. Weimer Winery.

Wasabi
Peas

Braised
Bok Choy
and Chicken
in a
Ginger Sauce

Fluffy
White Rice

Mixed
Fresh Fruit

Green
Tea

Braised Chicken with Artichokes and Greek Olives

Make this skillet dinner in a handsome porcelain-clad cast-iron skillet, or your grandmother's old black cast-iron skillet, and you'll have a meal in one container that you can bring right to the table. It looks good. It tastes good.

All the Trimmings

Bring the skillet to the table and watch your guests' mouths water as you spoon individual servings into rimmed soup bowls. Sprinkle with chopped parsley. Pass the tangerine sections with crushed pistachios. The orange and green colors will be a feast for the eyes.

PREPARATION TIME: 15 MINUTES   MAKES 8 SERVINGS
COOKING TIME: 1 HOUR

Cook this at your convenience, up to a day ahead, then cover and refrigerate it. Reheat in the skillet over medium heat until bubbling, about 3 to 4 minutes.

- 2 TABLESPOONS OLIVE OIL
- 8 BONELESS, SKINLESS CHICKEN THIGHS (ABOUT 2 POUNDS)
- 1 LARGE YELLOW ONION, CHOPPED
- 4 CLOVES GARLIC, SMASHED
- 3/4 POUND LARGE BROWN MUSHROOMS, CUT INTO QUARTERS
- 3/4 CUP CHICKEN BROTH
- 3/4 CUP DRY RED WINE
- 3 TABLESPOONS BALSAMIC VINEGAR
- 2 TABLESPOONS TOMATO PASTE
- 2 TEASPOONS FRESH THYME LEAVES, OR 1 TEASPOON DRIED
- 1 (16-OUNCE) CAN ARTICHOKE HEARTS, DRAINED AND QUARTERED
- 2 CUPS HALVED SMALL RED POTATOES (ABOUT 1 1/2 POUNDS)
- 1/2 CUP GREEK OLIVES
- 1/2 CUP FINELY MINCED FRESH FLAT-LEAF PARSLEY, FOR GARNISH
- 1/2 TEASPOON KOSHER SALT
- CRACKED PEPPER TO TASTE

Preheat a 12-inch skillet over medium-high heat, then add the oil. When the oil is hot, brown the chicken thighs on all sides, from 3 to 5 minutes per side. Remove the chicken pieces to a warmed platter.

Add the onion, garlic, and mushrooms to the pan and sauté until the onion begins to look translucent, 5 to 10 minutes. Stir in about 1/4 cup of the broth and 1/4 cup of the red wine, deglazing the pan by stirring up the browned bits from the bottom. Now stir in the vinegar and tomato paste. Once this mixture has boiled, return the chicken to the pan, add the remaining broth and red wine, and the thyme. Nestle the artichoke pieces, potatoes, and

48   STYLISH ONE-DISH DINNERS

olives in amongst the chicken pieces, cover, and bring to a boil. Season with the salt and pepper. Reduce the heat and simmer, uncovered, until the chicken and potatoes are cooked through and tender when pierced—35 to 40 minutes.

Taste and adjust the seasoning with additional salt and pepper. Garnish individual servings with chopped parsley as you serve.

Romaine, Walnut, and Watercress Salad with Garlic Vinaigrette

Braised Chicken with Artichokes and Greek Olives

Crusty Country Bread with Butter and Apricot Jam

Hot Mango Chutney

Tangerine Sections Drizzled with Honey, Fresh Mint, and Crushed Pistachios

Some chicken dishes work well with red wines, and this is a good example. Try a Petite Sirah from the Languedoc region of France or from California. The bitterness of the olives are a good foil for the fruitiness of this red wine.

Beer-Braised Pork Chops
with Onions, Apples, Cabbage, and Currants

Believe us, you can have this savory winter skillet dinner ready for the oven in less time than it takes to order out. The rich flavors of succulent pork chops, autumn apples, and sweet yellow onions are punctuated by little explosions of taste from the currants.

PREPARATION TIME: 15 MINUTES   MAKES 4 SERVINGS
COOKING TIME: 1 HOUR

Make and serve this dish in an hour. To save the leftovers, transfer them to a refrigerator dish, cover, and save for up to 3 days. Reheat in a skillet on top of the stove in 5 minutes or less.

1 TEASPOON GROUND GINGER

1/2 TEASPOON KOSHER SALT

FRESHLY GROUND
    BLACK PEPPER TO TASTE

1 TABLESPOON
    ALL-PURPOSE FLOUR

4 LARGE, BONE-IN, DOUBLE-CUT
    (1-TO-2-INCH-THICK)
    LOIN PORK CHOPS

3 TABLESPOONS BUTTER

1 LARGE YELLOW ONION,
    THINLY SLICED

4 SMALL, TART APPLES, CORED
    AND CUT INTO EIGHTHS

2 TEASPOONS BROWN SUGAR

1 SMALL HEAD RED CABBAGE,
    CORED AND CUT INTO EIGHTHS

JUICE AND ZEST OF 1/2 LEMON

2 WHOLE CLOVES

1/2 CUP CURRANTS

1 (12-OUNCE) CAN
    PILSNER-STYLE BEER
    (SUCH AS HEINEKEN)

Preheat the oven to 350°F.

Rub ginger, salt, pepper, and flour into both sides of the pork chops. Heat a 12-inch ovenproof skillet over medium heat, then add the butter. Tip the skillet to coat the bottom, then brown the chops well on both sides, about 4 to 5 minutes. Remove them to a plate and add the onion to the pan. Cook until it looks translucent, about 3 minutes. Add the apples and continue cooking until they begin to soften, about 5 minutes, adding the brown sugar to aid the browning.

Return the chops to the skillet along with the cabbage and top with the lemon juice and zest, the cloves, currants, and beer. Cover the skillet with foil or a lid and place it in the preheated oven. Bake for 30 minutes, then remove the lid and raise the temperature to 400°. Roast for an additional 15 minutes. Serve hot from the stove on warmed dinner plates.

We suggest beer with this meal.
If you feel like getting fancy, go for a
German Riesling. The fruity flavors of this wine will
marry well with this German-influenced recipe.

Pretzels,
Peanuts, and Beer

Beer-Braised
Pork Chops
with Onions,
Apples, Cabbage,
and Currants

Red New Potatoes
Tossed in Butter and
Seeded Mustard

Ginger Snap–Vanilla
Ice Cream
Sandwiches

Broccoli Rabe
with Italian Sausage, Tortellini, and Fresh Cherry Tomatoes

Italian flavors all seem to complement one another. This meal takes advantage of that general principle. After all, the flavors of the foods developed together for the last few hundred years. The bitter broccoli rabe and spicy sausage are a great foil for the rich cheese course.

All the Trimmings

We usually serve the olives and sliced fennel very informally in the living room with a starter glass of wine, like maybe Prosecco, our favorite Italian sparkler. A stack of cocktail napkins will be all you need to serve the first course. Don't forget a small bowl for the olive pits. Preset the table with the rather brothy broccoli rabe, Italian sausage, and tortellini in rimmed soup bowls set atop a dinner plate or charger just before serving. Shave the Parmigiano-Reggiano on top of each bowl of broth. Set the table with a side plate for the bread and later the cheese, fruit, and nuts. This simple meal is simply a knock-out. Your guests will be amazed and you will have used only one pot!

PREPARATION TIME: 10 MINUTES
COOKING TIME: 15 MINUTES

MAKES 4 SERVINGS

2 TABLESPOONS OLIVE OIL

1 POUND ITALIAN TURKEY SAUSAGE, HOT OR SWEET, OUTER SKIN REMOVED (SEE NOTES)

1 ONION, COARSELY CHOPPED

2 CLOVES GARLIC, FINELY CHOPPED

2 (13-OUNCE) CANS CHICKEN BROTH

2 CUPS WATER

1 POUND FRESH TORTELLINI FILLED WITH SAUSAGE OR CHEESE

1 BUNCH BROCCOLI RABE, CHOPPED AND WITHOUT STEMS

15 CHERRY TOMATOES, HALVED

SALT AND FRESHLY GROUND BLACK PEPPER TO TASTE

FRESHLY SHAVED PARMESAN CHEESE CURLS (SEE NOTES)

How to cook terrific tortellini:

Cooking tortellini in a broth works like a charm. Tortellini needs to cook no more than 5 to 10 minutes, or else they turn to mush. So watch the time!

In a 12-inch skillet, heat the olive oil and sauté the turkey sausage and onion for 5 minutes. Add the garlic and sauté for 2 minutes more. Remove from the pan and deglaze the pan with the chicken broth and water, scraping up all of the bits from the bottom.

In a large sauce pot, bring the broth and water to a boil, add the tortellini, and cook for 5 minutes, then drain.

Return the sausage, onion, and garlic to the skillet, add the broccoli rabe and tomatoes, and cook for 5 minutes more. Top with the shaved Parmesan curls and serve at once.

NOTE: We have also used Italian pork sausage, or the fancy chicken and apple sausages, or sun-dried tomato sausages. Whatever you are in the mood for or have on hand will work.

NOTE: Use a potato peeler to shave Parmigiano-Reggiano cheese into curls.

Sliced
Fennel
and Olives

Broccoli Rabe with
Italian Sausage,
Tortellini, and
Fresh Cherry Tomatoes

Italian Baguette

An Italian Cheese Plate—
Pecorino Tuscano, Fontina,
Gorganzola, and/or
Parmigiano-Reggiano

Grapes, Dried Fruit,
Nuts

**Try a Barbera d'Alba.
This light red wine is a
classic with most Italian meals.**

Stracotto (Parma Pot Roast with Pasta)

Visiting Parma, Italy, home of Parmigiano-Reggiano cheese, Linda learned there is more to pot roast than her mother let on. Sunday dinner in Parma starts on Saturday with Mama in the kitchen slow-cooking a pot roast on top of the stove with a cracked plate filled with wine set over the meat, the wine seeping through the cracks and slowly infusing the meat with the flavor of red wine. After the meat cooks a day and a half, Mama makes and stuffs ravioli with Parmigiano-Reggiano. She rolls out the pasta on a board using a 2-foot-long rolling pin that no one else is allowed to touch. She cooks the ravioli in the broth from the meat and serves the meal in two courses—pasta with just a little cheese and butter first, followed by the meat and broth. The flavors are fantastic. What can Americans do? Use a pressure cooker. You'll get that same mama's-in-the-kitchen flavor, and in just over an hour. If you want to try it the old way, see Lynn Kasper's great book, *The Splendid Table*, which provided inspiration for our streamlined version. Don't be surprised if your guests burst into arias after they've tasted this. It's that good. Thank you, Parma mothers. And grandmothers.

All the Trimmings

Italian meals are served differently from American ones in that each course is given equal measure. Serve the prosciutto in paper-thin slices with 3 to 4 figs on a plate, then whisk that away and replace it with a plate containing a few ravioli dressed only with butter and a whiff of freshly grated Parmigiano-Reggiano. Follow this with a rimmed soup bowl containing a modest serving of meat and broth, and finish the dinner with Italian-style ice cream and butter cookies. The vegetables are in the broth. The flavor is in every course—comforting, and there to make you feel at home.

PREPARATION TIME: 15 MINUTES
COOKING TIME:
1¼ HOURS USING A
PRESSURE COOKER;
3 TO 4 HOURS ON TOP OF
THE STOVE

MAKES 6 SERVINGS

You may cook and refrigerate the meat and broth at your convenience, up to 2 days ahead, then reheat the dish on top of the stove to a good rolling boil. Cook the ravioli in the broth at the last minute.

1 (2½-POUND) BEEF ROUND RUMP ROAST

½ TEASPOON KOSHER SALT

FRESHLY GROUND BLACK PEPPER TO TASTE

3 TABLESPOONS BUTTER

1 LARGE YELLOW ONION, THINLY SLICED

4 CLOVES GARLIC, THINLY SLICED

1 STALK CELERY, CHOPPED

1 MEDIUM CARROT, CHOPPED

1 MEDIUM TOMATO, CUT INTO 8 WEDGES

1 TABLESPOON ROSEMARY NEEDLES

3 WHOLE CLOVES

2 TEASPOONS IMPORTED TOMATO PASTE

2 CUPS BEEF BROTH

1 CUP DRY RED WINE (LIKE A CHIANTI)

12 OUNCES FRESH CHEESE RAVIOLI

½ CUP MINCED FRESH FLAT-LEAF PARSLEY

FRESHLY GRATED PARMIGIANO-REGGIANO CHEESE, FOR SPRINKLING

So what's the story on pressure cookers?

If you don't have a pressure cooker, the big question is: Why not? This new-again idea makes slow cooking fast, and once you try it, you'll love it. However, if you don't have one, just remember, most dishes that are cooked in a pressure cooker can also be cooked over the flame—it just takes 3 to 4 times longer. So just because a recipe calls for a pressure cooker and you don't have one, do not be deterred. Just give yourself a peaceful, lazy Saturday, and simmer the dish slowly. You may have to add a little more broth and wine as the time goes by to keep the right amount of liquid, but you'll get a good result. In fact, given enough time, say, a day and a half, you'll get the same result as those Italian mamas who live in their kitchens.

Season the meat generously with the salt and pepper. Heat the butter in the bottom of a pressure cooker until it foams. Brown the meat on all sides, adding the onion and garlic after you have turned the meat once. After 5 minutes, add the celery, and carrot, and cook for 5 minutes. Add the tomato, rosemary, cloves, tomato paste, broth, and wine. Close the pressure cooker and raise the temperature to the second ring. Pressure cook for 45 minutes to 1 hour, or until the meat is fork-tender. (Alternatively, cook the meat over low heat until tender in a covered Dutch oven, 3 to 4 hours.) Remove the meat from the broth and slice thin.

Bring the broth to a boil and add the ravioli. Cook until tender, following the package directions, from 5 to 8 minutes.

To serve as a one-dish dinner, place a few slices of meat in a rimmed soup bowl, add 3 to 4 ravioli, and spoon the broth over all. Add a sprinkling of minced parsley and sprinkle generously with freshly grated Parmigiano-Reggiano. Serve hot.

Prosciutto
and Figs

Cheese Ravioli
with Butter
and
Parmigiano-Reggiano

Stracotto
in Broth

Chocolate Gelato
with
Butter Cookies

**Start off with Prosecco or
Malvasia sparkling wine.
Next, offer a full-flavored Chianti.
And don't forget tiny cups of espresso
and maybe a shot of grappa to end the dinner.**

Braised Herbes de Provence Beef in Burgundy Wine

From Mama's pot roast to boeuf Bourguignonne, a slow-cooked mixture of beef with vegetables and potatoes has drawn people to the Sunday dinner table in both America and Europe for hundreds of years. The differences in flavor depend upon both ingredients and technique. We simply adore the full-flavored chuck roast with ordinary potatoes, onions, and carrots that our grandmamas made, but we do add a few twists to make this old-fashioned Sunday dinner our own. We even like those precooked pot roasts in the butcher case.

First, we cut the fat and bone away from the meat. Then, we season everything with herbes de Provence. We simmer the roast in hearty red wine. It makes this dish meltingly delicious.

PREPARATION TIME: 20 MINUTES   MAKES 8 GENEROUS SERVINGS
COOKING TIME: 3 HOURS

All the Trimmings

Start with the pickled beets and walnuts as an appetizer, preset at the table. Serve the braised beef on a large platter to be set in the center of the table. Pass the polenta disks. For an intimate dessert course, bring the whole pears and cheese to the table on a wooden cutting board. Make each guest a plate with a few slices of pear and blue cheese.

Only have 20 minutes?
Begin with a fully cooked pot roast from the butcher. Brown the vegetables in oil, then add the beef and wine. Cover and cook until vegetables are tender. Serve at once.

May be made ahead and refrigerated for up to 2 days. It tastes great reheated the next day by placing the pan on the stovetop and heating slowly until it bubbles.

1 (3- TO 4-POUND) CHUCK ROAST, FAT AND BONES REMOVED AND RESERVED, MEAT CUBED

½ CUP ALL-PURPOSE FLOUR

SALT AND FRESHLY GROUND BLACK PEPPER TO TASTE

3 TABLESPOONS OLIVE OIL

1 LARGE YELLOW ONION, CUT INTO THICK SLICES

1 POUND BABY CARROTS

1 CUP CREMINI MUSHROOMS, CUT IN HALF

15 CLOVES GARLIC, UNPEELED

6 LARGE RUSSET POTATOES, PEELED

1 TABLESPOON HERBES DE PROVENCE

1 FIFTH OF HEARTY RED BURGUNDY WINE

Place the beef cubes on a sheet of wax paper and coat them with the flour, salt and pepper. Reserve the flour remaining on the wax paper. Turn and dredge the pieces to coat them thoroughly.

Heat the oil in a large Dutch oven over medium-high heat, then brown the meat until it is light golden brown on every side. Lift the meat with a fork and slip the onion underneath. Brown the onion until it is golden, 5 to 10 minutes, then add the carrots, mushrooms, and garlic cloves. Continue to brown, about 3 to 4 more minutes.

Meanwhile, put the bones and fat you have trimmed from the meat into a large saucepan. Cover with cold water, add a little salt, and bring to a boil over high heat. Lower the heat to medium-low and simmer for about 1 hour. Lift out the bones, cool the broth, then skim off the fat. This will make a wonderful full-flavored beef broth for the sauce, and you'll have enough to freeze some for pumping up the flavors of soups you make at another time.

While these items are browning, toss the potatoes in the flour remaining on the wax paper and season them generously with salt and pepper. Add them to the beef cooking pot. Sprinkle the herbes de Provence over all. Pour in the wine and bring to a boil. Reduce the heat to medium-low, cover, and simmer until the meat is meltingly tender, about 3 hours. The finished dish may be set aside to cool and reheated to serve, or it may be served immediately.

To serve: Arrange the meat in the middle of a large platter and surround it with the vegetables and potatoes.

Make a sauce from the pan drippings by adding a couple of tablespoons of flour to the bottom of the pan, cooking and stirring over medium-high heat to make a roux. Then add 2 cups of the beef broth and stir to combine. Reduce until the sauce is thick, about 5 minutes, then season to taste with salt and pepper. Serve on the side in a gravy boat.

**Try a red Châteauneuf-du-Pape
from the southern region of France.
This earthy wine with its strong herbal note
will go nicely with the herbes de Provence and beef.**

Pickled Beets
and
Toasted Walnuts in
Vinaigrette

Braised Herbes
de Provence
Beef in Burgundy Wine

Grilled Polenta Disks
with Olive Oil and
Red Pepper Flakes

Hot Baguettes

Perfectly Ripe Comice
Pears and Blue
Cheese

Port

Zucchini Beef Bow-ties

Cooking pasta in broth not only means you get the meal done all in one pan, it also means the pasta will be infused with the perfumed broth as it cooks. For best results, choose pasta imported from Italy and made with durum wheat. Purchase the best-quality ground sirloin and this simple dinner becomes good enough for company.

PREPARATION TIME: 15 MINUTES   MAKES 6 SERVINGS

COOKING TIME: 30 MINUTES

All the Trimmings

Simplicity works best with this colorful menu where the food is the star of the show. Preset the table with the pear salad, then serve the main dish in wide-rimmed soup bowls. We picked up a set of plain white, restaurant-quality bowls—the kind they use in Italian bistros—and find we use them over and over for dishes like this. Big, casual napkins tied in a knot, plenty of candles, and fresh flowers. Stand the bread sticks in a short barrel glass. And don't forget a wedge of Parmigiano-Reggiano on a plate with a hand grater for people to add additional cheese. It's an easy party for 2 couples to enjoy on a Friday night.

Make this a day ahead, cover, and refrigerate it, then reheat on the stovetop just to the boil.

1½ POUNDS GROUND SIRLOIN

1 LARGE YELLOW ONION, FINELY CHOPPED

4 CLOVES GARLIC, MASHED

½ TEASPOON SALT

2 CUPS BEEF OR CHICKEN BROTH

½ TEASPOON DRIED OREGANO

¼ TEASPOON DRIED THYME

½ TEASPOON RED PEPPER FLAKES

2 CUPS SLICED BABY ZUCCHINI

1 CUP UNCOOKED BOW-TIE PASTA

4 SMALL PLUM TOMATOES, QUARTERED

¼ CUP CHOPPED FRESH BASIL

½ CUP FRESHLY GRATED PARMIGIANO-REGGIANO CHEESE

Preheat a large skillet over high heat, then brown the ground sirloin along with the onion and garlic until the beef is no longer pink, about 10 minutes. Lift from the skillet with a slotted spoon to a warm serving platter, cover, and set aside.

Pour out any remaining fat from the skillet and add the broth, oregano, thyme, red pepper flakes, zucchini, and pasta. Use the

Bow-Ties

Italian

English

How to choose and prepare ground beef:

You may wonder why the meat is removed from the pan before the broth is added. We believe the best flavor can be obtained from this dish when the meat is sautéed at a high temperature in an open pan with no added fat, then drained and reserved, only to be added back at the very end. In this way, every bite gives you the splendid caramelized taste of well-seared beef, as well as the complexity that comes from pasta cooked in an aromatic, seasoned broth.

When choosing ground beef, look for bright, cherry red meat. We buy either ground sirloin, or ground beef with 15 percent fat. Either cook it or freeze it when you get home. Thaw it in the refrigerator for best results and don't put ground beef into the pan until that pan is thoroughly preheated. This makes the difference between dull gray meat and mouthwatering mahogany. Cook and stir the meat until no pink remains. That's how you know you've cooked ground beef to the safe temperature, 160°. Then complete the recipe as directed.

back of your spoon to submerge all the bow-ties. Bring to a boil, then reduce the heat to medium. Simmer, uncovered, stirring occasionally, for 15 minutes, or until the pasta is tender.

Return the beef to the skillet, add the tomatoes and basil, and heat through. Sprinkle with the cheese and serve in wide-rimmed soup bowls.

Ripe
Bartlett
Pear Halves
with Shaved
Parmigiano-Reggiano
and Balsamic Vinaigrette
on a Bed of Baby Greens

Zucchini Beef Bow-ties

Bread Sticks

Cannoli
and
Other Assorted
Italian Pastries

Espresso

**Try a Côtes du Rhône.
The herbal, earthy flavors
of the wines from this region will
pick up the herbal flavor of the zucchini
while complementing the earthy flavor of the beef.**

Tequila-Braised Chicken with Two Kinds of Peaches

Stephan Pyles makes a high-heeled version of this dish in his Star Canyon Restaurant in Dallas. He uses farm-raised pheasant, which works well, but you'll be happy with a plain old roasting chicken. We've also used this method with quail and partridge, and with doves—creating Paloma tequila. It's your basic spirit-braised poultry dish, punched up with summer fruit.

All the Trimmings

Summer in the South means meals taken outside. Serve this dinner in your backyard or at the park. Use a checkered tablecloth, turn on the sprinkler so the kids can run through it while you're getting dinner on the table, and take advantage of every time-saver you have: Use the microwave to cook the corn. Too easy. Throw the ears in the microwave, shucks and all, and cook for 4 minutes per ear (or 24 minutes for 6 ears), then put the ears on a cutting board, whack off the ends, and peel the shucks and silks off. We like this meal served in wide-rimmed soup plates. Serve the chicken at the head of the table and ask Dad to cut it into pieces. Add to each bowl a dollop of rice and black beans, a pickled peach, and finish with the gravy. Sprinkle cilantro over the top of each helping and serve. All you need to complete this menu is a fly swatter. You know how it is when you sit outside in the summertime.

PREPARATION TIME: 30 MINUTES   MAKES 6 SERVINGS
COOKING TIME: 1½ HOURS

Like most braised dishes, this one tastes good the first day and even better the second. Cover and refrigerate overnight, then reheat it on the stovetop before serving.

1 (5-POUND) ROASTING CHICKEN
   OR 2 PHEASANTS
2 NAVEL ORANGES, PEELED
SALT AND FRESHLY GROUND
   BLACK PEPPER TO TASTE
2 TABLESPOONS OLIVE OIL
2 TABLESPOONS BUTTER
1 TABLESPOON CHOPPED FRESH
   ROSEMARY
1 TABLESPOON CHOPPED FRESH
   THYME
1 BAY LEAF, CRUMBLED
1 MEDIUM YELLOW ONION,
   CHOPPED
8 CLOVES GARLIC

2 TABLESPOONS FLOUR
1 CUP GOLD TEQUILA
1 CUP CHICKEN BROTH
1 (12-OUNCE) PACKAGE FROZEN
   PEACHES
1 (16-OUNCE) CAN PICKLED
   PEACHES
1 CUP DRY RED WINE
3 CLOVES
2 TABLESPOONS SUGAR
½ TEASPOON CAYENNE
½ CUP FINELY CHOPPED FRESH
   CILANTRO, FOR GARNISH

Stuff the chicken with the oranges, then season it with salt and pepper. Tie the chicken legs together with cotton string.

In a large Dutch oven, heat 1 tablespoon each oil and butter over medium-high heat, then brown the bird on all sides, 10 to 15 minutes, turning as needed. Remove the chicken to a plate and sprinkle it with the herbs.

Sauté the onion and garlic in the remaining oil and butter until onion turns golden, 3 to 4 minutes; sprinkle with the flour; then cook and stir another minute. Add half the tequila and all the chicken broth, stirring until it thickens, about 3 to 4 minutes.

How to make spicy black beans in a hurry:

Simply open a couple of cans of black beans, rinse and drain them, then add them to a saucepan with ½ cup orange juice. Add ½ teaspoon ground allspice and ½ teaspoon ground cloves. Simmer a few minutes, then finish with curls of orange zest.

Adjust the seasonings with salt and pepper. Add the frozen peaches, then return the chicken to the pan. Cover and cook in a 375° oven for 50 minutes to 1 hour 15 minutes, or until the chicken is tender. An instant-read thermometer inserted into the thickest part of the thigh should read 170°. Lift the cooked bird from the juices to a warmed serving platter, arrange the pickled peaches around the bird, cover, and set it aside.

To make the sauce, add the wine, cloves, and sugar to the pan juices. Raise the heat to high and boil about 3 to 4 minutes to reduce the sauce a little and to thicken it. Add the cayenne and adjust the salt and pepper as needed. Pour the sauce into a gravy boat and serve it along with the chicken. Sprinkle cilantro over each helping.

Texas
Pickled Okra

Tequila-Braised Chicken
with
Two Kinds of Peaches

Fluffy White Rice
and
Spicy Black Beans

Corn on the Cob

Country Rolls
and
Sweet Butter

Blackberry
Pie

**Iced tea with mint and sugar
or an Oregon Pinot Noir
marry well with this rich, full-flavored dish.**

The Fast and Fabulous Egg

Lox-Tarragon Omelet

Just the 4 of you? What could be more satisfactory than a French-style omelet with croissants, baked apples, and a Belgian endive salad? Yes, you'll have to make the omelets one at a time, but you'll be there in the kitchen together, sipping champagne and making the most of your Sunday.

PREPARATION TIME: 10 MINUTES MAKES 4 SERVINGS
COOKING TIME: 3–5 MINUTES
PER OMELET

All the Trimmings

Intimate entertaining, where the cook makes every omelet individually, calls for the diners to be gathered as close to the stove as possible. Perch your guests on stools in the kitchen and give them a glass of champagne while you make the omelets. Follow these with a bitter endive salad and a baked apple to finish. Don't forget to have on hand both plain and chocolate croissants, and do buy 2 for each guest. You know how people are on Sunday mornings.

Don't even think about making omelets ahead or reheating them. This meal is about comfort and taking care of those you love. Make and serve each omelet right off the stovetop, and your grateful loved ones will eat them up in a minute.

½ CUP SOUR CREAM

2 TABLESPOONS COARSE-GRAINED DIJON MUSTARD

8 LARGE EGGS

¼ CUP WATER

¼ CUP CHOPPED FRESH CHIVES OR GREEN ONION TOPS

3 TABLESPOONS MINCED FRESH TARRAGON

SALT AND FRESHLY GROUND BLACK PEPPER TO TASTE

4 TEASPOONS BUTTER

¼ POUND LOX, CUT INTO STRIPS

MINCED PARSLEY FOR GARNISH

In a small bowl, whisk the sour cream and mustard together and set it aside. In a large bowl, combine the eggs, water, chives, and tarragon, and whisk to blend. Season with salt and pepper.

Warm 4 plates in the oven. Melt 1 teaspoon of the butter in a 7- to 8-inch carbon steel or non-stick omelet pan or skillet. Add about ⅓ cup of the egg mixture to the pan and stir briefly. Let the eggs begin to set at the edges, about a minute, then use your spatula to lift the edges and tilt the pan so that the uncooked

How to make a perfect omelet:

Choose a 7- to 8-inch omelet pan with sloping sides made of carbon steel or with non-stick coating. Break all the eggs into a bowl, adding a shot of salt, pepper, and Tabasco if you wish, plus about 1 tablespoon water per egg. Whisk the eggs vigorously to mix the whites and yolks.

Preheat the pan thoroughly, then melt the butter in it, tilting the pan just until the butter foams and begins to color up. Use a 3-ounce ladle or ⅓ cup liquid measure to add the eggs.

Hold the pan handle with your left thumb on top of the handle and start sliding the pan back and forth rapidly over the heat. Hold the fork in your right hand and stir the eggs quickly, spreading them over the bottom of the pan as they thicken. Within about 20 seconds, you'll see the mixture become a soft, light custard. Add any fillings now to half the pan.

Lift the handle to tilt the pan at a 45-degree angle over the heat and gather the eggs at the far lip of the pan with the back of your fork. Hold the pan for a few seconds more, then fold it in half with a spatula and turn the omelet onto the plate by inverting the pan over the plate. The finished omelet should be golden with just a hint of browning around the edges. Finish with a sprinkling of parsley or more of the filling and serve.

portion flows underneath. Cook just until the eggs are set but still moist, about 1 minute. Spread a tablespoon of the mustard mixture on half the top, then add a quarter of the salmon strips. Use the spatula to fold the unfilled portion over the filling as you slide the omelet onto a plate and serve. Repeat, until you have made 4 omelets.

Fresh-Squeezed
Orange Juice

Lox-Tarragon Omelet

Hot Croissants,
both Plain and Chocolate

Belgian Endive Salad
with a
Three-Citrus Vinaigrette
(page 25)

Baked Apples
with Whipped Cream

Espresso

**Prosecco with its bubbly texture
and dry flavor will marry perfectly
with an omelet. You can add orange juice
and make an Italian version of a Mimosa.**

Herbes de Provence Lettuce Frittata

This dish is a French classic. We think it is a great recipe and demonstrates the true parsimonious nature of French cooks. The frittata is simple and delicious.

PREPARATION TIME: 10 MINUTES
COOKING TIME: 8–10 MINUTES

MAKES 4 SERVINGS

All the Trimmings

Preset the table with a thin slab of pâté over a piece of lettuce set on a salad plate. The French serve it this way and just eat it with a fork and knife before a meal. If you must, you can serve it with a piece of bread, but there is no need to. Stack the dinner plates next to the host. Ask people to the table as you put the frittata in the oven.

When the timer rings, bring in the frittata and serve people large, pie-shaped pieces. Pass the bread, butter, and honey. End with the fruit and coffee. What a simple and elegant meal.

2 TABLESPOONS BUTTER

2 CUPS COARSELY CHOPPED ROMAINE, BUTTER, RED-TIP, OR ICEBERG LETTUCE

4 EGGS, LIGHTLY BEATEN

1 TEASPOON HERBES DE PROVENCE

1 TABLESPOON WATER

1/4 TEASPOON SALT

FRESHLY GROUND BLACK PEPPER TO TASTE

1/2 CUP GRATED EMMENTALER OR SWISS CHEESE

PAPRIKA

Preheat the broiler to a full broil. In a 10-inch, non-reactive skillet, heat the butter over medium heat. Add the lettuce and cook, stirring for 1 to 2 minutes. In a bowl, combine the eggs, herbes de Provence, water, salt, and pepper and beat slightly. Reduce the heat to medium-low and pour the egg mixture over the lettuce leaves. Lift the edges to let the raw eggs run under the lettuce a bit and cook until the eggs are just nearly done. The eggs will cook in 3 to 4 minutes. Once the top is shiny, with no large pools of raw egg, sprinkle with the cheese and paprika and run the frittata under the broiler for 2 minutes, until the cheese and eggs begin to puff up and brown slightly. Serve at once.

What is herbes de Provence?

Herbes de Provence is a wonderful mixture of herbs that originates from the south of France. A pinch of herbes de Provence is an easy way to add complex flavor to a simple dish. It is basically a mixture of thyme, lavender, marjoram, and other goodies. Don't bother to try and make your own. Just keep it on hand. You will soon find yourself using it to season many things. It is great as a rub on a chicken to be roasted. And when you visit the Provençal area of France, take a deep breath. The air is perfumed with the same herbs.

Try a rosé from the Provençal region of France. These pinks are nothing like most American rosés, which are sweeter than pancake syrup. The drier pinks from France (and now some from California) were developed in the same region that developed herbes de Provence, so, not surprisingly, the flavors complement one another.

Sliced
Country Pâté

Herbes de Provence
Lettuce Frittata

Crusty French
Baguette
with
Butter and Honey

Grapes
and Apples

Good
Coffee

Spring Frittata
with Flat-Leaf Parsley, Baby Leeks, Green Onions, and a Touch of Balsamic Vinegar

A golden, green-flecked wedge of frittata makes a terrific lunch alongside a green salad or a thick slice of red tomato. The addition of mere drops of balsamic vinegar showcases both the balsamic and the most delicate spring vegetables. Great for an Easter brunch.

All the Trimmings

Serve the frittata on a platter to be passed around. Pass a salad to complement the dish.
What a great, simple brunch.

PREPARATION TIME: 10 MINUTES   MAKES 6 SERVINGS

COOKING TIME: 15 MINUTES

Delicious warm or at room temperature. You can make this dish as much as an hour before serving time, then cover and hold it until you're ready to go. Or, store it covered in the refrigerator overnight and warm it in a skillet a moment or two before serving.

3 TABLESPOONS OLIVE OIL

6 GREEN ONIONS WITH TOPS, CHOPPED

1 BABY LEEK, SPLIT, WASHED THOROUGHLY, AND CHOPPED

6 LARGE EGGS

1/2 CUP (6 OUNCES) PART SKIM MILK RICOTTA, CRUMBLED

2 TABLESPOONS FRESHLY GRATED PARMESAN CHEESE

1/2 CUP CHOPPED FRESH FLAT-LEAF PARSLEY

2 TABLESPOONS SKIM MILK

1/2 TEASPOON SALT

1/4 TEASPOON CAYENNE

FRESHLY GROUND BLACK PEPPER TO TASTE

1 TABLESPOON BEST-QUALITY BALSAMIC VINEGAR

SPRIGS OF FRESH, FLAT-LEAF PARSLEY, FOR GARNISH

In a 12-inch, broiler-proof, non-stick skillet, heat 1 tablespoon of the oil over medium heat. Add the green onions and leek and sauté until they're golden, 3 to 5 minutes. Transfer the vegetables to a large bowl and mix in the eggs, cheeses, chopped parsley, milk, salt, cayenne, and black pepper.

Preheat the broiler. Heat the remaining 2 tablespoons oil in the same skillet over medium-high heat. Pour in the egg mixture. Cook, using a rubber spatula to lift the edges of cooked egg so that the raw part can flow onto the hot skillet, just until the top is beginning to set, about 3 to 4 minutes. Reduce the heat to low,

How to prepare frittatas:

If you think of the frittata as an open-faced omelet, you'll immediately see how you can translate this version into another by using the fillings of your choice. The basic principle remains the same: Precook any meats or vegetables in fat in the pan, then transfer them to a warmed container and add more butter and/or olive oil to the sauté pan. Whisk the eggs with flavorings and cooked meats and veggies, then pour into the preheated pan. Stir the mixture gently until the eggs begin to set up, then simply lift the edge of the egg and tilt the pan so that the uncooked egg runs underneath to hit the hot pan and cook. Finish the frittata under the broiler or in a hot oven to brown it. Slide it onto a serving dish and, *voilá*, it's done.

cover and cook until the frittata is set, about 9 more minutes. Transfer the skillet to the broiler and brown the top, about 3 minutes. Sprinkle with the balsamic vinegar. Run the spatula around the edges to loosen the frittata, then slide it onto a platter and cut it into wedges to serve. Garnish with sprigs of Italian parsley.

Antipasti:
Mortadella, Salami,
Coppa, Prosciutto

Spring Frittata
with Flat-Leaf Parsley,
Baby Leeks,
Green Onions, and a
Touch of Balsamic Vinegar

Ciabatta Bread

Tossed Greens,
Edible Flowers,
and Herb Salad

Cheese Board and
Fruit of the
Season

**The texture of eggs
and the texture of icy Prosecco
go very well together. The bubbly
Italian wine will surely dress up this meal.**

Lemon Madras Egg Curry

Quick as a flash, made from ingredients found in the pantry, brightly flavored and attractive on the plate, that's a curry made for eggs, served on English muffins. Haul out the chutneys from the fridge, serve up bowls of coconut, cilantro, raisins, and peanuts, and you've got a meal that can be served from brunch to midnight supper.

PREPARATION TIME: 20 MINUTES   MAKES 4 SERVINGS

COOKING TIME: 25–30 MINUTES

All the Trimmings

Now's the time for plate service. All you need to do is preheat the plates in the oven while you're making the curry, then plate up the curry on the muffins and add a side of mango slices with a wedge of lime juice. Serve all the condiments in small bowls for guests to help themselves.

Make the sauce and hard-cook the eggs as much as half a day ahead, refrigerate covered, then reheat on the stovetop just to boiling. Serve hot.

6 LARGE EGGS

2 TABLESPOONS BUTTER

1 SMALL YELLOW ONION, CHOPPED

2 CLOVES GARLIC, MINCED

1½ TABLESPOONS MADRAS
    CURRY POWDER

2 TABLESPOONS TOMATO PASTE

1 CUP WATER

SALT AND FRESHLY GROUND
    BLACK PEPPER TO TASTE

JUICE AND ZEST OF ½ LEMON

4 ENGLISH MUFFINS,
    SPLIT AND TOASTED,
    THEN BUTTERED

Place the eggs in a medium saucepan and cover them with cold water. Bring to a gentle boil and gently cook for 12 minutes. Do not allow the water to boil rapidly. Rinse the eggs under cold water, drain, remove the shells, and cut them in half.

In the same pan you cooked the eggs, melt the butter over medium-low heat. Add the onion and cook until it's translucent, about 5 minutes. Add the garlic, and cook for 2 minutes. Add the curry powder and cook, stirring, 2 to 3 minutes. Stir in the tomato paste and cook for 2 minutes. Add the water and bring the sauce to a boil. Cook for about 10 minutes, or until the sauce thickens. Season with salt and pepper. Add the lemon juice and zest. Lay the eggs, cut side up, into the sauce and let them heat.

To serve, lay a toasted muffin on a warmed dinner plate and spoon the curry and eggs over it.

How to customize grocery store curries

Commercial curry powder is a blend of spices that probably includes turmeric, coriander, pepper, cloves, cumin, cardamom, mace, fenugreek, cayenne, and other spices and herbs. If you would like to punch-up the flavor of the brand in your pantry, add a shot of cayenne. If you'd like it to be more Asian, as in Garam Masala, throw in a pinch of ground cloves and/or cinnamon. If you have available more than one brand, look for Sun Brand Madras Curry Powder. It's what we've used here and is a reliable brand.

Mango Slices
with
Lime Wedges

Lemon Madras
Egg Curry

Tamarind
(and other)
Chutneys

Bowls of
Coconut, Raisins,
Chopped Peanuts,
Cilantro

Darjeeling
Tea

**Using the opposites rule,
the spicy flavor of the curry
is perfectly foiled by a fruity Riesling.
Try one from South Africa.**

Poblano Pepper Chilequiles

This wonderful Mexican dish was a favorite of Katherine's in college. Not only could it be made in one pot, but it fit the college student's budget! We have updated it using a smoky poblano pepper to give it more depth of flavor.

PREPARATION TIME: 15 MINUTES
COOKING TIME: 10 MINUTES

MAKES 4 SERVINGS

All the Trimmings

Arrange the avocado, grapefruit, and pomegranate seeds on a platter in a pinwheel design. This not only looks good, but it allows people to take what they want. We love the drama of bringing the chilequiles to the table in the black skillet. Serve the refried beans in a nice bowl. We usually open a can of refried beans and microwave them in the serving bowl. To spruce them up, add ¼ cup of salsa. We love Pace mild! Pan dulce, or Mexican bread pastries, which are usually beautifully colored, unworldly pinks, blues, and yellows, can be purchased at any Mexican grocery store. Warm and serve them on a big platter. We like to cut them in half so that people can taste the pink ones *and* the blue ones!

2 TABLESPOONS OLIVE OIL

2 SLICES BACON, CHOPPED

6 CORN TORTILLAS, CUT INTO TRIANGLES

1 SMALL YELLOW ONION, COARSELY CHOPPED

1 POBLANO PEPPER, FINELY CHOPPED

1 CLOVE GARLIC, CHOPPED

1 (12-OUNCE) CAN STEWED TOMATOES, DRAINED AND CUT UP; OR 2 VERY RIPE FRESH TOMATOES, CHOPPED

½ TEASPOON SALT

4 EGGS

1 CUP GRATED MONTEREY JACK OR MILD LONGHORN CHEESE

SOUR CREAM, FOR GARNISH

Preheat a heavy skillet, preferably cast-iron, on medium-high for 1 minute. Add the olive oil and bacon. Cook just until the bacon is limp. Remove it from the oil with a slotted spoon. Add the tortilla triangles and cook for 1 to 2 minutes per side. Remove the tortillas and drain all but 1 tablespoon of the grease from the pan. Add the onion and poblano pepper to the pan and cook for 3 minutes. Add the garlic and cook for 1 to 2 minutes more. Over the vegetables in the pan, layer the corn tortillas, then the bacon bits, the tomatoes, then the 4 eggs broken individually, like fried eggs. Season with the salt. Reduce heat and cook, covered, for 2 to 3 more minutes. Cover with the cheese and let stand until the cheese has melted. Serve with a dollop of sour cream, taking care to give each person an egg.

How to prepare tortillas:

For those folks who don't have much experience cooking with tortillas, either flour or corn, one of the most common mistakes is serving tortillas raw. If they are not fried or cooked in a dry skillet, corn tortillas will have a distinct lime (as in the mineral, not the fruit) flavor, and flour tortillas will taste like paste. Microwaving or just steaming them does not adequately cook either one. No wonder many people think they don't like corn tortillas. Never skip the fry or dry skillet fry step when cooking with tortillas. Even if they are meant to be cooked a bit more later in the recipe, this step is vital.

This hot and spicy meal is best complemented by a good Mexican beer.

Chips and Salsa

Avocado,
Pomegranate Seed,
and
Grapefruit Salad

Poblano Pepper
Chilequiles

Refried Beans

Pan Dulce

And Don't Forget the Much Maligned Microwave

Asparagus, Ham, and Rice Casserole

The flavor of fresh dill juxtaposed with the asparagus and ham will fill your house with a wonderful aroma matched only by the flavor.

All the Trimmings

Casseroles are great comfort foods meant to be shared among close friends and family. This meal should be served casually. We suggest buffet style, with the salad and rice casserole served on the main dinner plate. Pass the bread and butter. The strawberries can go in the middle of the table. People can dip their own strawberries into the crème fraîche followed by the brown sugar.

PREPARATION TIME: 10 MINUTES MAKES 4 SERVINGS
MICROWAVE COOKING TIME:
45–50 MINUTES

Make this 2 to 3 days ahead, cover, and refrigerate it. Reheat it in the microwave until hot, about 1 to 3 minutes on high (100% power), or in the oven at 350° for 10 to 15 minutes.

2 TABLESPOONS BUTTER

2 TABLESPOONS OLIVE OIL

1 MEDIUM ONION, CHOPPED

1 CLOVE GARLIC, CHOPPED

1 (1-POUND) BUNCH ASPARAGUS,
  CUT INTO 3-INCH SECTIONS,
  TOUGH PART OF STEMS
  REMOVED

1 POUND BLACK FOREST HAM,
  CUBED

2 CUPS UNCOOKED
  LONG GRAIN RICE

2 (15-OUNCE) CANS CHICKEN
  BROTH

1 CUP WATER

JUICE OF 1 LEMON

4 EGGS

1 CUP MILK

3/4 CUP LOOSELY PACKED FRESH
  DILL, PLUS CHOPPED
  FRESH DILL FOR GARNISH

1 1/2 CUPS GRATED EMMENTALER
  OR SWISS CHEESE

In a 10-X-6-inch microwavable glass baking dish, combine the butter and olive oil. Microwave on high (100% power) for 1 minute. Add the onion and microwave on high for 3 minutes. Add the garlic, asparagus, ham, and rice and microwave on high

How to make a compound butter:

To make lemon-pecan butter, simply cream ½ cup butter (1 stick) with 2 teaspoons fresh lemon juice and ¼ cup finely chopped pecans. Spread the butter mixture onto a piece of wax paper and role like a cigar. Refrigerate it for at least 30 minutes to an hour. Cut into thick pats and serve. The sky's the limit on different flavors for compound butters: basil and lemon, tarragon and almonds, and many more.

for 8 minutes. Add the broth and the water, cover with microwavable plastic wrap, pricking a few holes in the wrap to let out some steam and microwave on high for 25 minutes. Remove the pan from the microwave and let it sit for about 5 minutes to cool slightly.

Meanwhile, combine the eggs, milk, and ¾ cup of dill in a bowl. Add the egg mixture, along with lemon juice, to the rice and stir thoroughly. Return to the microwave and cook on high for 5 minutes more. Remove from the microwave and top with the grated cheese. Run under the broiler for 1 to 2 minutes more to melt and brown the cheese. Garnish with the chopped dill.

Dried
Italian Salami,
Crackers, and Dijon
Mustard

Asparagus, Ham,
and Rice Casserole

Romaine Lettuce Salad
with a
Balsamic Vinaigrette

French Bread and Lemon-
Pecan Butter

Strawberries Dipped in
Crème Fraîche
and
Brown Sugar

A fruity Petite Sirah from Australia will complement the salty quality of the ham in this dish. Look for David Wynn vineyards.

Polenta with Chicken Apple Sausage, Apples, and Fontina Cheese

You know, of course, that polenta is nothing more than the Italian word for *cornmeal*. Comfort food is made comforting for the cook when cooked in the microwave. We say use the microwave whenever appropriate, such as for cooking grains.

PREPARATION TIME: 10 MINUTES   BAKING TIME: 15 MINUTES
MICROWAVE COOKING TIME: MAKES 6 SERVINGS
    12 MINUTES

All the Trimmings

This menu includes some of fall's best flavors: cranberries, apples, ginger, and pumpkin. The main course is best served family-style. We just bring the polenta to the table in the baking dish. Stack the dinner plates at the designated server's seat and pass around portions of the polenta. The salad and bread can be passed. A family-style dinner with some pass-around items is casual and comfortable. There is something very symbolic in our culture about passing food around the table.

Of course, a smart cook will find a good bakery for the gingerbread and pumpkin bread. Okay, if you're in the mood, make it from scratch. The house will smell great. However, a close approximation can be made by toasting the bought dessert. Always make fresh whipped cream. The stuff in a can bears little resemblance to the real thing, and is better for noncooking uses!

This can be made up to the point just before baking, covered, refrigerated, and held for a day. Bring to room temperature before baking.

2 TABLESPOONS OLIVE OIL

2 CLOVES GARLIC, CHOPPED

1 POUND CHICKEN APPLE SAUSAGE, SKIN REMOVED, CUT INTO SMALL CHUNKS

1 1/2 CUPS COARSE YELLOW CORNMEAL

4 CUPS WATER

2 TEASPOONS SALT

4 TABLESPOONS BUTTER, CUT INTO CHUNKS

1/4 CUP FRESHLY GRATED PARMESAN CHEESE

2 TART APPLES (GRANNY SMITH, WINESAP, OR MACOUN), CORED AND CHOPPED

1/2 POUND FONTINA CHEESE, GRATED (2 CUPS)

Preheat the oven to 350°F. Meanwhile, in a 12-×-8-×-2-inch glass baking dish, combine the olive oil, chopped garlic, and sausage. Cook in the microwave on high (100% power) for 2 minutes. Add the cornmeal, water, and salt, then let sit for 3 minutes. Cook covered in the microwave on high (100% power) for 6 minutes. Stir in the butter and Parmesan cheese and microwave for 6 minutes more. Add the apples and Fontina cheese. Bake in the oven for 10 to 15 minutes, or until the cheese melts.

How to prepare an appetizer in a hurry:

Serve the appetizer in the living room. Arrange the sliced salami and Swiss cheese around a bowl of Dijon mustard. Serve the crackers in a basket on the side. Guests should each have a small dessert plate for the hors d'oeuvre course. This is a little too messy to get away with just napkins. Slice it before you serve it. Never ask guests to slice hard salami or hard cheeses. It's just too cumbersome and not very appetizing.

Hard
Salami, Swiss
Cheese, and Dijon
Mustard, with
Crackers

Mesclun Salad with
Balsamic Vinaigrette and
Dried Cranberries

Polenta with Chicken Apple
Sausage, Apples,
and Fontina Cheese

Baguette and Butter

Warm Gingerbread and
Pumpkin Bread with
Fresh Whipped
Cream

Try a Pinot Blanc from France's Loire Valley. The fruit and honey overtones to the wine will nicely complement the sausage.

Risotto with Apples and Sausage

Nothing says fall like a tart apple and good sausage. Try this dish in the fall or any time you can get your hands on good apples.

All the Trimmings

Risotto is very conducive either to plate service or to being served on a large platter. In either case, traditionally, Italians eat risotto from the outer edge, which is cooler, toward the inner mound, which cools as the outer edge is eaten away. Serve the salad on a side plate. The walnut bread is great with both the main course and the cheese course. A purist would set out bread plates for the bread and cheese course. Morbier is such a divine cow's milk cheese that it deserves its own plate. The cheese is divided by a thin layer of ash. The top cheese is the morning cheese, the bottom is the afternoon. Long debates can evolve from trying to taste the difference between one and the other. We can't tell the difference, but some people say they can. What we notice is a very compelling nutty, fruity cheese.

PREPARATION TIME: 10 MINUTES   MAKES 6 SERVINGS
MICROWAVE COOKING TIME:
  30–35 MINUTES

This may be made 1 day in advance and reheated in the microwave a minute or so, or on the stovetop until hot, about 2 to 3 minutes.

3 TABLESPOONS OLIVE OIL

1 MEDIUM ONION, CHOPPED

2 CUPS ARBORIO RICE

1 (15-OUNCE) CAN
  CHICKEN BROTH

$\frac{1}{2}$ CUP WHITE WINE

$2\frac{1}{2}$ CUPS HOT TAP WATER

$\frac{3}{4}$ CUP ITALIAN TURKEY SAUSAGE

3 APPLES, CUT INTO
  1-INCH PIECES

$\frac{1}{4}$ CUP FRESHLY GRATED
  PARMIGIANO-REGGIANO
  CHEESE

SALT AND FRESHLY GROUND
  BLACK PEPPER TO TASTE

In a ceramic microwavable bowl, combine the olive oil, onion, and rice, and heat uncovered in the microwave on high (100% power) for 5 minutes. Stir in the chicken broth and white wine and microwave uncovered for 12 minutes on high (100% power). Stir in the water and sausage, and microwave for 12 minutes more on high (100% power). Add the apples and Parmesan cheese, salt, and pepper. Add additional water if the rice appears too sticky or dry. Consistency should be creamy. Microwave for 3 minutes uncovered on high (100% power). If you have a small 400-watt microwave, you may need to cook the risotto a minute or so longer at each step.

How to select apples:

For a dish like this, you will want to pick a tart, crunchy apple. From early fall through the winter try to buy Rome, Northern Spy, McIntosh, or Macoun. They are all wonderful for this and other baked dishes. In a pinch, Granny Smith is always a dependable choice.

**A fruity and rich
Beaujolais is a classic with sausage,
and the acidity of this wine will work
nicely against the creamy texture of the risotto.**

Spinach
and Bacon
Salad

Risotto
with Apples
and Sausage

Whole-Wheat
Raisin and Walnut
Bread

Morbier Cheese

Butter Cookies
and
Fruit

Risotto with Ham, Corn, and Red Peppers

Risotto has become a regular on many restaurant menus. While delicious, it's time consuming when made the Old World way. This microwave version is much simpler. The bright flavors of ham, corn, and peppers are wonderful in combination.

All the Trimmings

This casual menu starts out with a classic: tomato slices in balsamic vinegar and extra-virgin olive oil. We usually do about half and half olive oil and balsamic vinegar, with plenty of salt and pepper. The tomato slices get better after at least 30 minutes of marinating in the basil, vinegar, and oil. Just dress them on the serving plate and let them stand. Serve this appetizer at the table because it is messy. Bring the risotto to the table in the bowl in which it was cooked. Stack the dinner plates at the "designated risotto server's" seat. Spoon the risotto onto individual plates. Eating risotto slowly, from the outside in, extends the time one spends at the table, a wonderful Italian ritual, and one Americans could afford to adopt. For dessert, just arrange washed strawberries on a platter with a bowl of chocolate syrup in the middle. This is simply elegant, and an intimate way to enjoy dessert with friends. Don't even talk about how easy it is.

PREPARATION TIME: 10 MINUTES

MICROWAVE COOKING TIME: 30–35 MINUTES

MAKES 6 SERVINGS

This may be made 1 day in advance and reheated in the microwave in a minute or so, or on the stovetop in 3 or 4 minutes.

3 TABLESPOONS OLIVE OIL

1 MEDIUM ONION, CHOPPED

2 CUPS ARBORIO RICE

1 (15-OUNCE) CAN CHICKEN BROTH

1/2 CUP WHITE WINE

2 1/2 CUPS HOT TAP WATER

4 OZ. (3/4 CUP) BLACK FOREST HAM, CUT INTO STRIPS

3/4 CUP FROZEN CORN KERNELS

2 RED BELL PEPPERS, SEEDED AND COARSELY CHOPPED

1/4 CUP FRESH GRATED PROVOLONE

1/4 CUP FRESHLY GRATED PARMIGIANO-REGGIANO CHEESE

SALT AND FRESHLY GROUND BLACK PEPPER TO TASTE

1/2 CUP CHOPPED FRESH FLAT-LEAF PARSLEY

In a microwavable bowl, combine the olive oil, onion, and rice, and heat uncovered in the microwave on high (100% power) for 5 minutes. Stir in the chicken broth and white wine and microwave uncovered for 12 minutes on high (100% power). Stir in the water and ham, and microwave for 12 minutes more on high (100% power). Add the corn, peppers, and cheeses. Season with salt and pepper. Consistency should be creamy; add more water if needed. Cook for 3 minutes uncovered on high (100% power). Stir in the parsley just before serving. If you have a small 400 watt microwave you may need to cook the risotto a minute or so longer at each step.

How to make proper risotto either the old-fashioned way or the easy way:

About risotto: Use only Arborio rice. Using long-grain or short-grain rice will yield rice paste or something that won't hang together at all. Arborio is a patented variety of Italian rice, though there are some producers of an American version of this particular nutty-tasting variety. Because risotto has become so popular, most supermarket gourmet sections will have Arborio. Although there are many variations in the ingredients and broth used in a risotto, the method for cooking it stays roughly the same. All risotto is started in oil and finished with constant stirring in a broth. We have found that the microwave does a great job of making risotto with almost no stirring. Though cooking the risotto in the microwave doesn't actually reduce the time, it does eliminate the constant stirring and attention you must give the rice when made on the stovetop.

Sliced
Tomatoes with
Fresh Basil Chiffonade,
Balsamic Vinegar, and
Extra-Virgin Olive Oil

Italian Baguette
or Ciabatta Bread

Risotto
with Ham, Corn,
and Red Peppers

Fresh Strawberries
Dipped in
Chocolate
Sauce

Try an Italian Barbaresco.
The slightly acidic quality of the wine
will marry well with the creamy texture of the risotto.

PART II

Out of the Dutch Oven

Chilies, Soups, and Stews

CHAPTER 6

Chili from Texas, Cincinnati, and the White Breast of a Chicken

Real Texas Chili

And the debate rages on in the great state of Texas (which some admit is more of a state of mind): Is chili cooked with or without beans? We vehemently side with the no-beans crowd. Who would want those starchy little things sapping the flavor of real beef! Okay, so cook a pot of beans, or even open a can of them to make a bed for the chili, but never cook the beans with the chili!

All the Trimmings

This is a perfect buffet meal. Leave the chili on the stove, in true Texas tradition, with the condiments laid out next to it. Let people help themselves to corn bread right out of the black skillet. The pie and ice cream can be bought, of course.

PREPARATION TIME: 30 MINUTES   MAKES 10–12 SERVINGS

COOKING TIME: 2–2½ HOURS

This only gets better with age. Make it a day, a week, or a month ahead. Refrigerate it covered for up to 3 days; freeze it for up to a year. Defrost and reheat on the stovetop or in the microwave to boiling, by the bowlful or the panful, from 1 to 10 minutes depending on vessel volume and heat source.

CONDIMENTS:

Chopped jalapeños	Pinto beans
Chopped flat-leaf parsley	Salsa or pico de gallo
Chopped green onions	Saltines
Fritos	Sour cream
Grated Cheddar cheese	Tabasco sauce
	Tortilla chips

How to make corny corn bread fast:

Corny corn bread is just 2 boxes of Jiffy Corn Bread mix made according to package directions with 1 cup of frozen corn kernels added to the batter. For best results, preheat the oven and a black skillet greased with bacon grease or shortening. Then add the batter. This will ensure that you have a nice crust. You can also add jalapeños and Cheddar cheese to the batter. We like to make a sunburst pattern on top of the batter with slivers of jalapeño.

¼ CUP VEGETABLE OIL

1 GREEN BELL PEPPER,
    SEEDED AND CHOPPED

3 YELLOW ONIONS, CHOPPED

1 JALAPEÑO PEPPER,
    SEEDED AND CHOPPED

2 CLOVES GARLIC,
    FINELY CHOPPED

1 STALK CELERY, CHOPPED

4 POUNDS CHUCK ROAST,
    CUT INTO LARGE CHUNKS

½ CUP CHILI POWDER

1 CAN BEER (WE LIKE PEARL OR
    LONE STAR)

1 TEASPOON GROUND CUMIN

3 DASHES TABASCO SAUCE

1 (7-OUNCE) CAN GREEN
    CHILE PEPPERS

1 (14-OUNCE) CAN TOMATOES
    WITH JUICE

1 (15-OUNCE) CAN TOMATO SAUCE

1 CUP WATER

SALT AND FRESHLY GROUND
    BLACK PEPPER TO TASTE

In a large Dutch oven over medium heat, heat the vegetable oil for 1 minute. Add the green pepper, onions, jalapeño, garlic, and celery. Cook for 5 minutes. Toss the chunks of chuck roast in the chili powder, add them to the vegetable mixture, and cook until the meat is brown on all sides, 5 minutes more. Now add the can of beer, deglazing the pan by scraping up all of the browned bits from the bottom. Add the cumin, Tabasco, green chiles, tomatoes, tomato sauce, water, and salt and pepper. Cook uncovered for 2 hours. Add more water if the mixture becomes too thick. The stew should be soupy but not watery. Adjust the seasonings with additional salt and pepper. Serve with some or all of the suggested condiments on the side.

For an authentic Texas experience, go for Shiner Bock beer. If you can't get it, try Lone Star or Pearl.

Chips
and Salsa

Real
Texas Chili

Corny
Corn Bread

Sliced
Sweet Onions

Fruit Pie
and
Ice Cream

Cincinnati-Style Chili

We Texans usually refuse to acknowledge the existence of chili from Ohio! Only recently have we even given it a chance. As it turns out, it is wonderful and quite different, with a totally different set of spices. As Texpatriates, we risk our reputation by recommending this recipe, but our love for food overrules our love of the Great Lone Star State. In Cincinnati they always add spaghetti and may serve it "three ways" with oyster crackers, chopped onions, and cheese, or "five ways," adding beans and more Cheddar cheese.

All the Trimmings

Like so many one-pot dinners, this is another chance to entertain very informally. With a party of 8 it is sometimes fun to serve the appetizer in the living room or den, then set up a buffet and continue the meal on your lap. This style party has the distinct advantage of promoting mingling among the guests. It also has the advantage that people bus their own dishes and is less trouble for the host to clean up.

PREPARATION TIME: 10 MINUTES
COOKING TIME: 2 HOURS

MAKES 8–10 GENEROUS SERVINGS

3 TABLESPOONS VEGETABLE OIL
3 YELLOW ONIONS, CHOPPED
4 CLOVES GARLIC, CHOPPED
4 POUNDS GROUND BEEF CHUCK
1/3 CUP CHILI POWDER
2 TABLESPOONS PAPRIKA
2 TEASPOONS GROUND CUMIN
1 TEASPOON GROUND CORIANDER
1 TEASPOON GROUND ALLSPICE
1 TEASPOON DRIED OREGANO
1/4–1/2 TEASPOON CAYENNE
1/2 TEASPOON CINNAMON
1/2 TEASPOON GROUND CLOVES
1/2 TEASPOON GRATED NUTMEG
1 BAY LEAF
5 CUPS WATER
1 (16-OUNCE) CAN TOMATO SAUCE
2 TABLESPOONS WINE VINEGAR
2 TABLESPOONS DARK MOLASSES
1/2 POUND SPAGHETTI
CONDIMENTS:
  Grated Cheddar cheese
  Chopped onion
  Kidney beans
  Oyster crackers

In a large Dutch oven over medium heat, heat the oil and sauté the onions for 4 to 5 minutes, until the onions begin to turn translucent. Add the garlic and cook 1 minute more. Add the beef and all the seasonings except the bay leaf. Cook until the beef is brown, about 10 minutes. Add the bay leaf, water, tomato sauce, vinegar, and molasses, and simmer, stirring occasionally, for 1 1/2 hours. Add more water as needed so that the chili remains soupy. Fifteen minutes before serving time, throw in the spaghetti. Add more water if needed, as the pasta will soak up some of the liquid. Cook until the pasta is al dente and serve at once.

How to prepare blue cheese dip:

Making blue cheese dip is embarrassingly easy, and people are so impressed with your efforts. You can get decent stuff readymade, but it really isn't as good as homemade. Just take 1 cup mayonnaise, the juice of ½ lemon, and 4 ounces of blue cheese and pulse in the food processor. You can refrigerate the mixture for a few days or serve it at once.

Celery Sticks
and
Blue Cheese Dip

Cincinnati-Style
Chili

Baked Apples
Stuffed with
Golden Raisins

Butter
Cookies

**The unique blend of spices
in this chili begs for dark beers.**

Kaki's White Chicken Chili for Sissies

Our cousin Kaki brought this recipe back from Athens, . . . Georgia, that is, and she takes it to sick friends. Sure made us feel better.

PREPARATION TIME: 15 MINUTES   MAKES 6–8 SERVINGS
COOKING TIME: 40 MINUTES

All the Trimmings

Preset the table with the corn bread, salad, and chili condiments. Invite your guests into the kitchen to eat the quesadillas hot out of the pan. After the appetizer, serve bowls of the chicken chili in the kitchen and invite them to the dining room to add their condiments. Pick up a carrot cake at the bakery.

Make this an hour, a day, or a month ahead. Cover and refrigerate it for up to 3 days. It will freeze for a month. Reheat it by the bowl or panful to boiling on the stovetop or in the microwave.

3 TABLESPOONS OLIVE OIL

1 LARGE ONION, CHOPPED

2–3 CLOVES GARLIC, MINCED

4 (4-OZ.) BONELESS, SKINLESS CHICKEN BREASTS, CUT INTO STRIPS

1 TABLESPOON GROUND CUMIN

1/2 TEASPOON DRIED OREGANO

2 (15-OUNCE) CANS SALTED CHICKEN BROTH

1 1/2 CUPS WATER

2 (15-OUNCE) CANS WHITE BEANS (GREAT NORTHERN OR CANNELLINI), DRAINED AND RINSED

2 (4-OUNCE) CANS MILD GREEN CHILES, DICED

SALT AND FRESHLY GROUND BLACK PEPPER TO TASTE

CONDIMENTS:

Sour cream

Salsa

Diced jalapeño peppers

Chopped cilantro

Heat the oil in a Dutch oven over high heat. Add the onion and garlic and sauté for 2 minutes. Add the chicken, cumin, and the oregano, rubbed between your palms. Cook until the chicken is brown at the edges, about 5 minutes. Add 1 can of the chicken broth and deglaze the pan, scraping up the browned bits on the bottom. Add the beans, green chiles, the remaining broth and water. Simmer for 30 minutes. Add salt and pepper.

Serve in bowls topped with dollops of salsa and sour cream side by side. Garnish with diced jalapeños and chopped cilantro.

How to make a quesadilla:

To cook a quesadilla, heat a black iron skillet until hot (add no oil or butter). If the pan begins to smoke, turn down the heat. Place a corn or flour tortilla on the skillet and cook it for 15 seconds on each side. Repeat this process with a second tortilla. When the second tortilla is done, top it with grated cheese, shredded lettuce, salsa, or whatever you like. Place the first tortilla on top and cook until the cheese melts. Flip the quesadilla and cook it for 15 seconds more. Remove it from the pan, cut it into quarters, and serve.

Quesadillas
with
Cheddar Cheese

Kaki's
White Chicken
Chili for Sissies

Corny
Corn Bread
(page 83)

Iceberg Lettuce
and
Tomato Salad

Carrot Cake

What else? White wine!
This is Chardonnay food. Riesling food.

CHAPTER 7

Soups and Stews Made from Real Red Meat

Tamarind Beef and Bean Stew with Pineapple and Bananas

Traditional Mexican cowboys cook beef and beans with tropical fruits as a way of both enhancing the flavor and tenderizing the meat. Look for tamarind paste in Mexican or Asian markets.

PREPARATION TIME: 20 MINUTES

COOKING TIME: 30 MINUTES IF
   YOU'RE USING A PRESSURE
   COOKER; 2 HOURS ON THE
   STOVETOP

MAKES 10–12 SERVINGS

All the Trimmings

We like to serve this stew from a big earthenware pot. A basket of flour tortillas, a mound of fluffy rice, and we let our guests make up their own bowls. Preset the table with salads, mini cactuses for a centerpiece, and turn on the salsa music. The scent of candles, their golden light, and good friends, that's all it takes to make this meal a celebration.

As with all stews, this tastes even better the second day. Store it covered in the refrigerator and reheat it gently on the stovetop until it bubbles slowly.

1 CUP DRIED PINTO BEANS

5 DRIED CHIPOTLE CHILE PEPPERS

2 POUNDS BEEF STEWING MEAT OR
   BEEF CHUCK, TRIMMED AND
   CUT INTO SMALL CUBES

1/4 CUP ALL-PURPOSE FLOUR

1/2 TEASPOON GROUND CUMIN

1/2 TEASPOON CAYENNE

1 TEASPOON KOSHER SALT

2 TABLESPOONS OLIVE OIL

1 LARGE YELLOW ONION, CHOPPED

1 YELLOW BELL PEPPER, SEEDED
   AND CHOPPED

3 LARGE CARROTS, CHOPPED

6 CLOVES GARLIC, SMASHED

1 QUART BEEF STOCK

1 (20-OUNCE) CAN PINEAPPLE
   CHUNKS WITH THEIR JUICE

2 BANANAS, PEELED AND CHOPPED

1/4 TEASPOON GROUND CINNAMON

1 TABLESPOON TAMARIND PASTE,
   OR 1/2 CUP TAMARIND CHUTNEY

1 CUP LOOSELY PACKED CILANTRO
   LEAVES

SOUR CREAM

Combine the beans and dried peppers in a bowl and cover them with water. Set them aside to soak.

Shake the meat in a bag with the flour, cumin, cayenne, and salt.

Heat the oil in a stockpot or pressure cooker and brown the beef over high heat in batches, then transfer it to a plate. Brown the onion, bell pepper, carrots, and garlic until they're golden, cooking each for a few moments before adding the next, stirring, taking your time. When all the vegetables have browned, pour in a little stock. Loosen up any brown bits from the bottom. Now drain the beans and dried chiles and add them to the pot along with the browned beef and the rest of the stock. Cover, and if using a pressure cooker, bring the pressure to the second red ring over high heat. Adjust the heat to stabilize the pressure and cook for 15 minutes. Alternatively, cook uncovered over medium-low heat in a stew pot until the meat is tender, from 1½ to 2 hours.

Cool to room temperature. If you cooked the meat in a pressure cooker, transfer it to a pot. Fish out the floating dried peppers and combine with 1 cup of the cooking liquid in the blender or food processor and puree. Pour this back into the meat and vegetables and add the pineapple and juice, the bananas, cinnamon, and tamarind. Bring to a simmer and cook for about 15 minutes, adjusting the seasonings with additional salt if needed. Sprinkle the cilantro over all and serve in rimmed soup bowls with a jot of sour cream.

This spicy dish cries out for ice cold beer.

Pickled Okra and Cocktail Onions

Tamarind Beef and Bean Stew with Pineapple and Bananas

Fluffy White Rice

Hot Flour Tortillas

Avocado, Grapefruit, and Pomegranate Seeds on a Bed of Greens with Three-Citrus Vinaigrette (page 25)

Chocolate Cake and Vanilla Bean Ice Cream

Hot Coffee with Cinnamon

Barbara Bradley's
Green Chile Stew with Beef and Pork

Ordering a bowl of green chili stew in the dining room of the La Fonda Hotel in Santa Fe was our first introduction to the "State Dish of New Mexico." Deceptively green and tame looking, the stew is more fiery than most Texas chilies. Our friend Barbara Bradley soon gave us a lesson in her Albuquerque kitchen. She keeps her freezer stocked with green chiles that she roasts herself although grocery stores in New Mexico and Arizona routinely sell frozen roasted green chiles. You can use either fresh chiles that you roast yourself, frozen chiles, or the canned variety and get good results.

All the Trimmings

Because this is an almost pure Pueblo Indian recipe, brought forward and modified by the various invaders to New Mexico, it should be served with the proper respect for its origins. Bring the stew pot straight from the stove to the dining table. Stack soup bowls beside the host, and spoon out a serving for each guest. Pass the hot flour tortillas, butter, and apricot preserves right from the beginning. Have plenty of beer and iced tea on hand—this dish is *hot*. A warm fruit pie from the bakery, topped with a dollop of vanilla ice cream, will finish this meal off nicely.

PREPARATION TIME: 30 MINUTES
COOKING TIME:
    APPROXIMATELY 2 HOURS

MAKES 8–10 SERVINGS

Make this as much as 3 days before serving, cover, and refrigerate, then reheat it on the stovetop over medium heat and serve hot.

1 CUP FRESH OR FROZEN ROASTED GREEN CHILES, CUT INTO STRIPS, OR 3 (7-OUNCE) CANS, DRAINED (SEE NOTE)

1/4 CUP OLIVE OIL

2 POUNDS BEEF STEWING MEAT, CUT INTO CHUNKS

1 POUND PORK STEWING MEAT, CUT INTO CHUNKS

2 CUPS CHOPPED YELLOW ONIONS

1 TEASPOON SUGAR

3 OR MORE JALAPEÑO PEPPERS (TO TASTE), SEEDED AND MINCED

6 CLOVES GARLIC, MINCED

1 TABLESPOON DRIED OREGANO, CRUMBLED

1 QUART DOUBLE-STRENGTH BEEF BROTH (THREE 10 1/2-OUNCE CANS PLUS WATER AS NEEDED)

1 (28-OUNCE) CAN ITALIAN-STYLE PLUM TOMATOES AND THEIR JUICE

2 POUNDS (ABOUT 4) YELLOW FIN POTATOES, PEELED AND CUT INTO 1-INCH CHUNKS

2 TEASPOONS KOSHER SALT, OR TO TASTE

FRESHLY GROUND BLACK PEPPER, TO TASTE

JUICE AND ZEST OF 1 LEMON

6 GREEN ONIONS WITH TOPS, MINCED, FOR GARNISH

SOUR CREAM, FOR GARNISH

In a large Dutch oven, heat 2 tablespoons of the oil over medium-high heat. Lay the meat out on paper towels and pat it dry. Brown the meat in batches, adding more oil as necessary, until all is well browned, 7 to 10 minutes per batch. Transfer the cooked meat to a bowl. Add the remaining oil to the pan and brown the onions, sprinkling them with the sugar, then stir in the chiles, jalapeños, garlic, and oregano and cook, covered, until browned, about 5 minutes. Scrape up any bits from the bottom of the pan and stir in the beef broth a little at a time, deglazing the pan. Add the tomatoes and potatoes, return the meat to the pan, and season with the salt. Bring the stew to a boil, then cover and cook for about 1½ hours, stirring from time to time, until the potatoes and meat are tender and the stew has thickened slightly. Add lemon juice and zest. Adjust the seasonings with additional salt and the pepper and serve immediately sprinkled with the green onions and topped with a dollop of sour cream.

NOTE: If you are starting with fresh green chiles (try a mixture of long greens and poblanos), roast them in a 450°F oven until they're blackened on both sides, then pop them into a paper bag until cool. Rub away and discard the burned skin. Stem and seed them, then cut them into ¼-inch strips and set them aside.

Pico de Gallo
with
Blue Corn Tostadas

Barbara Bradley's
Green Chile Stew
with Beef and Pork

Warmed
Flour Tortillas,
Butter, and Apricot
Preserves

Peach Pie and
Vanilla Ice Cream

Iced Tea

**Try a nice cold lager beer
with this wonderful stew.**

Peppery Italian Beef Stew on Grilled Polenta Rounds

This is simple Italian home cooking. Yes, you need to start the day before, marinating the beef. But the gift of time will reward you. The depth and complexity of this hearty beef dish will warm your heart.

PREPARATION TIME: 30 MINUTES
MARINATING TIME: 6–24 HOURS
COOKING TIME: 2½–3 HOURS,
    UNATTENDED

MAKES 6 SERVINGS

All the Trimmings

Why not pretend you're in a '50s-style Italian restaurant? Red checkered tablecloth, candle stuck in a straw-covered Chianti bottle, Dean Martin music. Preset the table and don't forget the daisies. At each place put a bread plate to the left of the dinner plate at the tip of the dinner fork. Make a ring of extra-virgin olive oil and put a drop of balsamic vinegar in the middle. Heat the bread. Now show people how to tear off a piece of hot bread and dip it into the oil, then the vinegar.

Make this stew as much as 2 days before serving, cover, and refrigerate, then simply reheat to boiling on the stovetop or in the microwave.

2 TABLESPOONS BLACK PEPPERCORNS

2 TABLESPOONS FRESH THYME LEAVES (2 TEASPOONS DRIED)

½ CUP EXTRA-VIRGIN OLIVE OIL, PLUS ADDITIONAL FOR THE POLENTA

3 POUNDS BONELESS BEEF CHUCK ROAST, FAT REMOVED, CUT INTO BITE-SIZE CHUNKS

4 PIECES PANCETTA, FINELY CHOPPED; OR 4 THICK SLICES BACON, CHOPPED

1 LARGE YELLOW ONION, CHOPPED

8 CLOVES GARLIC, SMASHED

4 LARGE ROMA TOMATOES, CUT LENGTHWISE INTO 6 STRIPS

2 BAY LEAVES

2 CUPS BEEF STOCK

2 CUPS CHIANTI OR OTHER DRY RED WINE

1 TABLESPOON BALSAMIC VINEGAR

1 TEASPOON KOSHER SALT, OR TO TASTE

6 THICKLY SLICED POLENTA ROUNDS

FRESH FLAT-LEAF PARSLEY LEAVES, FOR GARNISH

Place the peppercorns in a plastic bag and crush them with the side of a rolling pin or the bottom of a glass. Transfer them to a medium bowl and combine with the thyme leaves and olive oil. Add the meat and stir to mix thoroughly. Cover and refrigerate from 6 hours to overnight.

About 3 hours before serving time, lift the meat from the marinade onto paper towels, and pat it dry. Heat half the remaining marinade in a large stew pot over medium-high heat and brown the meat, in batches, stirring frequently, until it is golden on all sides, 3 to 5 minutes. Transfer the meat to a bowl and reserve.

How to sear meat:

When browning meat, poultry, or fish, you want to make sure you don't steam it. Simply dry the meat between sheets of paper toweling before putting it into the pan. Make sure the pan is preheated until a drop of water jumps off it when flicked onto the surface, and add the oil *after* the pan is preheated. Add the meat to the pan and don't move it for 45 to 60 seconds, so that the surface sears (seals). Now you can turn it. This will seal in the moisture, caramelize the surface, and guarantee a good finished product.

Lower the heat to medium and add the chopped pancetta (or bacon) to the pan. Cook and stir until the fat is rendered, 2 to 3 minutes. Add the onion and cook until it is translucent and beginning to brown, about 5 minutes. Add the garlic and cook about 2 minutes. Now return the beef to the pan, along with tomatoes, bay leaves, remaining marinade, stock, and red wine. Bring the stew to a boil, stirring to mix well, then cover and reduce the heat to medium-low. Cook until the beef is tender, 2 or more hours. During the cooking, add more stock or wine if the stew seems dry.

To serve, discard the bay leaves, stir in the balsamic vinegar, taste, and add salt as needed. Grill the cooked polenta with a bit of olive oil in a hot skillet. Serve the stew on a grilled polenta round in a rimmed soup plate. Garnish with the parsley leaves.

Chianti,
Chianti,
Chianti.

Antipasti:
Italian Peppers,
Thin-Sliced Dry
Salami, Carrot and
Celery Sticks

Mixed
Mediterranean Olives

Peppery Italian Beef Stew
on Grilled Polenta Rounds

Hot Italian Bread with
Extra-Virgin Olive Oil
and Balsamic Vinegar

Mesclun with Three-Citrus
Vinaigrette (page 25)

Spumoni and Cookies

Espresso

Beef Bigos

This dish originated in Eastern Europe, where it went by a variety of names: Bigos, hunter's stew, paprikash. Basically, the idea is that you can cook the meats that are available along with sauerkraut, season it with ever-ready caraway seeds and sweet, hot Hungarian paprika, and you'll have a good stick-to-the-ribs dinner. This dish is very forgiving. Don't have enough beef? Add extra kielbasa. Short of sauerkraut? Cut up an apple or two and cook it right in the pan. Think of this as peasant cooking—made from one pot and meant to feed the masses—and you'll be right on the money. We like to use top-quality sirloin or one of those precooked roasts because it means we can turn this dinner out in an hour or so. If you prefer the flavor of less tender cuts, as, for example, chuck, by all means make this dish anyway: Just give it a couple of hours to simmer away and tenderize the meat. Whatever combination of meats you choose, it makes a great autumn dinner.

PREPARATION TIME: 20 MINUTES   MAKES 10–12 SERVINGS
COOKING TIME: 1 HOUR

All the Trimmings

Preset the table with a tray of celery and baby carrots, cream cheese, and bowls of pickled beets and dill pickles. This is dinner not only from one pot, but served on one plate. It's easy to present all at once. You can even make the dessert the decoration. Make a mountain of crisp, shiny pears and apples in the middle of the table, with wedges of cheese and whole nuts around it.

Make this at your convenience the day you plan to serve, then cover and set it aside until dinnertime. Bring to a boil on the stovetop. The leftovers, covered and refrigerated, may be reheated to sizzling on the stovetop for a lovely lunch the next day.

$1\frac{1}{2}$ OUNCES DRIED WILD
    MUSHROOMS (CEPES, PORCINI,
    CHANTERELLES)

$1\frac{1}{2}$ POUNDS BONELESS BEEF TOP
    SIRLOIN, CUT 1 INCH THICK

4 TABLESPOONS OLIVE OIL

$\frac{1}{2}$ TEASPOON KOSHER SALT

$\frac{1}{2}$ TEASPOON CRACKED
    PEPPERCORNS

3 THICK SLICES BACON, CHOPPED

2 MEDIUM YELLOW ONIONS,
    THINLY SLICED

1 KIELBASA RING
    (ABOUT 1 POUND),
    CUT INTO $\frac{1}{2}$-INCH SLICES

1 (16-OUNCE) PACKAGE
    SAUERKRAUT, THOROUGHLY
    RINSED AND DRAINED

2 TABLESPOONS HUNGARIAN
    SWEET PAPRIKA

2 CUPS BEEF BROTH
    (ONE $14\frac{1}{2}$-OUNCE CAN)

$\frac{1}{4}$ CUP TOMATO PASTE
    (HALF A 6-OUNCE CAN)

1 TABLESPOON CARAWAY SEEDS

$\frac{1}{4}$ TEASPOON CAYENNE, OR TO
    TASTE

2 BAY LEAVES

1 CUP CHOPPED FRESH
    FLAT-LEAF PARSLEY

$\frac{1}{2}$ CUP SOUR CREAM

In a bowl, cover the mushrooms with hot water and set them aside to soak for about 20 minutes. Lift them from the water and chop coarsely. Save the perfumed water.

Trim and discard the fat from the beef. Cut the beef into bite-size chunks and season it with the salt and pepper. Heat 2 table-

How to precook meat:

Old-fashioned recipes for bigos were made with less tender cuts of beef and cooked slowly for a long time. However, if you begin with a tender cut of beef, such as sirloin, you can turn this meal out in about an hour. Just take some care with the meat cookery and you will like it. Because the sirloin is a tender cut, you don't need to do more than brown the outside of each piece. Thoroughly preheat the skillet and the fat. The way to tell if it's the correct temperature is to float a little piece of bread in the fat. It should color up and look golden right away. Now, add the meat, a few pieces at a time, taking care not to overcrowd the skillet, and brown the pieces quickly. Lift them from the hot fat with a slotted spoon and transfer them to a waiting, warmed bowl. Work quickly, keeping the heat up, and you'll soon have the meat all precooked. This is a great technique to learn and one that you can apply to a variety of meats. Try it with venison, chicken cutlets, or pork chops. You'll get equally good results.

spoons of the oil in a large, heavy skillet over medium-high heat, then brown the beef pieces, a few at a time, just until the meat is no longer pink on the outside, 3 to 5 minutes, adding more oil as needed to keep the pan moist. Remove the beef from the pan with a slotted spoon to a warm serving bowl. Cover and set it aside.

Heat the pan over medium-high heat, add the chopped bacon, and cook until most of the fat is rendered, then add the onions and cook for 3 to 4 minutes, until they begin to turn golden. Add the kielbasa and cook for 2 to 3 minutes. Add the sauerkraut, chopped mushrooms, paprika, and about ½ cup of the mushroom soaking water. Bring to a boil, then cook and stir for about 3 minutes. Stir in the broth, another ½ cup of the mushroom soaking water, the tomato paste, caraway seeds, bay leaves, and cayenne. Bring it to a boil, reduce the heat to medium, and simmer for 30 minutes. At this point you may cover and set the stew aside until serving time.

At serving time, add the browned beef chunks, and reheat just until hot. Transfer the mixture to a large serving bowl and serve sprinkled with the parsley. Pass the sour cream separately.

Gewürztraminer
and dark micro-brewed beer.

Crisp
Celery Ribs
and Baby Carrots
with
Flavored Cream Cheese

Beef Bigos

Buttered Noodles

Cold Pickled Beets
and Crisp Dill Pickles

Assorted Black Breads

Selection of Cheeses
with Autumn Fruits:
Pears, Apples,
Pomegranates

German Spiced Beef with Root Vegetables

Think of this as a tuned-up version of corned beef and cabbage. Adding root vegetables and additional spices makes this flavorful mixture of meats and vegetables suitable for company. We cooked this in a pressure cooker first and were happy with the perfumed broth. Not that this is anything new. M.F.K. Fisher was raving about pressure cookers in the '40s. We just found out about them again. Safer, made of stainless steel, we are in love with our Swiss Kuhn Rikon pressure cookers. Instead of taking 3 to 4 hours to make tough brisket tender, the entire meal was ready for the table in 1¼ hours. Cooked in one pan it was no trouble at all.

PREPARATION TIME: 10 MINUTES   MAKES 6–8 SERVINGS

COOK TIME: 1¼ HOURS IN A
   PRESSURE COOKER;
   OR 3–4 HOURS SIMMERED ON
THE STOVETOP

All the Trimmings

Serve this homey meal family style. Preset the table with soup bowls, and spoon hot broth into each one. Pass the black bread and sweet butter. This does exactly what an hors d'oeuvre is supposed to do—it whets the diners' appetites for the hearty dinner to come. After the soup course, pass the soup bowls to the head of the table and remove them, then bring on that steaming platter of meat and vegetables. It's a meal-in-one that requires nothing more than some coleslaw from the deli and a side of pickled peaches from a can. Pick up a pot of mums from the store, light the candles, put on some soft music. This is a dinner that's relaxing for the cook and the guests.

Make this dish at your leisure, cover, and store in the refrigerator. Reheat it to boiling when ready to serve. It will keep up to 3 or 4 days, refrigerated.

1 (3- TO 4-POUND) CORNED BEEF BRISKET WITH SPICES AND PACKAGE JUICES

4 CUPS WATER

1 TEASPOON SALT

1 LARGE ONION, QUARTERED

4 CLOVES, STUCK INTO THE ONION QUARTERS

6 JUNIPER BERRIES

1 TEASPOON WHOLE BLACK PEPPERCORNS

2 BAY LEAVES

2 STALKS CELERY, CUT INTO LARGE PIECES

½ CUP FLAT-LEAF PARSLEY LEAVES

1 SMALL HEAD RED CABBAGE, CORED AND CUT INTO 6 WEDGES

6 FINGERLING YELLOW FINN POTATOES

3 MEDIUM CARROTS, PEELED AND CUT INTO LARGE PIECES

2 PARSNIPS, PEELED AND CUT INTO LARGE PIECES

1 MEDIUM RUTABAGA, PEELED AND QUARTERED

1 MEDIUM TURNIP, PEELED AND QUARTERED

Place the brisket along with juices and spice packet in a large Dutch oven. Do not rinse the meat. Add the water, the clove-studded onion quarters, juniper berries, peppercorns, bay leaves, celery, and parsley.

Bring the water to a boil over high heat. Skim the foam from the surface. Close the lid. If using a pressure cooker, bring the pressure up to the second red ring over high heat and cook for

How to make horseradish sauce:

So many things don't really require a recipe. Take this horseradish sauce, for example. Pick up some creamed horseradish and stir it into equal parts mayonnaise and sour cream. Taste it and add more horseradish if you like the sauce hotter. Sprinkle the top with paprika. Easy, isn't it?

1 hour, stabilizing the pressure by adjusting the heat downward as needed. If you're cooking on the stovetop, cook covered until the meat is tender, 2 to 3 hours.

Remove the pan from the heat and allow the meat to cool. Remove the brisket to a cutting board and set it aside.

Add the remaining ingredients to the pan. Remove broth as needed so that the pan is no more than two thirds full. Close the lid. For a pressure cooker, bring the pressure up to the second red ring and cook for 5 minutes. Cool down before opening the lid. Alternatively, cook the vegetables, covered, in boiling broth until tender, up to 40 minutes.

To serve, cut the brisket across the grain into thin slices and arrange them down the middle of a warm platter. Using a slotted spoon, remove the vegetables from the pan and arrange them around the beef. Spoon a little broth over the meat and vegetables. Serve with horseradish sauce (see above). And don't forget that marvelous broth. We like to serve it as a separate course. It's that delicious. And we pray there's some left over for lunch the next day.

**The German spice mixture
goes with Beck's or another German beer.
Or, try a Germandry or semi-dry Riesling.
We try to get Rieslings from the Mosel region with a
low alcohol content so they don't compete with the food.**

Hot
Spiced Beef Broth

Black Bread
and Sweet Butter

German Spiced Beef
with
Root Vegetables

Horseradish Sauce

Cole Slaw

Pickled Peaches

Apple Pie
and Vanilla
Ice Cream

Pork Paprikash over Rice

This Hungarian-inspired menu says autumn—the richness of the stew and the crisp pears for dessert. All you need is a football game to make a perfect Saturday.

PREPARATION TIME: 20 MINUTES   MAKES 4 SERVINGS
COOKING TIME: ABOUT 30 MINUTES

All the Trimmings

Preset the table with the paprikash served in soup bowls over rice. This is a very rich stew. The lemony salad will help clear the palate after the main course. For added drama, bring the whole pears on a cutting board and the cake with a stack of dessert plates to the table. As your guests are talking, cut the pears into wedges and serve them with a piece of cake to each diner.

This can be made 1 day in advance up to the point of adding the fresh parsley, and rewarmed before serving.

1 POUND PORK TENDERLOIN MEDALLIONS

SALT AND FRESHLY GROUND BLACK PEPPER

2 TABLESPOONS DIJON-STYLE MUSTARD

3 TABLESPOONS PEANUT OIL

6 TABLESPOONS BUTTER, CUT INTO 3 CHUNKS

2 MEDIUM ONIONS, SLICED

4 ITALIAN WAX (FRYING) PEPPERS, SEEDED AND CUT INTO THIN STRIPS

1 STALK CELERY, COARSELY CHOPPED

10 OUNCES MUSHROOMS, SLICED

4 CLOVES GARLIC, CHOPPED

2 LARGE TOMATOES, SEEDED AND CHOPPED

2 TABLESPOONS HUNGARIAN PAPRIKA

1 TEASPOON DRIED THYME, OR 1 TABLESPOON FRESH

$1/8$ TEASPOON CAYENNE, OR TO TASTE

1 CUP BEEF BROTH

$1/3$ CUP RED WINE

JUICE OF 1 LEMON, (ABOUT $1/4$ CUP)

$1/4$ CUP CHOPPED FRESH FLAT-LEAF PARSLEY

3 CUPS COOKED RICE

Salt and pepper the pork tenderloin medallions and place them in a large bowl. Coat each medallion with mustard. Preheat a 12- to 14-inch skillet for 2 minutes. Add 1 tablespoon of the peanut oil and 2 tablespoons of the butter and heat for 1 minute more. Using tongs, place each medallion in the skillet. Cook for 2 minutes and turn to cook for 2 more minutes on the other side. The meat will still be pink inside, but will finish cooking in the stew. Remove the pork from the pan and set it aside in the same bowl you used to coat the medallions with mustard. Don't worry about the brown stuff sticking to the bottom of the pan. It will give your stew deep flavor. The juices from the vegetables will begin to help deglaze the pan.

What to do with pears:

Pears are tricky. Most are eaten under-ripe, and usually the wrong variety is served. For best results, buy either Comice or Bosc, both available only in the fall and winter. These are not the most beautiful varieties, but they are definitely the most flavorful. Buy them at least 3 days before you plan to serve them. Bring them home and place them in a brown paper bag or box in a relatively cool spot. When they become just soft to the touch, they are ready to emerge from the darkness. We slice them with a slicer that both cores them and slices them into 8 sections with one downward motion.

Add 1 more tablespoon of peanut oil and 2 more tablespoons of butter, the onions, peppers, and celery. Sauté for 6 minutes, until the onions are translucent. Remove the vegetables from the pan and add them to the bowl with the meat. Add the remaining tablespoon of peanut oil and the remaining 2 tablespoons of butter, and sauté the mushrooms and garlic for 4 minutes, or until the mushrooms are limp. Stir, scraping up the browned bits from the bottom of the pan. Remove the vegetables and add them to the bowl. Add the tomatoes, paprika, and thyme, and continue to stir, scraping up the browned bits from the bottom of the pan. Add the cayenne, and continue to sauté the tomatoes for 5 minutes more. Add the broth, wine, and all of the ingredients that have been set aside in the bowl. Stir well and cook for 30 minutes more, stirring occasionally. Add the lemon juice and fresh parsley. Serve over rice.

Pork Paprikash
over Rice

Baby Romaine Lettuce
with Lemony
Salad Dressing

French Bread

Pears and
Butter Cake

Earl Gray Tea
with
Milk and Sugar

Try a red Perequita from the Estremadura region of Portugal. These dry red wines will go nicely with the paprika in this dish.

Uzbekistan Lamb Stew
with Cilantro, Dried Fruit, and Pine Nuts

Irena Guloskvy, a wonderfully cultured woman from the former Soviet Union, gave us this recipe. While she is not from Uzbekistan, she explained that the cuisine from this region is one of the most interesting in all of the former Soviet States. Traditionally on the spice trade routes, Uzbekistan combines some Middle Eastern flavors with more Western techniques. An ancient "fusion" cuisine.

PREPARATION TIME: 15 MINUTES   MAKES 4 SERVINGS
COOKING TIME: 1¼ HOURS

All the Trimmings

Family style and nothing else. Present the stew in the pot you cooked in after you've served the hot pita triangles with babaganoush and hummus from the deli in the living room along with the olives and peppers.

Brew the coffee after dinner and serve it with that bakery baklava. Anyone for grappa after dessert?

This dish may be made as much as 2 days ahead up to the point of adding the cilantro and pine nuts.

2 POUNDS LAMB SHOULDER CHOPS, DEBONED AND CUT INTO BITE-SIZE CHUNKS, BONES DISCARDED

2 TABLESPOONS FLOUR

SALT TO TASTE

FRESHLY GROUND BLACK PEPPER TO TASTE

⅓ CUP OLIVE OIL

2 ONIONS, COARSELY CHOPPED

2 CARROTS, COARSELY CHOPPED

4 CLOVES GARLIC, FINELY CHOPPED

1 TABLESPOON TOMATO PASTE

6 BLACK PEPPERCORNS

¾ TEASPOON GROUND CUMIN

1 TEASPOON GROUND CORIANDER

1 TEASPOON PAPRIKA

¼ TEASPOON CAYENNE

2 (14-OUNCE) CANS BEEF BROTH

1 CUP WATER (MORE IF NECESSARY)

2 POTATOES, PEELED AND CUT INTO LARGE CUBES

½ CUP CHOPPED DATES

½ CUP CHOPPED APRICOTS

¼ CUP PINE NUTS

½ CUP FINELY CHOPPED FRESH CILANTRO (RESERVE SOME SPRIGS FOR GARNISH)

Dust the lamb with flour, salt, and pepper. Preheat a Dutch oven for 2 minutes, then add the olive oil. Brown the lamb in the olive oil in 4 small batches, about 3 minutes per batch. Remove each batch to a large bowl as it is done. The lamb will be browned only and will finish cooking in the stew. Add the onions, carrots, garlic, tomato paste, black peppercorns, cumin, coriander, paprika, and cayenne. Sauté on medium until the onions begin to turn translucent, about 5 minutes. Deglaze the pan by adding the beef broth and water, and scraping up the browned bits from the

How to make strong coffee:

Until very recently, the difference between American and European coffee was as profound as the difference between dishwater and a hot fudge sundae. Now, thanks to the influence of Starbucks, Illy, and others, Americans are beginning to get it. Want strong coffee? Start with the best-quality dark roasted beans. Grind them right before making the coffee. Use good, very hot water just at the boil. Mr. Coffee's lukewarm water just doesn't cut it. Katherine prefers a Melitta drip system when there is no espresso machine available. Linda uses a French press, drip, or espresso pot. Start with boiling water, great beans, and the system of choice. Soon you'll have that rich, deep, aromatic, bitter perfume so profound you'll begin to see why the Europeans add the sugar. Great coffee is meant to be bittersweet. Want to silken that? Add hot or foamed milk, and you've got cappuccino.

bottom. Return the lamb to the pan, along with the potatoes, dates, and apricots. Reduce the heat and cook uncovered for 1 hour. Stir occasionally and add more water if the stew becomes too thick. (It can be made 2 days in advance up to this point.) Remove from the heat and toss in the pine nuts and cilantro. Stir and serve at once, garnished with a few whole cilantro sprigs.

Hot
Pita Triangles
with Babaganoush
and Hummus

Olives
and Peperoncini

Uzbekistan
Lamb Stew
with
Cilantro, Dried Fruit,
and Pine Nuts

Baklava

Strong
Coffee

**A Petite Sirah,
with its fruity overtones,
will pick up the dried fruit in this dish
and complement the gaminess of the lamb.**

Lamb and Sweet Potato Curry Stew

Developed by Sylvia Kristal, a great entertainer who knows the value of time, this is a wonderfully aromatic and colorful dish that's ready to eat in 1 hour.

All the Trimmings

Plate service is best for this. Mound the couscous in the middle of a rimmed soup plate, then pour a serving of stew around the edges, like a moat.

The stew may be made up to 24 hours in advance. The couscous is best prepared just before serving.

2 TABLESPOONS PEANUT OIL

2 POUNDS LAMB, CUBED

2 SMALL ONIONS, CHOPPED

4 CARROTS, PEELED AND SLICED

1 GREEN BELL PEPPER,
    SEEDED AND CHOPPED

2 TABLESPOONS GROUND CUMIN

1 TEASPOON CURRY POWDER

1/2 TEASPOON GROUND TURMERIC

4 TOMATOES, CHOPPED

2 SWEET POTATOES,
    PEELED AND CHOPPED

1 (12-OUNCE) CAN
    GARBANZO BEANS

1 (15-OUNCE) CAN
    CHICKEN BROTH

FRESHLY GROUND BLACK PEPPER
    TO TASTE

1 (12-OUNCE) BOX COUSCOUS,
    COOKED ACCORDING TO
    PACKAGE DIRECTIONS

Preheat a large Dutch oven for 1 to 2 minutes. When hot, add the peanut oil and heat for 30 seconds, then add the lamb cubes. Cook the lamb for 5 minutes, just until seared on all sides. The lamb will finish cooking in the stew. Remove the lamb from the Dutch oven and set it aside. Add the onions, carrots, green pepper, cumin, curry, and turmeric and sauté for 5 minutes. Return the lamb to the pan, along with the tomatoes, potatoes, garbanzo beans, and chicken broth. Season with pepper. Cover and simmer for 35 minutes. Serve over the couscous.

How to make a bracing good salad:

The romaine, mint, and parsley salad is a great foil to the lamb and sweet potato curry stew. In the bottom of the salad bowl, make the dressing. That is 2 parts extra-virgin olive oil and 1 part lemon juice with a dash of white wine vinegar, salt, and pepper. Stir well, then add the greens. The ideal mix is 2 parts romaine, 1 part mint leaves, and 1 part flat-leaf parsley. Remove mint and parsley leaves from their woody stems. Place all the greens in the bowl to be tossed just before serving. This can be done several hours in advance. Just before serving, cut a few pieces of pita bread into bite-size triangles, toast, and toss them with the salad.

A dry or semi-dry Riesling is our choice to best complement the curry.

Almonds,
Olives,
Stuffed Grape Leaves

Romaine, Mint,
and Parsley Salad
with
Lemon Vinaigrette
and Pita Triangles

Lamb and
Sweet Potato
Curry Stew

Couscous

Baklava

CHAPTER 8

Seafood and Shellfish Soups and Stews

Fennel and Pernod Shellfish Stew

The subtle, licorice-like flavor of fennel and Pernod complements the sweetness of shellfish in this quick-to-fix stew. Call the neighbors. This is too good *not* to have company.

PREPARATION TIME: 15 MINUTES

COOKING TIME: 30 MINUTES

MAKES 4 SERVINGS

All the Trimmings

Serve the stew in a tureen with the toasted bread in a basket on the side. This ethereal Mediterranean-style stew will pleasantly complement the tasty pâté appetizer and the blockbuster dessert.

1/4 CUP OLIVE OIL

2 CUPS CHOPPED ONIONS

1 BULB FENNEL, CHOPPED

2 TEASPOONS FENNEL SEEDS

2 CLOVES GARLIC, CHOPPED

2 CUPS DRY WHITE WINE

1 (28-OUNCE) CAN PLUM TOMATOES, DRAINED AND CHOPPED; OR 6 PLUM TOMATOES, SEEDED AND CHOPPED

2 TABLESPOONS PERNOD (FRENCH ANISE LIQUOR)

1 DOZEN CLAMS

1 (8-OUNCE) BOTTLE CLAM JUICE

1/2 POUND RAW, SHELLED AND DEVEINED MEDIUM SHRIMP

1/2 POUND SEA SCALLOPS

4 SLICES TOASTED WHITE OR WHEAT COUNTRY BREAD

SPRIGS OF CURLY PARSLEY, FOR GARNISH

In a large Dutch oven, heat the oil over medium-high heat, and sauté the onions, fennel, fennel seed, and garlic for 10 minutes, until the brown caramel coats the bottom of the pan. Add the white wine and deglaze the pan, scraping up the brown bits from the bottom. Boil the wine for 8 minutes, or until it is reduced by half. Stir in the tomatoes and Pernod and simmer for 5 minutes.

Add the clams and the clam juice, and let the mixture return to a boil, and cook for 4 minutes. Add the shrimp and scallops, cook for 3 minutes, and turn off the heat. Serve over toasted bread, preferably country white or wheat, and garnish with sprigs of parsley.

Country Pâté
and
Water Crackers

Mesclun Salad
with Orange Slices

Fennel and Pernod
Shellfish Stew

Toasted
Country Bread

Chocolate Mousse
Cake

**Try an Arneis
from the Piemonte region of Italy.
This grape varietal gives the wine a slightly anise
flavor, which will pick up the anise flavor of the Pernod.**

Shrimp and Ginger Soup

Feel a cold coming on? Whip up this "Chinese penicillin." Hey, why wait for a cold? You'll be doing well to wait for dinner. It's that good.

PREPARATION TIME: 10 MINUTES
COOKING TIME: 10–15 MINUTES

MAKES 4 SERVINGS

All the Trimmings

Pass a big platter of dumplings around the table, followed by the salad. Abundance is the theme with most Chinese dishes. Divide the dipping sauce into small bowls and set one between every 2 people. Stack the soup bowls next to the host. When the salad/dumpling plates have been cleared, have the host serve each guest the soup. When the bowls of soup are dished up by the host and then passed down the table, the aroma will be sublime. Pass the mango and papaya sections and fortune cookies.

1 TABLESPOON PEANUT OIL

1 CLOVE GARLIC, CHOPPED

2 TABLESPOONS CHOPPED FRESH GINGER

20 MEDIUM SHRIMP, SHELLED AND DEVEINED

2 (15-OUNCE) CANS CHICKEN BROTH

2 CUPS WATER

1 POUND ASIAN EGG NOODLES

1 POUND CAKE TOFU, DICED (OPTIONAL)

10 SPINACH LEAVES, STEMS REMOVED

SOY SAUCE TO TASTE

2 GREEN ONIONS WITH TOPS, CHOPPED, FOR GARNISH

Heat the peanut oil in a Dutch oven. Add the garlic and ginger and sauté for 2 minutes. Add the shrimp and sauté just until it turns pink, about 4 minutes. Add the broth, water, and noodles and bring to a boil. Add the tofu and spinach, and cook for 3 minutes more. Add soy sauce and serve with the green onion garnish.

How to prepare Chinese dumplings:

Chinese dumplings, also sometimes called "pot stickers," are easily found in the frozen section of most Asian markets. We once asked our friend Lorraine Leong, who is a fabulous cook, why her dumplings were always so perfect. She shared an old Chinese trick. Bring a medium-sized pot of water to a boil. Add the dumplings, and return to the boil, then add a cup of cold water and bring to a boil once more. Repeat the cold water step twice more, then remove the dumplings. The cold water makes the dumplings tender, but not mushy. For pot stickers, you can *then* fry them in a little salted peanut oil. Or just serve them with a sauce composed of soy sauce, chicken broth, and a dash of rice wine vinegar, garnished with chopped green onions. Dumplings are the perfect comfort food.

Chinese
Dumplings

Mesclun Greens
with Sesame Seeds
and
Sesame Vinaigrette

Shrimp and
Ginger Soup

Mango and Papaya
Sections

Fortune
Cookies

Gewürztraminer,
a spicy, yet fruity wine,
will complement the ginger in the stew.

Oregon Bouillabaisse

Our nurse friend, Eileen, makes this for family and friends. It's healthy. It's easy. It's French by way of Oregon. It goes together in a flash, and is certainly hearty enough to be offered as a main course. We like to serve this in the autumn, when all the ingredients are ripe and in season.

PREPARATION TIME: 15 MINUTES
COOKING TIME: 15–20 MINUTES

MAKES 8 SERVINGS

All the Trimmings

Set the table with brilliant fall leaves, nuts, and berries strewn across the top. Serve the soup from your grandest tureen and don't forget to light the candles. The aroma of burning candles makes even the simplest dinner taste better.

This can be made 1 day ahead, covered, and refrigerated until serving time. Reheat it on the stovetop, or microwave it to just under the boil.

- 1 LARGE SWEET POTATO (OR YAM)
- 2 TABLESPOONS EXTRA-VIRGIN OLIVE OIL
- 2 MEDIUM ONIONS, CHOPPED
- 1 TEASPOON CHOPPED GARLIC
- 3 CUPS CHICKEN BROTH
- 2 CUPS DRY WHITE WINE
- 1 (14½-OUNCE) CAN CHOPPED TOMATOES WITH THEIR JUICE
- ZEST OF ½ ORANGE
- 1 TEASPOON DRIED THYME, CRUSHED
- 1 TEASPOON FENNEL SEEDS
- ¼ TEASPOON SAFFRON

- 1 POUND CODFISH (OR OTHER FIRM, WHITE-FLESHED FISH: HALIBUT, GROUPER, SNAPPER, HADDOCK), CUT INTO BITE-SIZE CHUNKS
- ½ POUND ROCK SHRIMP (OR PEELED, DEVEINED MEDIUM SHRIMP WITH TAILS)
- 24 MUSSELS AND/OR CLAMS IN THEIR SHELLS
- SALT AND FRESHLY GROUND BLACK PEPPER TO TASTE
- 1 LOAF FRENCH BREAD, CUT INTO THICK SLICES AND TOASTED

Cook the sweet potato until tender (5 to 6 minutes) in the microwave on high (100% power) or 20 to 30 minutes in a pot of boiling water. Peel and cut into bite-size pieces.

Meanwhile, in a large stewpot, heat the oil over medium heat, then sauté the onions until they turn translucent, about 5 minutes. Add the garlic and sauté for 2 minutes more. Pour in the chicken broth, wine, tomatoes and juice, orange zest, thyme, fennel, and saffron. Bring to a boil, then add the fish, shrimp, and mussels. Return to a boil, then reduce the heat and simmer, covered, 3 to 5 minutes. Add the sweet potatoes. Season with salt and pepper.

To serve, place a piece of toasted French bread at the bottom of a rimmed soup bowl and ladle the soup over it. Serve at once.

How to make a spinach and bacon salad:

You don't really need a recipe to make a spinach and bacon salad. Place a bagful of washed spinach leaves in a large salad bowl. Now, simply cook a couple of slices of thick bacon until crisp, then crumble it over the spinach. Pour some cider vinegar into the bacon grease and bring it to a boil. Pour this mixture over the spinach leaves and crumbled bacon. Oh, you might need to add a little salt and pepper, but what could be simpler? Toss in some red onion rings if you have them, and croutons if they're around. This is meant to be an ad-lib salad, made from what's on hand.

Pâté Maison
with
Cornichons

Spinach and Bacon
Salad with
Hot Vinaigrette

Oregon Bouillabaisse

Hot French Bread
and
Sweet Butter

French Apple Pie and
Vanilla Ice Cream

Espresso

This spicy, bold-flavored bouillabaisse stands up well to an Oregon Pinot Noir.

Gulf Chowder

This chowder has the Southern distinction of being perked up by a pinch of chili powder and sugar, which make the flavors sing. The soup is made quickly—a nod to hot Southern kitchens and the wish to get in and out of them in a hurry.

PREPARATION TIME: 15 MINUTES   MAKES 6 SERVINGS
COOKING TIME: 15 MINUTES

All the Trimmings

As long as you're paying homage to the South, you might as well cover the table with a checked cloth, serve the iced tea in mason jars, and add a bouquet of yellow daisies in its own mason jar. Southerners might skip the candles—perhaps it's all the light that glows almost year round. You do what you want about the lighting. But keep it friendly. After all, hospitality is the watchword in the South.

Start with the okra and stuffed olives in the living room. Spoon the Gulf chowder into rimmed soup bowls. Pass the corn bread and butter. Buy a great pecan pie from a local bakery or farmers' market. Always whip your own cream.

Best if made and eaten the same day, but it can be made a few hours in advance and stored in the refrigerator, covered until ready to serve. Reheat it on the stovetop to just under the boil.

3 TABLESPOONS EXTRA-VIRGIN OLIVE OIL

1 MEDIUM YELLOW ONION, FINELY CHOPPED

1 STALK CELERY, MINCED

1 TEASPOON CHILI POWDER

1 (16-OUNCE) CAN TOMATOES WITH THEIR JUICE, CHOPPED

3/4 CUP WATER

1 TEASPOON SALT

1 TEASPOON SUGAR

1 TABLESPOON WORCESTERSHIRE SAUCE

1 1/2 POUNDS FILLET OF FIRM-FLESHED FISH (COD, HALIBUT, BLUEFISH, GROUPER, SALMON, SNAPPER, ROCKFISH), CUT INTO BITE-SIZE CHUNKS

1/4 CUP MINCED FRESH FLAT-LEAF PARSLEY

Heat the oil in a heavy soup pot over medium heat. Add the chopped onion, celery, and chili powder. Sauté until the onion is translucent, about 3 to 4 minutes. Stir in the tomatoes and juice, the water, salt, sugar, and Worcestershire sauce, and bring to a rolling boil. Add the fish to the boiling mixture. Reduce the heat and simmer until the fish turns opaque, up to 15 minutes. Sprinkle with the parsley. Transfer to a soup tureen until serving time.

How to cut a canned tomato quickly:

Rather than having tomatoes floating around whole in our soup, we prefer to cut them bite size. The easiest way to cut up canned tomatoes is with a pair of scissors right in the can. Kitchen shears work well, but we find that any scissors are fine. We keep a few pairs in the kitchen to avoid that frustrating moment when a favorite pair goes missing.

Pickled Okra
and
Stuffed Olives

Gulf Chowder

Corny
Corn Bread
(page 83)
and Sweet Butter

Pecan Pie
and
Whipped Cream

Iced Tea

We can't imagine this Gulf Coast classic with anything but ice-cold beer. Haul out the Sam Adams. Okay, we know it's from Boston, but it's one of the best.

Caldo Mariscos y Chipotle

This quickly made fish soup is meant to be eaten at once. Believe us—with the lively flavors of sea bass, smoky chipotles, bitter spinach, and sweet mango all swimming in a punched-up limey broth, you'll wish there were some to eat the next day.

All the Trimmings

Preset the table with the hot tortilla chips, salsa, and guacamole. Set salad plates on the side and a charger or dinner plate to hold the soup bowl. Colorful napkins tied in a knot, candles, some salsa music, and a white-cloth-wrapped basket of hot rolls will make this table complete. Compose the salad on the plates and sprinkle each serving with your favorite vinaigrette. Light the candles. Call the diners to the table. Serve the soup in wide-rimmed soup bowls. The vanilla ice cream with caramel will cool down the spicy main course. Painless entertaining, a party you can put together in less than a half hour.

PREPARATION TIME: 15 MINUTES   MAKES 6 SERVINGS
COOKING TIME: 20 MINUTES

This soup is so quick and easy to make, you won't be able to resist finishing it at once, but should you have some left over, cover and refrigerate it, then reheat it on the stovetop to just under the boil. It will keep no longer than 2 days in the refrigerator.

1/4 CUP OLIVE OIL	2 LARGE PLUM TOMATOES, CUT INTO THIN STRIPS
6 (6-OUNCE) SEA BASS FILLETS WITH SKIN, CUT INTO BIG CHUNKS (SEE NOTES)	1 DRIED CHIPOTLE PEPPER (SEE NOTES)
1/2 TEASPOON KOSHER SALT	1 CUP DRY WHITE WINE
1/2 TEASPOON FRESHLY GROUND BLACK PEPPER	1 CUP CHICKEN BROTH OR CLAM JUICE
1/4 TEASPOON CAYENNE	2 LIMES, 1 CUT INTO 8 WEDGES
1 MEDIUM YELLOW ONION, THINLY SLICED	1 CUP FRESH OR FROZEN SPINACH LEAVES
6 CLOVES GARLIC, THINLY SLICED	1/4 CUP LOOSELY PACKED FRESH CILANTRO LEAVES
1 MEDIUM RIPE MANGO, CHOPPED	

In a 12-inch heavy iron-clad skillet, heat the oil over medium-high heat. Season the fish with the salt and peppers, then sauté it, skin side up, until nicely browned—about 1 minute. Now turn and brown the other side. The fish should be barely opaque throughout; it takes no more than a couple of minutes. Transfer it to a warmed plate, cover, and reserve.

Add the onion to the skillet and cook over medium-high heat until the onion browns, about 4 minutes. Raise the heat to high and add the garlic, mango, tomatoes, and chipotle pepper. Cook until fragrant, about 2 minutes. Add the wine, and cook until reduced by half, about 3 minutes. Add the broth and bring it to a boil. Reduce the heat and simmer for about 2 minutes. Squeeze the juice of 1 lime into the broth and float the lime wedges in the broth along with the reserved fish and the spinach. Cover and cook until the fish is opaque throughout, from 1 to 3 minutes. Taste and adjust the seasonings with salt and pepper. Transfer the fish and vegetables to wide-rimmed soup plates. Distribute the broth evenly among the bowls and serve at once, sprinkled with cilantro leaves.

NOTE: If sea bass is not sold in your market, substitute halibut, cod, or other firm-fleshed, lean, white fish fillets, cut into big chunks.

NOTE: Chipotles are dried, smoked jalapeños and can be purchased as is (Mo Hotta, Mo Betta 1-800-462-3220 or on with World Wide Web at mohotta.com) or canned. If you are desperate to do the recipe today and can't find chipotles, substitute fresh jalapeños, but remember to remove the seeds, unless you are a real chile head. If you want to kick up the flavor, mince the chipotles into the soup. Otherwise, for a more subtly hot, smoky hit, leave the pepper whole.

Hot
Tortilla Chips
with Fresh Salsa
and Guacamole

Caldo Mariscos
y Chipotle

Bolillos (Hot Rolls)
and Sweet Butter

Salad of Jicama
and Tangerines
with Cilantro

Vanilla Ice Cream
with
Hot Caramel
Sauce

The smoky flavored chipotle is well complemented by a Mexican beer such as Dos XX.

Louisiana Swampland Shellfish Gumbo

This is a classic gumbo recipe that we have been using for years. The filé and okra give gumbo its thickness and texture. Your guests will love it.

PREPARATION TIME: 15 MINUTES   MAKES 8 SERVINGS
COOKING TIME: 1½ HOURS

All the Trimmings

Gumbo is best served straight from the stove. You can either set up a buffet in the kitchen or make up plates for your guests. Pass around the Tabasco for those who want a truly fiery Louisiana experience. We suggest the salad be served after the main course to clear the palate. Cajuns love a tart lemon pie for dessert. Find a good one at the bakery.

The gumbo tastes even better the second day. Cover and refrigerate it for up to 3 days, then reheat it on the stovetop until boiling, or by the bowl in a microwave for a minute or so.

¼ CUP VEGETABLE OIL

¼ POUND HAM, DICED

1 POUND OKRA, SLICED

2 LARGE YELLOW ONIONS, CHOPPED

2 STALKS CELERY, CHOPPED

2 CLOVES GARLIC, FINELY CHOPPED

2 TABLESPOONS FLOUR

1 LARGE GREEN BELL PEPPER, SEEDED AND CHOPPED

½ CUP FINELY CHOPPED FRESH FLAT-LEAF PARSLEY

2 BAY LEAVES

1 TABLESPOON FRESH THYME, OR 1 TEASPOON DRIED

1 (8-OUNCE CAN) TOMATO SAUCE

2 QUARTS WATER

1 (15½-OUNCE) CAN TOMATOES WITH THEIR JUICE

4 CHICKEN THIGHS

½ TEASPOON SALT

¼ TEASPOON CAYENNE

1 POUND LUMP CRABMEAT, PICKED OVER FOR SHELLS

2 POUNDS MEDIUM SHRIMP, SHELLED AND DEVEINED

2 PINTS OYSTERS AND THEIR LIQUOR

2 TABLESPOONS GUMBO FILÉ (SEE NOTE)

TABASCO, TO BE ADDED INDIVIDUALLY

8 CUPS COOKED FLUFFY WHITE RICE

In a large stockpot, heat the oil and sauté the ham, okra, onions, celery, and garlic for 5 minutes. Add the flour and continue to cook until the flour turns dark brown, from 5 to 10 minutes. This is the roux. Add the bell pepper, parsley, bay leaves, thyme, tomato sauce, and water, stirring to scrape up the browned bits from the bottom of the pan. Add the tomatoes and juice, the chicken thighs, salt, and cayenne. Cook for 1½ hours over medium-low heat, uncovered. Taste and adjust the seasonings. The gumbo can be made up to this point 3 days in advance. About

How to pick a good fish:

Picking good fish is important for any fish dish. A whole fish should have clear eyes that are not sunken in. The fish should never smell fishy or like ammonia. The sniff test also works with shellfish. There will be a smell of the sea, but not a fishy or briny smell. We always ask the fishmonger to let us smell the fish.

10 minutes before serving, add the crabmeat and shrimp. In the last 5 minutes, add the oysters and their liquor. Add the filé and stir. Serve over fluffy white rice. Let each person add his or her own Tabasco sauce.

NOTE: Gumbo filé is a spice mixture that can be purchased in most major supermarkets.

Crackers
and
Cream Cheese
with
PickaPepper Sauce
(page 43)

Louisiana Swampland
Shellfish Gumbo

Romaine Lettuce Salad
with
Red Wine Vinaigrette

French Bread

Tart
Lemon Pie

**Ice-cold beer
will wash down this fiery
Louisiana classic admirably.**

CHAPTER
9

Poultry in the Pot

Chicken Pot-au-Feu

French farm wives made their reputation with this simple stew that gains its reputation from the excellence of the ingredients as well as technique. The classic version is made with a mixture of beef and veal, but the method can be applied to other good ingredients: fish, pork, or chicken.

We like to use chicken because it reduces the cooking time. And we believe the best way to imitate that good country cook is to start with great vegetables and a fresh kosher chicken, if you can get it. The first day you simmer, then refrigerate the aromatic broth. On the second day, about 1½ hours before you're ready to serve, caramelize the vegetables and add them to the broth one by one, so that nothing is overcooked, and everything is perfect.

All the Trimmings

The ceremony comes at the table, when you bring in the Dutch oven and remove the lid, revealing the hot, perfumed, smoky liquid brimming with chicken; chunks of carrot, celery, and pearl onions; bright green peas; and wedges of pale green cabbage.

It's a family feast you can serve in courses, offering first a bowl of aromatic broth, followed by vegetables and chicken, or you can dish up the whole thing at once and set it before your guests—mysterious, complex, and nourishing as family life.

PREPARATION TIME: 45 MINUTES
TOTAL, DIVIDED BETWEEN 2 DAYS
COOKING TIME: 1 HOUR THE FIRST
DAY; 1 HOUR THE SECOND DAY

MAKES 10–12 SERVINGS

Pray for leftovers! This is one dish that tastes better the second and third time you serve it. Be sure to refrigerate both the broth and the pot-au-feu, covered. You can reheat it in the microwave, and you can—if you like—freeze the leftovers for some dark night when you need a little comfort in a wide-rimmed bowl.

THE BROTH:

- 3 thick bacon slices, coarsely chopped
- 2 quarts water
- 1 (4- to 5-pound) chicken, cut into serving pieces, including back and neck
- 1 leek, thoroughly rinsed and chopped into ½-inch pieces, both white and green parts
- 1 carrot, cut into ½-inch pieces
- 1 stalk celery, cut into ½-inch pieces
- 3 sprigs flat-leaf parsley
- 1 tablespoon black peppercorns
- 1 tablespoon kosher salt

THE POT-AU-FEU:

- 3 tablespoons unsalted butter
- 1 medium onion, finely chopped
- 1 leek, thoroughly rinsed and cut into 2-inch pieces, both white and green parts
- 1 green onion with top, cut into 2-inch pieces
- 1 large carrot, scraped and finely chopped
- 1 turnip, peeled and finely chopped
- 1 rutabaga, peeled and finely chopped
- 1 teaspoon brown sugar
- 2 stalks celery, cut diagonally into thin slices
- 8 shiitake (or brown cremini) mushrooms, quartered
- 1 medium head green cabbage, cored and cut into 8 wedges
- 1 cup fresh or frozen green peas
- 1 cup fresh or frozen peeled pearl onions
- ½ cup finely chopped fresh flat-leaf parsley
- Salt and freshly ground black pepper to taste

To make the broth, in the bottom of a 5-quart Dutch oven over medium heat, sauté the bacon until crisp, about 3 to 5 minutes. Add the remaining broth ingredients. Bring to a boil, cover, and reduce the heat. Simmer for about 40 minutes, or until the chicken is tender. Taste the broth and adjust the seasonings. Cool the chicken in the broth, covered, then strain, discarding the neck and back. Refrigerate the chicken and broth together until the next day.

To make the pot-au-feu, about 1½ hours before serving, melt the butter in a large skillet set over medium heat. Add each vegetable to the pan in the order it's listed, stirring in the sugar after adding the rutabaga to enhance the caramelization and release the natural vegetable sugars. Add the celery and mushrooms last, after the other vegetables have been cooking 15 or 20 minutes.

Meanwhile, lift off and discard the fats collected on top of the chilled broth, then reheat the broth to a simmer over medium heat. Add the cabbage, then the sweated vegetables to the broth and cook for 15 to 20 minutes, adding the peas and onions at the last minute. Just before serving, stir in the chopped parsley and adjust the seasonings with salt and pepper.

Serve the broth first, followed by the chicken and vegetables, or serve it all at once in wide-rimmed soup bowls.

Pâté Forestier
with
Crusty French Bread
and
Thin-Sliced Red Onion

Chicken
Pot-Au-Feu

Small Pots of Coarse Salt,
Various Mustards,
and Gherkins

Chocolate Mousse
Cake

How to make a perfect pot-au-feu:

Good broth is the basis for a great pot-au-feu. Cold water, meat and bones, plus simple vegetables (known as mirepoix), salt, and pepper are all that's required. The bones are vital. Don't toss out the neck and back of the chicken until you've made and strained the broth. They are the literal backbone of a flavorful broth (which differs from a stock in that it is made with bones AND meat).

Since chicken broth is quick to make, chop the vegetables fine to yield the most flavor. After the broth is made, the seasonings adjusted, and the mixture cooled, carefully strain the broth through a chinois or cheese-cloth-lined colander so the broth will be crystal clear. Refrigerate, covered, overnight, then lift off the solid-ified fats from the top before finishing the dish.

Caramelizing vegetables is a French technique guaranteed to yield every ounce of flavor. Instead of just dumping vegetables into liquid, begin by cutting them into small, uniform pieces—we like to use a big chef's knife or Chinese cleaver—then adding them to a large skillet filmed with butter and set over medium heat. Stir and brown them, adding a little sugar to ensure the final result. Take your time here. No rush, you're try-ing to condense the vegetables' flavor by browning their natural sugars and evaporating the water from them before you add them to the stockpot.

The secret to a perfect pot-au-feu is adding the vegetables at the appropriate time so that they are cooked, but not gray, in the final dish. Add the cabbage too soon and it becomes ghastly. Get impatient and toss in the peas before the last minute, and they'll lose their bright green color. Always mince and add the parsley at the very instant before you're ready to serve. The bright, fresh flavor of the herb will brighten the flavor of the whole dish.

This subtly-flavored
French classic is a wonderful
opportunity to show off a fine
French wine. Ask your wine merchant
to recommend his best white
Butlery Chardonnays
or a Burgundy, which is
made from a Chardonnay grape,
or a blend including Chardonnay.

Tortilla Chicken Soup

Viva Mexico! Here is a traditional answer to the Mexican cook's question of how to make one bird feed a family. Naturally, we gringos use only the chicken parts we like best—in our case the thighs. In Mexico, this soup was meant to clean out the pantry and the hen house.

PREPARATION TIME: 15 MINUTES
COOKING TIME: 1 HOUR

MAKES 4 SERVINGS

All the Trimmings

Serve the chips and salsa with a beverage in the living room. Preset the table with the layered mesclun, black bean, and red bell pepper salad. Stack wide-rimmed soup bowls next to the host, and bring the soup to the table in the pot. The host will serve up portions for each guest to garnish individually. Pass the warmed tortillas and the honey butter mixture. Finish this warm, winter meal with a Mexican classic—hot chocolate with cinnamon and cookies.
Don't forget the mariachi music.

3 TABLESPOONS PEANUT OIL

6 CHICKEN THIGHS
(OR BREASTS, IF YOU PREFER)

3 ONIONS, SLICED

1 STALK CELERY, CHOPPED

3 CLOVES GARLIC, CHOPPED

3 (15-OUNCE) CANS
CHICKEN BROTH

1 CUP WATER

1 (28-OUNCE) CAN TOMATOES,
DRAINED AND CUT UP

2 (7-OUNCE) CANS
CHILE PEPPERS

1 CUP FROZEN CORN KERNELS

1 PICKLED JALAPEÑO PEPPER,
SEEDED AND CHOPPED

1 TABLESPOON GROUND CUMIN

2 TABLESPOONS CHILI POWDER

4 CORN TORTILLAS,
CUT INTO TRIANGLES

SOUR CREAM
AND A SPRIG OF CILANTRO,
FOR GARNISH

Preheat a Dutch oven for 2 minutes, then add the peanut oil and heat for 30 seconds more. Add the chicken thighs and sauté for 3 minutes on each side, or until they're golden brown. The thighs will finish cooking in the stew. Remove the thighs from the pan and set them aside in a large bowl.

Add the onions and celery to the hot oil and sauté for 5 minutes, or until the onions are translucent. Add the garlic and cook for 2 minutes more. Deglaze the pan by adding the chicken broth, water, tomatoes, chile peppers, frozen corn, jalapeño pepper, cumin, and chili powder, scraping up any browned bits from the bottom. Simmer for at least 45 minutes. Stir in the tortilla triangles just 5 minutes before serving. Serve in rimmed soup plates with a dollop of sour cream and a sprig of cilantro.

How to complete the menu in a hurry:

For the salad, either make or buy your favorite vinaigrette. Toss the mesclun with a portion of the dressing and arrange a bunch of dressed greens on the plate. In a separate bowl, toss the rinsed black beans, chopped red pepper, and red onion with more vinaigrette. Lay this mixture on top of the greens.

For perfect tortillas, wrap them in damp dish towels or paper towels between 2 dinner plates and microwave on high for 2 minutes. Store them between layers of hot towels between 2 plates. If necessary to reheat, microwave all the cooked tortillas nestled between the plates for 2 minutes just before serving. Serve with a mixture of 2 parts butter combined with 1 part honey.

For dessert, slice oranges (all pith removed) and mangos (peeled) and layer on a large platter. Mix ½ cup of Dubonnet and a pinch of cayenne and drizzle. Cover and let sit. This can be made before dinner and served at room temperature.

Chips
and Salsa

Mesclun Salad
with Black Beans,
Red Bell Pepper, and
Red Onion Vinaigrette

Chicken Tortilla Soup

Warmed Flour Tortillas
with Honey Butter

Sliced Oranges
and Mangoes

Butter Cookies and
Hot Chocolate
with Cinnamon

**There's nothing like
an ice-cold beer to complement
the green chile flavor of this stew.**

Tarragon-Smothered Chicken with Pearl Onions and Mushrooms

The rich, creamy sauce that smothers these chicken pieces tastes so good you may want to eat it with a spoon. Place a generous serving of rustic European bread in the bottom of a rimmed soup plate, then top it with a plump chicken thigh and a generous spoonful of sauce jeweled with pearl onions and mushrooms.

Tarragon is one herb whose flavor you'll remember. Its hint of anise, clover, and pepper pumps up the flavor of the cream sauce. Once Linda planted a stand of French tarragon in her backyard herb garden and got a lifetime supply. The stuff grows like a weed. However, this herb also dries well, and a shot of the dried herb is good in most recipes.

PREPARATION TIME: 25 MINUTES   MAKES 8 SERVINGS
COOKING TIME: 45 MINUTES

All the Trimmings

Country French food is best served family style, the way French farmers do. Place the soup tureen at the head of the table, stack rimmed soup bowls to the left and hot French bread to the right, and ladle the chicken over bread for each diner.

When setting the table, preset the orange slices on salad plates to the left of the dinner plate, drizzle with oil, and sprinkle with capers.

The dish may be made ahead and refrigerated for up to 2 days. Store leftovers covered in the refrigerator. To reheat, zap it in the microwave for a minute or so, or heat it over low heat on the stovetop.

1 TABLESPOON OLIVE OIL

1 TABLESPOON BUTTER

16 CHICKEN THIGHS WITH SKIN AND BONES (ABOUT 4 POUNDS), OR AN EQUAL AMOUNT OF BREASTS, IF YOU PREFER

KOSHER SALT AND FRESHLY GROUND BLACK PEPPER, TO TASTE

2 CUPS SMALL CREMINI MUSHROOMS

1 MEDIUM SHALLOT, MINCED

2 CUPS PEARL ONIONS (FROZEN, PEELED ARE THE EASIEST TO USE)

1½ CUPS HEAVY CREAM

¾ CUP MARSALA WINE

1 TABLESPOON MINCED FRESH TARRAGON LEAVES, OR 1 TEASPOON DRIED

1 LOAF RUSTIC EUROPEAN BREAD, CUT INTO THICK SLICES

In a large Dutch oven over medium-high heat, heat the oil and butter. Season the chicken pieces generously with salt and pepper. Add them to the pan, skin side down, and sauté until they're browned, turning once, about 10 minutes altogether. Remove them to a large, deep bowl.

Pour out all but 2 tablespoons of fat from the skillet. Add the mushrooms and cook until they release their liquid, about 5 minutes. Raise the heat to high and continue cooking until the mushrooms are golden, about 3 minutes; remove them to the bowl with the chicken. Add the shallot and pearl onions to the skillet and cook for about 1 minute. Return the chicken and mushrooms to the skillet, arranging the chicken pieces, skin side up. Pour in the cream and marsala, sprinkle with the tarragon, and bring to a boil. Cover and simmer over low heat for 30 to 40 minutes. (The recipe may be completed ahead to this point, then covered until time to reheat it for dinner.)

Preheat a soup tureen, by pouring hot water into it and letting it heat up. Pour out the water at serving time. Remove the chicken, mushrooms, and onions to the warmed tureen. Cover and set it aside. Thicken the sauce by boiling it down for a few moments, stirring. Season with additional salt and pepper, then pour it over the chicken.

To serve, place a slice of bread in the bottom of a wide-rimmed soup bowl and ladle a portion of chicken over it, being sure each serving gets some of the mushrooms and onions.

Assorted
Oil-Cured
Green and Black
Olives

Orange Slices
with Extra-Virgin
Olive Oil and Capers

Tarragon-Smothered
Chicken with Pearl Onions
and Mushrooms

Hot French Bread

Assorted Bakery Pastries
and Ice Cream

Espresso and a Shot
of Irish Cream
Liqueur

How to select chicken:

Remember the most expensive chicken is still a bargain. Choosing chicken parts instead of a whole chicken ensures that the cooking time will be the same for every piece. Choosing the best chicken available is critical. Out West, we buy Shelton organic chickens—either whole or in parts. In the East, kosher chickens are readily available.

We prefer chicken pieces with both skin and bones. The flavor comes from the bone, and the meat is protected from drying out by the skin. Chickens store their fat in the skin, and if you wish, you can skin the pieces before cooking, but you'll have to be responsible for the loss of flavor. Diners may always remove the chicken skin before eating and place it on the plate beside the bone. That guarantees the best flavor and leaves most of the fat on the plate.

Whatever your choice, buy the best-quality, locally grown chicken you see. Cook it within a day or two of purchase, and don't freeze it. That ruptures the cells and causes the bird to dry out when cooked.

In the East, consumers seem to prefer their chickens to look yellow, so the chicken feed is dyed yellow. In the West, the consumer sees yellow and thinks fat. Westerners seem to like their birds' skin pure white. The truth is, there's not much difference in taste. It's just a matter of choice. But if you move from one part of the country to the other, you can be disconcerted by the difference.

To ensure a plump, juicy bird, you can brine it yourself—as kosher birds are brined before being sold. In a nonreactive bowl (glass or plastic), dissolve ¼ cup kosher salt in a quart of cold water, and place the chicken in the brine. Cover and refrigerate it for 6 hours or overnight. Remove the bird from the brine, rinse it with cold water, and pat it dry with paper towels. Then proceed with the cooking.

A dry French Vouvray,
with its classic herbal note,
or Sauvignon Blanc and its
earthy flavors, will complement
the earthy, herbal flavor of the tarragon.

Jerry Thompson's Costa Rican Tropical Stew

Jerry Thompson retired to Costa Rica for a slower, healthier lifestyle. In his other life, he practically invented Burger King franchising. In his house at 3,000 feet elevation above San José, Jerry has created a paradise. He's never really stopped working. He has chickens, a vegetable garden, and over 300 Bird of Paradise plants. At any one time, he has 20 projects in the works. He never could lose that Midwest farmboy work ethic. This is a recipe he learned from his Costa Rican friends.

All the Trimmings

Start in the living room with the chips and mango-pineapple salsa. Preset the table with large bowls brimming with soup. Don't worry, people will want seconds. Serve the tortillas between 2 plates and 2 damp cloth napkins that have been microwaved to keep the tortillas hot (see page 121). Invite everyone into the kitchen as you sauté the bananas in butter, adding a splash of rum at the end. Get a volunteer to scoop out the ice cream as the bananas come off the skillet!

PREPARATION TIME: 20 MINUTES
COOKING TIME: 1 HOUR

MAKES 6–8 SERVINGS

3 TABLESPOONS OLIVE OIL

4 CLOVES GARLIC, FINELY CHOPPED

1 TEASPOON GROUND CUMIN

1 TEASPOON GROUND GINGER

1 TEASPOON COARSELY GROUND BLACK PEPPER

2½ POUNDS BONELESS, SKINLESS CHICKEN BREASTS, CUT INTO 1-INCH JULIENNE STRIPS

1 GREEN OR RED BELL PEPPER, SEEDED AND JULIENNED

2 (15-OUNCE) CANS CHICKEN BROTH

2 CUPS WATER

½ POUND NEW POTATOES, PEELED AND CUBED

½ POUND CHAYOTE, ENDS SLICED OFF, PEELED AND CUBED (SEE NOTE)

½ POUND YUCCA ROOT, PEELED AND CUBED TO THE SAME SIZE AS THE POTATOES (SEE NOTE)

½ POUND BABY CARROTS, CUT IN HALF LENGTHWISE

2 (6-OUNCE) CANS BUTTON MUSHROOMS, DRAINED

1 (12-OUNCE) CAN GARBANZO BEANS, DRAINED

1 (8-OUNCE) CAN GREEN PEAS

¾ CUP HONEY

1 (18-OUNCE) CAN TOMATO SAUCE

1 (16-OUNCE) CAN PINEAPPLE CHUNKS WITH THEIR JUICE

In a large Dutch oven or stockpot, heat the olive oil and sauté the garlic, cumin, ginger, black pepper, chicken strips, and bell pepper until the chicken is browned, about 5 to 8 minutes. Remove the chicken, pepper, and spices to a bowl.

Add the chicken broth and water to the pan, scraping up any browned bits from the bottom. Then, to make the sauce, add the potatoes, chayote, yucca, baby carrots, button mushrooms, garbanzo beans, peas, honey, and tomato sauce. Simmer for 30 minutes. Return the chicken, spices, and peppers to the pan, add the pineapple chunks and juice, and simmer for 15 minutes more. Serve in large-rimmed soup bowls.

NOTE: Chayote is an ancient Central American squashlike crossover fruit-vegetable. Its roots lie deep in Mayan cuisine, and the odd-shaped green chayote is now a favorite of Latin America and the Caribbean. The flavor is like a peppery cucumber with the texture of an apple. Yucca is a starchy tuber that looks like elephants' knees. Look for both chayote and yucca in Caribbean or Latin markets.

Mango-Pineapple
Salsa and
Plantain Chips

Jerry Thompson's
Costa Rican
Tropical Stew

Flour Tortillas
and Butter

Sautéed Bananas
with Rum
and
Ice Cream

**Do as the
Costa Ricans do—drink beer!**

Beans, Rice, and Posole

Debra Pucci's Super-Quick White Bean and Escarole Soup

If your local market doesn't carry canned beans called cannellini, choose Great Northern or navy beans instead. Our friend Debbi Pucci serves this soup every week, figuring on two 1-pound cans of beans and 1 head of escarole for a 4-serving dinner that's on the table in less than 20 minutes. This is one of those great, forgiving recipes that will blow up to feed the masses, a hearty rich winter soup that is ready to serve quickly and will also stand on a sideboard in a crockpot or soup tureen and wait until you're ready.

Debbi's mother starts with dried beans, of course. Should you wish to start this way, cook up a pound of dried beans in salted water the day before, following package directions, then, just before the party, proceed with the recipe as given.

All the Trimmings

This works well when served from the stove. Make it a complete do-it-yourself dinner. All you need do is set the table, stack the plates and bowls, and stand out of the way. It's placemat and paper napkin food at its best. Heck, we don't even serve the beer in a glass, except by special request.

PREPARATION TIME: 10 MINUTES   MAKES 6 SERVINGS
COOKING TIME: 15 MINUTES

This soup can be made a few hours ahead. It just gets better with time.

¼ CUP EXTRA-VIRGIN OLIVE OIL

4 CLOVES GARLIC, CHOPPED

½ TEASPOON CRUSHED
   RED PEPPER FLAKES,
   OR TO TASTE

3 (1-POUND) CANS
   CANNELLINI BEANS,
   OR 6 CUPS COOKED
   GREAT NORTHERN BEANS
   IN THEIR LIQUID

1 LARGE HEAD ESCAROLE,
   WASHED, DRAINED,
   AND CHOPPED

SALT AND FRESHLY GROUND
   BLACK PEPPER TO TASTE

FRESHLY GRATED
   PARMIGIANO-REGGIANO
   (PARMESAN) CHEESE

Place 2 soup pots on the stove—one filled three quarters full with barely salted water. Bring the water to a boil.

How to cook beans from scratch:

Okay, so you want to cook beans from scratch. In a pot, start by covering the dry beans with cold water by at least an inch. Bring the water to a quick boil over high heat, then turn off the stove, cover, and let the beans stand for an hour or so to quick-soak. Now drain off the water, add fresh water to cover the beans by an inch again, season with a teaspoon or so of salt, maybe a piece of bacon, and let the beans boil gently until they're tender. If you're really in a hurry, skip the quick-soak altogether and just throw everything into the pot at once, boiling gently until the beans are tender. How long this takes depends upon several factors, not the least of which is altitude. The higher you are, the longer it takes. For most of us, hugging the coasts, dry white beans will cook in 2 hours or less. If you live on the high plains or in the mountains, 5,000 feet or more above sea level, you'll need to add a couple of hours or so, and for you, we definitely recommend soaking, even as long as overnight.

Meanwhile, in the other pot, heat the oil and barely brown the garlic over medium heat, about 3 minutes, then toss in the red pepper flakes and stir. Now add all the cooked beans and liquid and bring to a boil.

Drop the escarole into the pot of boiling water and cook until the greens are tender, about 10 minutes. Using a large slotted spoon, scoop the escarole into the bean pot. Stir, then add enough of the escarole cooking water to maintain a thick, soupy consistency (usually 2 to 3 cups). Taste, and adjust the seasonings with salt and pepper.

Transfer the soup to a preheated crockpot or tureen, cover, and place it on the sideboard, or just serve it from the stove. Let diners scoop out individual bowls of soup, and have a bowl of grated Parmesan cheese handy.

A good Chianti, of course.
Ask your wine dealer for a suggestion.

Antipasti:
Pickled Peppers,
Carrot and
Celery Sticks,
Thin-Sliced Pepperoni

Deli Meat and Cheese
Focaccia Sandwiches

Debra Pucci's
Super-Quick
White Bean and
Escarole Soup

Chocolate
Cake

Red Beans and Rice

This Cajun specialty, with its unique blend of spices, defined Cajun cooking before blackened red fish was invented. Any real Cajun will tell you. An old standby comfort food in our house, we even serve it to guests!

PREPARATION TIME: 10 MINUTES

COOKING TIME: 1 HOUR

MAKES 6 SERVINGS

All the Trimmings

After the mint julep course, everyone will dive into the shrimp. Serve each person 4 or 5 shrimp. Better grocery stores sell very good shrimp precooked and shelled. Serve them wedged over the edge of a bowl with a small amount of red cocktail sauce, also available at better grocery stores. Clear the shrimp cocktail bowls and pass the salad, to be served on individual plates. Serve the red beans and rice from the kitchen in rimmed soup bowls.

For dessert, bring the ice cream and a stack of bowls to the table with the bourbon. Let the host prepare each person's serving. This slows dinner down to a nice pace. Pass the pralines for the hard-core Cajuns who still have room.

2 SLICES BACON, CHOPPED

1 POUND ANDOUILLE SAUSAGE, SLICED $\frac{1}{2}$ INCH THICK (OR SUBSTITUTE HOT ITALIAN SAUSAGE)

1 LARGE ONION, CHOPPED

3 STALKS CELERY, CHOPPED

$1\frac{1}{2}$ TEASPOONS DRIED THYME

2 TEASPOONS DRIED OREGANO

$\frac{3}{4}$ TEASPOON GROUND CLOVES

$\frac{3}{4}$ TEASPOON GROUND ALLSPICE

$\frac{3}{4}$ TEASPOON FRESHLY GROUND BLACK PEPPER

4 CLOVES GARLIC, CHOPPED

2 (15-OUNCE) CANS CHICKEN BROTH

4 BAY LEAVES

3 TEASPOONS TABASCO, OR TO TASTE

2 (15-OUNCE) CANS RED KIDNEY BEANS, DRAINED AND RINSED

6 CUPS COOKED FLUFFY WHITE RICE

Preheat a large Dutch oven for 2 minutes. Add the bacon and sausage and sauté on medium-high for 5 minutes. Remove the bacon and sausage from the pan and set them aside. Add the onion, celery, thyme, oregano, cloves, allspice, black pepper, and garlic, and sauté on medium-high for 3 minutes. Return the sausage and bacon to the pan and add the chicken broth, bay leaves, Tabasco, and beans. Simmer uncovered for 45 minutes. Serve over rice.

How to make a mint julep:

A perfect mint julep is made by combining the best-quality bourbon with mint syrup, then serving it in silver julep cups over crushed ice. But don't worry about the silver cups—mint juleps taste great in 10-ounce tumblers.

Start by making the mint syrup: In a saucepan, simmer 2 cups sugar and 1 cup water for about 5 minutes, then combine with 1 cup chopped mint leaves. Cool 15 minutes or so and strain.

For each julep, fill a tumbler with crushed ice, then freeze for 6 hours or so. Remove it from the freezer and pour about ½ cup bourbon and ¼ cup mint syrup over the ice. Stick a sprig of mint and 2 straws into the glass, and retire to the verandah. You do have a verandah, don't you? Rent *The Long Hot Summer* for further instructions. Big Daddy knew how to sip those mint juleps.

This down-home dish cries out for ice-cold beer.

Mint Juleps

Individual
Shrimp Cocktails
with Red Sauce

Red Beans and Rice

Romaine Lettuce
with
Garlic Vinaigrette

Vanilla Ice Cream
with a
Splash of Bourbon
and
Pralines

Spinach and Sugar Snap Risotto with Parmigiano-Reggiano

In Italy, risotto is served in wide-rimmed soup bowls to hold the heat in. Eat around the edges first, then every last bite will still be hot once you get to it. This golden, creamy rice dish with flecks of bright green spinach and whole pea pods, is accented by purple sage, which gives a grassy flavor that plays well against the bitterness of spinach, sweetness of peas, and creamy comfort of perfectly cooked risotto.

PREPARATION TIME:
30 MINUTES TO STIR THE RICE
FROM TIME TO TIME

COOKING TIME:
THE SAME 30 MINUTES
MAKES 4 MAIN-DISH SERVINGS

All the Trimmings

Wouldn't you like to reprise the fifties once in a while? Red-checkered tablecloth, Frank Sinatra, of course. Okay, so you don't want to revisit *all* the aspects of this decade. You can at least stick the breadsticks in a tumbler and set a lone candle on the table.

The risotto may be made early in the day, covered, and held until dinnertime. Store leftovers covered in the refrigerator and reheat them in the microwave in a minute or on the stovetop in 2 or 3.

2 TABLESPOONS OLIVE OIL

1 SMALL ONION,
    FINELY CHOPPED

1/4 TEASPOON SUGAR

1 CLOVE GARLIC, MINCED

3 CUPS SPINACH LEAVES,
    WASHED, DRAINED,
    STEMMED, AND CHOPPED

1 CUP SUGAR PEA PODS
    (OR SNOW PEAS),
    BLOSSOM ENDS SNAPPED OFF

3 TABLESPOONS MINCED FRESH
    SAGE, OR 1 TABLESPOON DRIED

1/2 TEASPOON KOSHER SALT

FRESHLY GROUND BLACK PEPPER,
    TO TASTE

2 TABLESPOONS BUTTER

1 CUP ARBORIO (ITALIAN
    SHORT-GRAIN) RICE

1/4 CUP DRY WHITE WINE

2 1/2 CUPS WARMED
    CHICKEN BROTH

1/2 CUP FRESHLY GRATED
    PARMIGIANO-REGGIANO
    CHEESE

In a 5-quart Dutch oven or a saucepot, heat 1 tablespoon of the olive oil over medium-high heat. Sauté the onion until it's golden, about 5 minutes, adding the sugar to aid the browning. Stir in the garlic, spinach, pea pods, sage, salt, and pepper and sauté until the spinach wilts, a minute or so. Transfer the vegetables to a large warmed serving bowl, cover, and set aside.

Leave the browned bits of onion in the bottom of the pot and add the remaining 1 tablespoon of oil and the butter. Add the rice, cooking and stirring it for 2 to 3 minutes, until the grains begin to look translucent but not brown. Add the wine and deglaze the pan, scraping up any browned bits from the bottom. Reduce the heat to medium-low and cook until all the liquid is absorbed, 2 or 3 minutes. Then add the chicken broth, ½ cup at a time, stirring after each addition until the liquid is absorbed (about 20 minutes total). Once you add the last ½ cup, cover and cook for 5 to 8 minutes, or until the rice is tender but firm. Return the vegetables to the pot and heat thoroughly. The rice should be creamy, tender, and firm. Off the heat, stir in the Parmigiano-Reggiano. Cover and let the risotto stand for 5 minutes, then serve. Or you can adapt this recipe to the microwave risotto method. (See page 78.)

Skewered and
Grilled Scampi

Spinach and
Sugar Snap Risotto
with Parmigiano-Reggiano

Breadsticks

Orange Slices and
Red Pepper Flakes with a
Touch of Balsamic Vinegar
and
Extra-Virgin Olive Oil
on a Bed of Radicchio

Gelato

Espresso

**A dry Vouvray
with its herbal flavors
will complement the
vegetables in this wonderful dish.**

Barbara Bradley's Posole

Christmas Eve wouldn't be Christmas Eve in New Mexico without steaming bowls of posole. It's the kind of one-dish dinner you can make at your leisure, then serve for midnight supper, or whenever it strikes your fancy to dine. The flavors are subtle, smooth, and inspiring. Posole is a dried corn product that's a second cousin to hominy. Both are limed-corn products with the corn kernel's covering removed so that you get springy, pure limed-corn taste in a preserved corn that was meant to keep all winter—long before people had refrigerators, freezers, or even cans. People in the South and the Southwest know how good this is. Yankees may have some trouble with the taste at first. Maybe it is one of those tastes you may have to grow up with to enjoy. But those of you from the South or Southwest will love it.

All the Trimmings

We love casual dinner service for this dish. Stack the plates and bowls near the stove and get out of the way. Pass the grapefruit and pomegranate seeds. The apricots and sweet cream will finish the meal perfectly.

PREPARATION TIME: 30 MINUTES

COOKING TIME: 1 1/2–2 HOURS

MAKES 10 SERVINGS

Make this as much as a week ahead, cover, and refrigerate it, then reheat by the potful on the stovetop, or one-bowl-at-a-time in the microwave to just under the boil.

1 POUND DRIED POSOLE,*
    SOAKED OVERNIGHT; OR 4
    (15-OUNCE) CANS WHITE
    HOMINY, DRAINED

4 TABLESPOONS OLIVE OIL

1 1/2 POUNDS PORK STEWING MEAT

1 1/2 POUNDS BEEF STEWING MEAT

FRESHLY GROUND BLACK PEPPER
    TO TASTE

2 LARGE YELLOW ONIONS,
    FINELY CHOPPED

1 TEASPOON SUGAR

4 GARLIC CLOVES,
    COARSELY CHOPPED

1 TEASPOON GROUND CUMIN

1/2 TEASPOON DRIED OREGANO

1/2 CUP CHOPPED FRESH CILANTRO

1 BAY LEAF

1/2 CUP CHILI POWDER

1 QUART HOT WATER,
    PLUS 1/2 CUP TO MOISTEN CHILI

1 TABLESPOON KOSHER SALT,
    OR TO TASTE

JUICE AND ZEST OF 1 LIME

CONDIMENTS:

    Chopped cilantro

    1 cup sliced radishes

    1 cup chopped green
        onions with tops

    1 cup grated Asadero or
        Cheddar cheese

    1 cup chopped fresh tomato

    1 cup finely
        chopped lettuce

    1 lime, cut into thin wedges

* TO ORDER POSOLE BY MAIL, CALL SANTA FE SCHOOL OF COOKING:
505-983-4511. OR WRITE: 116 W. SAN FRANCISCO STREET, SANTA FE, NM 87501.

How to stew dried apricots:

Nothing could be simpler than stewing dried fruits. Place a package of dried apricots in a medium saucepan and add about 1 cup of water. Sprinkle with a tablespoon or so of sugar, and heat slowly until the fruits plump up, about 10 minutes. If you wish, you may substitute apple juice for the water. Season with a pinch of cinnamon and serve warm, in a little pool of cream.

If you begin with dried posole, soak it overnight, then parboil it in a pot for about 25 minutes, or until it's tender. Drain. If you begin with canned hominy, simply open the cans and drain. Set it aside.

In a large stewpot, heat 2 tablespoons of the oil over medium-high heat. Lay the meat out on paper towels and pat it dry. Season with freshly ground black pepper. Brown the meat in batches until each piece is browned on all sides, about 5 minutes per batch. Transfer the meat to a warm bowl as it browns.

Add the remaining 2 tablespoons of oil to the pan and begin browning the onions, sprinkling them with sugar to hasten the browning. Once the onion is beginning to brown, add the garlic and cook, stirring about 30 seconds. Add the cumin, oregano, cilantro, and bay leaf. Cook and stir for another 2 minutes, then return the meat to the pan. Cook and stir for a couple minutes, then add the posole (or hominy). Cook and stir for a few minutes more.

Make a paste of the ground red chili and about ½ cup of water, then add it to the pot. Cook and stir for about 1 minute, then add the quart of water. Bring to a boil, then reduce to a simmer and cook for about 1 hour, or until the meat is tender. Adjust the seasonings with salt and additional pepper. Add the lime juice and zest and taste again.

Serve the posole directly from the pot with bowls of the various condiments set out for everyone to help themselves.

Beer, and plenty of it.
What else cools off the palate?
Well, there's Riesling,
and iced tea if you must have a choice.

Blue
Corn Chips
and
Green Olives

Barbara Bradley's
Posole

Sliced Grapefruit
Studded with
Pomegranate Seeds

Hot Flour Tortillas
with Butter

Stewed Apricots
with
Sweet Cream

Noodles and Dumplings

Paprika Chicken with Saffron Dumplings

This dressed-up version of a wonderful comfort dish will impress your guests and delight your palate. No need for bread or side vegetables. This meal has it all. The yellow dumplings against the red paprika makes for a smashing presentation. Start with a bottle of dry Spanish Albarino and you could invite the mayor!

PREPARATION TIME: 20 MINUTES   MAKES 4 GENEROUS SERVINGS

COOKING TIME: 1 HOUR

DUMPLING COOKING TIME:
    15 MINUTES

All the Trimmings

Plate service is easy. Preset the table with salad, silver, and glasses. Then, when the diners are seated, bring in rimmed bowls of paprika chicken and dumplings.

The chicken soup part of this dish can be made up to 3 days in advance. The dumplings are best if made just before serving. Store leftovers, covered, in the refrigerator. Reheat them on the stovetop over medium heat until bubbling.

1 TABLESPOON VEGETABLE OIL

10 CHICKEN THIGHS, OR YOU CAN
    USE BREASTS IF YOU PREFER

2 STALKS CELERY, CHOPPED

1 CARROT, CUT INTO
    MATCHSTICK JULIENNE

1 MEDIUM ONION, CHOPPED

2 CLOVES GARLIC,
    FINELY CHOPPED

3 TABLESPOONS PAPRIKA

2 (15¼-OUNCE) CANS
    CHICKEN BROTH

1 CUP WATER

FRESHLY GROUND BLACK PEPPER
    TO TASTE

DUMPLINGS:

⅓ cup milk

½ teaspoon saffron threads

1 cup pastry flour
    or soft-wheat
    all-purpose flour

1½ teaspoons
    baking powder

2 tablespoons vegetable
    shortening or margarine

½ cup finely chopped
    fresh flat-leaf parsley,
    for garnish

In a large Dutch oven, warm the oil over medium heat for 1 minute. Add the chicken thighs, skin side down, and brown for about 5 minutes per side. Remove them from the pan and add the celery, carrot, onion, garlic, and paprika. Cook for 5 minutes, or until the onion is translucent. Add the broth and water, then return the chicken to the pan. Pepper generously. Simmer, covered, for 45 minutes.

Meanwhile, make and refrigerate the dumpling dough. In a mug in the microwave, or on the stove over medium heat, warm the milk and saffron threads for 1 minute. The milk will turn yellow. In a food processor, or using your fingers, process the flour, baking powder, and shortening for 30 seconds. Remove the blade from the bowl and use a wooden spoon to gently mix in the saffron milk. Gather the dough into a ball and flatten it out to a 1-inch-thick disk. Cover it with plastic wrap and refrigerate it until 20 minutes before serving time. Place the dough on a lightly floured surface and use a sharp knife to cut it into 12 rectangular pieces.

Fifteen minutes before serving, slip the dumplings into the simmering soup. Cover and cook *just under the boil.* After about 15 minutes, the dumplings will float to the top, and will be puffed and cooked through. Carefully ladle the soup, 2 thighs, and 3 dumplings into each soup bowl. Garnish each serving with a little chopped parsley.

Try a dry Sauvignon Blanc
to complement the flavor of the paprika and saffron.

Crackers
with Hummus
Garnished
with a Raspberry
and Mint Leaf

Paprika Chicken
with
Saffron Dumplings

Mesclun Salad

Cookies and
Grapes

California Hot Pot

One-pot noodle dishes began in ancient China when cooks prepared everything over small charcoal fires. What you get in this version is a delicate, clear broth with noodles, cabbage, and seafood that yields surprising explosions of taste.

Learn to make this simple preparation and you'll soon be applying the technique to all kinds of ingredients. Don't have seafood? Substitute thin slices of Chinese barbecued pork. Don't have cabbage? Substitute spinach, bok choy, or other flavorful greens. Don't have homemade chicken stock? Start with a big can.

If you've added a crab, remember to offer nutcrackers so your guests can break open the legs and pick out the meat.

PREPARATION TIME: 20 MINUTES   MAKES 6 SERVINGS
COOKING TIME: 45–50 MINUTES

All the Trimmings

Make the soup the centerpiece on the table as well as the centerpiece of the menu. Place the hot pot or soup tureen in the middle and gather the diners around. Serve it in wide-rimmed soup bowls or deep noodle bowls. Chopsticks and ceramic soup spoons add an Asian note.

Make the soup as much as one day ahead, cover, and refrigerate, then reheat gently on the stovetop over medium heat.

2 1/2 (15-OUNCE) CANS CHICKEN BROTH, OR 5 CUPS HOMEMADE STOCK

1/4 POUND DRIED FETTUCCINE, UDON, OR OTHER FLAT NOODLES

1/2 PLUS 1/3 CUP CHINESE RICE WINE, SHIN MIRIN, OR SAKE

3 TABLESPOONS MINCED FRESH GINGER

1 TEASPOON MINCED GARLIC

1 TEASPOON TOASTED SESAME OIL

3/4 POUND FILLET OF FIRM-FLESHED WHITE FISH (COD, HADDOCK, HALIBUT, OR ORANGE ROUGHY), CUT INTO 1-INCH CHUNKS

1 POUND LARGE, PEELED AND DEVEINED SPOT PRAWNS, OR MEDIUM SHRIMP, PEELED AND DEVEINED

1 WHOLE COOKED DUNGENESS CRAB, CLEANED, BACK AND LEGS SEPARATED (OPTIONAL)

1 TABLESPOON PEANUT OIL

4 CLOVES GARLIC, SMASHED AND PEELED

1/2 SMALL NAPA CABBAGE, CUT INTO 2-INCH PIECES

1/2 RED BELL PEPPER, SEEDED AND CUT INTO LARGE CHUNKS

1 TEASPOON SALT, OR TO TASTE

1 CUP SNOW PEA OR SUGAR PEA PODS

2 TABLESPOONS MINCED GREEN ONIONS WITH TOPS

1 TEASPOON TOASTED SESAME SEEDS

MONGOLIAN SAUCE (SEE OPPOSITE)

In a large soup pot or flameproof casserole, bring the broth to a boil. Cook the noodles just until tender, from 5 to 8 minutes, then transfer the noodles and broth to a large bowl to keep warm in a warm oven.

In a large bowl, combine ½ cup of the rice wine, 2 tablespoons of the minced ginger, minced garlic, and the sesame oil. Add the fish, prawns, and crab (if using), turn to coat evenly, and set aside to marinate.

Add the peanut oil to the soup pot over medium-high heat and sauté the smashed garlic, cabbage, remaining ginger, and the pepper until the cabbage begins to wilt, about 2 minutes. Add the remaining ⅓ cup of rice wine, toss, and cover. Steam for about 2 minutes, then strain the reserved broth into the soup pot and bring to a boil. Reserve the noodles. Reduce the heat and simmer gently for about 30 minutes.

Taste and adjust the seasonings with salt. Add the pea pods, and marinated seafood, cover, and cook for about 5 minutes, or until the fish is opaque. Add the reserved noodles and heat through.

Serve from the pot and ladle into individual soup bowls, topping each serving with minced green onions and toasted sesame seeds.

Pass the Mongolian sauce.

Japanese
Rice Crackers
and
Hot Dried
Wasabi Peas

California Hot Pot

Assorted Fresh Fruits:
Melon, Grapes, Mangos,
Papaya, Bananas

Gingersnaps and
Fruit Sorbet

Hot Teas

**We love Rieslings with Asian dishes.
This is no exception. Also try a Chinese or Japanese beer.**

PART III

Vegetables onto the Middle of the Plate

Composed Salads and Vegetables Make a Meal

Baby Spinach and Strawberry Salad with Goat Cheese Disks

Here's a lovely lunch you can't forget. Serve the salad with a loaf of crusty French bread so that diners can spread the cheese on the bread or eat it with the salad, as they wish. A deep green, glistening salad sparked by strawberry hearts and flecked with poppy and sesame seeds as well as almonds, this dish gives you all the good tastes in one: sweet, puckery sour, bitter, and savory. Plus you'll get crunch and great presentation. Not only do we adore this in the summer when local berries are ripe to perfection, we also make it at Christmastime for a red and green entrée when the punched-up dressing cloaks those big cotton strawberries into some semblance of tasting as good as they look. Serve on clear glass plates and top each portion with a perfect whole strawberry.

All the Trimmings

Preset the table with the salad on chilled plates. Serve the gazpacho in balloon wineglasses in the living room or out on the terrace before you call your guests to the table.

PREPARATION TIME: 5 MINUTES   MAKES 6 SERVINGS

Although this salad is best made and eaten at once, you may find, as we do, that the leftovers make a fine supper with a bowl of soup on the side.

1 POUND (6 CUPS) BABY SPINACH LEAVES, WASHED, STEMMED, AND TORN INTO BITE-SIZE PIECES

1 PINT FRESH STRAWBERRIES, HULLED AND CUT IN HALF LENGTHWISE TO MAKE "HEARTS"

6 TABLESPOONS TOASTED SLIVERED ALMONDS

1 (3-OUNCE) LOG OF GOAT CHEESE, CUT INTO THIN DISKS

1 LOAF HOT CRUSTY FRENCH BREAD

How to toast almond slivers and sesame seeds:

An easy way to toast almond slivers and sesame seeds is to place either one in a dry skillet over medium heat. Shake the pan until the nuts or seeds begin to color up, a minute or 2, then transfer them immediately to a cool container. Seeds and nuts can go from toasty to burned very quickly, so watch them, and you'll have the job done quickly and easily. If in doubt, taste. Burned nuts and seeds taste bitter instead of rich and caramelized.

DRESSING:

- ½ cup sugar
- 2 teaspoons minced red onion
- ½ teaspoon sweet Hungarian paprika
- ¼ cup sherry vinegar
- ½ teaspoon kosher salt
- 2 tablespoons toasted sesame seeds
- ½ tablespoon poppy seeds
- ¼ cup extra-virgin olive oil

In a large salad bowl, combine the spinach and strawberry hearts, reserving 6 of the best-looking strawberries for garnish.

To make the dressing, combine all the ingredients in a jar with a tight-fitting lid and shake to mix. Drizzle over the salad and toss, then divide the salad among chilled plates and top each serving with the toasted almonds. Add 3 thin disks of goat cheese to each plate and serve with the French bread.

NOTE: For an impromptu gazpacho, soak 2 or 3 pieces of crustless bread in ice water, then toss into the blender or food processor with a couple of absolutely ripe tomatoes, half a cucumber, and a squeeze of lemon juice. Puree. Taste and add salt and pepper until it seems right. Serve in balloon wine glasses.

This light meal is perfectly complemented by a Brut Rosé, Yalumba from South Australia. This dry, bubbly rosé with its red fruit overtones will complement the strawberries. Besides, there is nothing more fun than icy cold bubblies.

Impromptu Gazpacho (see Note)

Baby Spinach
and
Strawberry Salad
with
Goat Cheese Disks

Hot Crusty
French Bread

Peach Iced Tea
and
Prosecco

Brownies

Bulgur, Tomato, and Feta Salad

For centuries, Middle Eastern cooks have stirred bulgur (a wheat berry that has had the bran removed, then been steamed and dried) with various flavorings—garlic, mint, tomatoes, and green onion. Here we offer a pungent, multicolored salad that adds a little zest to traditional tabbouleh. Cut the vegetables into uniform fine dice for the best taste and appearance.

Zip it up with sweet currants and you'll get little explosions of taste: salty feta, sweet currants, puckery tomatoes, sour-sweet rice vinegar, and hot and spicy mint and basil on a base of nutty bulgur. The flavor notes are heightened further when you serve the salad on a bed of bitter red radicchio.

All the Trimmings

Preset the table with the ham and cantaloupe slices arranged on salad plates and placed at the tip of the fork. Present the main dish salad on a dinner plate.

PREPARATION TIME: 15 MINUTES
MAKES 8 SERVINGS
MARINATING TIME: UP TO 24 HOURS
COOKING TIME: 20 MINUTES

Make this a day ahead and refrigerate it covered. Serve at room temperature.

2 CUPS VEGETABLE BROTH OR WATER

1 TEASPOON SALT, OR TO TASTE

1 CUP COARSELY GROUND BULGUR

ZEST OF 1 LEMON

1/4 CUP DRIED CURRANTS

12 CHERRY TOMATOES, QUARTERED

2 GREEN ONIONS WITH TOPS, MINCED

2 CLOVES GARLIC, MINCED

1/2 CUP MINCED MINT LEAVES

1 TABLESPOON CHOPPED FRESH BASIL

1/4 CUP RICE VINEGAR

1/4 CUP EXTRA-VIRGIN OLIVE OIL

1/2 TEASPOON CRACKED PEPPER, OR TO TASTE

6 OUNCES CRUMBLED FETA CHEESE WITH BASIL AND TOMATO (SEE NOTE)

1 HEAD RADICCHIO, WASHED AND DRIED, LEAVES SEPARATED

In a medium saucepan over high heat, combine the broth and 1/2 teaspoon of the salt and bring to a boil. Stir in the bulgur, reduce the heat, and simmer for 15 to 20 minutes, or until all the liquid is absorbed. Cover and set aside for 10 minutes. Fluff the bulgur with a fork.

Meanwhile, in a large salad bowl, combine the lemon zest, currants, tomatoes, green onions, garlic, mint, and basil. In a small bowl, whisk together the vinegar and oil, then season with the remaining salt and the pepper and toss with the bulgur. Combine the dressed bulgur with the salad ingredients and feta. Cover and refrigerate for up to 24 hours. Serve on a bed of crimson radicchio.

How to prepare bulgur:

Look for bulgur in a box or in the bulk section of a natural food store. Don't confuse it with cracked wheat, which requires longer cooking. Bulgur is sold in a fine grind, as in tabbouleh mixes, or in a medium grind in the bulk section.

To use bulgur in a salad, you need only soak it for a half hour or so, then fluff it up with a fork, or briefly cook it, as we recommend here, to infuse the nutty wheat grain with the essence of the broth.

NOTE: Feta with basil and tomato is available in the cheese section of most supermarkets.

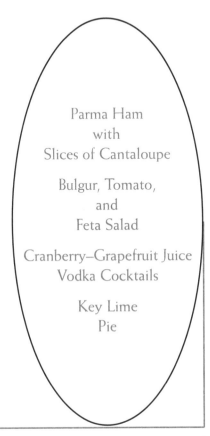

Parma Ham
with
Slices of Cantaloupe

Bulgur, Tomato,
and
Feta Salad

Cranberry–Grapefruit Juice
Vodka Cocktails

Key Lime
Pie

**Try a dry Vouvray.
The slightly acidic flavor of the wine
will go well with the tomatoes and will
cut the salty flavor of the feta.**

Bulgur, Chick-pea, and Tomato Pilaf

The beauty of this grain is that all you have to do is hydrate it and you have a splendid grain base for salads or pilafs. The nutty, chewy taste and golden color of the bulgur are most well-known in tabbouleh (sometimes spelled tabouli), but we like to make this main dish salad that calls for nothing more than pita bread to make a meal.

PREPARATION TIME: 10 MINUTES   COOKING TIME: 5 MINUTES
STANDING TIME: 30 MINUTES   MAKES 6 SERVINGS

All the Trimmings

As if you couldn't tell, it's a picnic. A take-to-the-park make-ahead that requires more time in the market than in the kitchen. Pack everything into your basket, then unfurl a quilt on the grass. Don't forget the wine bottle opener and real glass wine goblets. Zip up a washcloth or two in plastic bags for sticky fingers. And remember to pack some fizzy water and a roll of paper towels.

Make this dish early in the day, then cover and refrigerate. Serve it warm or chilled.

1 CUP BOILING CHICKEN BROTH

1 CUP BULGUR OR CRACKED WHEAT

6 MEDIUM RED OR YELLOW CHERRY TOMATOES, HALVED

6 SMALL GREEN ONIONS WITH TOPS, SLICED DIAGONALLY

1/2 CUP CHOPPED FRESH FLAT-LEAF PARSLEY

1/4 CUP FRESH LEMON JUICE, PLUS ZEST FROM 1/2 LEMON

1/4 CUP EXTRA-VIRGIN OLIVE OIL

1/2 TEASPOON KOSHER SALT

1/2 TEASPOON FRESHLY GROUND BLACK PEPPER

1/2 TEASPOON RED PEPPER FLAKES

1 (15-OUNCE) CAN CHICK-PEAS (GARBANZO BEANS), RINSED AND DRAINED

6 PITA BREAD ROUNDS, HEATED AND CUT INTO WEDGES

In a medium saucepan, heat the broth to boiling then add the bulgur. Cover and set aside for 30 minutes.

Meanwhile, in a salad bowl, combine the tomatoes, green onions, parsley, lemon juice and zest, olive oil, salt, peppers, and chick-peas. Toss to mix, then cover and set aside. Stir in the bulgur and serve warm or chilled, with warmed pita bread wedges.

How to hard-cook eggs:

If you've ever wondered about that annoying gray-green stuff covering hard-boiled egg yolks, the answer lies in the word *boil*. You'll have better results with eggs if you begin them in cold water to cover, bring the water to a gentle boil (plop, plop go the bubbles in the pan), and either cook the eggs for 12 minutes at this temperature, or simply cover them and remove them from the heat for a half hour or so. Cool the eggs under cold running water, drain, then roll them on the counter to loosen the shells. Now we guess you want to know why some egg shells seem infernally stuck to the eggs after they're cooked even when you've done everything right. Usually this results from really fresh eggs. Although there are long, complicated directions for how to prevent or get around the problem, we say just peel away, discard the egg shell—cooked egg white and all— and cover it all up with gravy.

Assorted
Pickles and Relishes

Hard-Cooked Eggs
and Deli Meats:
Ham, Roast Beef, Turkey

Bulgur, Chick-pea,
and Tomato Pilaf

Warmed Pita Bread Wedges

Fresh Fruit of the Season:
Cherries, Peaches,
Nectarines

Selection of Cheeses:
Parmigiano-Reggiano,
Gorgonzola,
Sharp Cheddar

**Try a soft German white wine,
Gewürztraminer or Riesling, with this meal.**

Orecchiette Puttanesca

Yes, this does mean the whore with the little ears, but it also refers to a quicker than greased lightning one-dish dinner you can make in the time it takes to boil pasta. The original puttanesca was developed by Rome's ladies of the night, who not only had to eat and run, but had to make something for themselves that would keep them up and running all night. By further simplifying the process, we've given the dish new life. While the ear-shaped pasta boils, make a cutting board sauce, finally stirring the whole dish together in the cooking pot.

PREPARATION TIME: 15 MINUTES

MAKES 8 SERVINGS

COOKING TIME:

   10 CONCURRENT MINUTES

All the Trimmings

Pasta works well served on a large platter in the middle of the table. Italian food, after all, is a family, kitchen-based cuisine meant for casual dining. Pass the Parmesan, serve the greens on a salad plate, and spoon the gelato into bowls at the table for a wonderful, intimate supper.

This is best if made and served at once. However, you may refrigerate the leftovers, covered, for a terrific lunch the next day.

8 QUARTS WATER

3 TABLESPOONS PLUS $\frac{1}{2}$ TEASPOON SALT, OR TO TASTE

1 POUND DRIED ORECCHIETTE (LITTLE EARS) PASTA

1 TABLESPOON CAPERS

10 KALAMATA OLIVES

$\frac{1}{2}$ CUP EXTRA-VIRGIN OLIVE OIL

3 TABLESPOONS FRESH LEMON JUICE, PLUS ZEST OF 1 LEMON

2 TABLESPOONS ANCHOVY PASTE

4 WHOLE ANCHOVIES

$\frac{1}{2}$ TEASPOON SALT

FRESHLY GROUND BLACK PEPPER TO TASTE

$1\frac{1}{2}$ POUNDS RIPE ROMA TOMATOES

2 TABLESPOONS CHOPPED RED ONION

2 TABLESPOONS CHOPPED FRESH BASIL LEAVES

$\frac{1}{2}$ CUP CHOPPED FRESH FLAT-LEAF PARSLEY

FRESHLY GRATED PARMESAN CHEESE

In a pot, bring the water to a boil, add the 3 tablespoons of salt, and cook the pasta, stirring occasionally, for about 11 minutes, or just until al dente. While the pasta boils, stir together in a small bowl the capers, olives, olive oil, lemon juice and zest, anchovy paste, anchovies, $\frac{1}{2}$ teaspoon of salt or more, to taste, and the pepper. Cover and set the mixture aside to marinate until the pasta is cooked and drained. Drain, and return the pasta to the cooking pot. Stir in the combined ingredients and the chopped vegetables and herbs. Cover and let it stand a few moments until you're ready to serve. Top each rimmed soup bowlful with grated Parmesan.

How to make a cutting board sauce:

Recently, somebody gave Linda a couple of those big (18-×-24-inch) flexible plastic cutting boards. We're finding this to be the perfect tool for making cutting board sauces. Basically, a cutting board sauce is an uncooked mixture of ingredients that are chopped and mixed on a board, using a chef's knife or cleaver to chop, then turning the blade sideways, to scoop the mixture with your hand onto the knife or cleaver blade and transfer the ingredients to a serving bowl. If you have a flexible plastic cutting board, pick it up and form a funnel, then dump the sauce into the pasta. Voilà.

Orecchiette
Puttanesca

Grilled Italian Bread

Bitter Greens and
Sliced Blood Oranges,
with
Three-Citrus Vinaigrette
(page 25)

Hazelnut Biscotti
and Gelato

Espresso

**Try a wonderful Italian Chianti.
Italian wines and Italian foods
always go well together.**

Orecchiette with Wild and Brown Mushrooms in a Balsamic Vinaigrette

In September, when the harvest is abundant and the season turns to autumn, you can make a grand picnic with a huge bowl of little ears and brown mushrooms combined in a dazzling salad with bright red and green lettuces—a bitter, sweet, rich salad that needs only a slice of cold country ham, some corn bread, and a bowlful of fresh peaches and figs for dessert.

PREPARATION TIME: 20 MINUTES

COOKING TIME: 15 MINUTES

CHILLING TIME:

30 MINUTES TO OVERNIGHT

MAKES 6 GENEROUS SERVINGS

All the Trimmings

Bring the beautiful salad to the table untossed. The layers will wow those around the table. Pass a chunk of Parmigiano-Reggiano with a potato peeler or cheese shaver so people can shave off curls of cheese to top their salad. Pass the sliced ham, focaccia, peaches, and figs.

Make the salad as much as 1 day ahead, cover, and refrigerate it in layers, then toss just before serving. This is best served at room temperature.

8 QUARTS WATER

3 TABLESPOONS SALT

1 POUND ORECCHIETTE (LITTLE EARS) PASTA

3 TABLESPOONS OLIVE OIL

3 TABLESPOONS PINE NUTS

6 CLOVES GARLIC, THINLY SLICED

3 CUPS MIXED BROWN AND WILD AUTUMN MUSHROOMS (PORCINI, OYSTER, CHANTERELLE, CEPES), QUARTERED

1 HEAD RADICCHIO, LEAVES WASHED AND DRIED

1 BUNCH ARUGULA, WASHED AND DRIED

1/2 CUP BASIL LEAVES, WASHED AND DRIED

1 CUP FLAT-LEAF PARSLEY LEAVES

1/2 TEASPOON KOSHER SALT

FRESHLY GROUND BLACK PEPPER, OR TO TASTE

2 TABLESPOONS EXTRA-VIRGIN OLIVE OIL

3 TABLESPOONS BALSAMIC VINEGAR, OR TO TASTE

FRESHLY SHAVED PARMIGIANO-REGGIANO CHEESE TO TASTE

In a pot, bring the water to a boil, add the 3 tablespoons of salt, and cook the pasta until al dente, 8 to 10 minutes. Drain, rinse thoroughly in cold water, then drain again and place in the bottom of a large clear glass salad bowl.

Meanwhile, in a skillet, heat the oil. Sauté the pine nuts and garlic over high heat until they're golden, about 2 minutes, then add the mushrooms and toss until the mushrooms begin to color up, about 5 minutes. Toss this mixture with the hot pasta.

Layer the salad greens in the bowl over the pasta-mushroom mixture, beginning with the deep magenta radicchio leaves, then the dark green arugula, the basil, and finally a layer of bright green parsley. Cover and refrigerate from 30 minutes to overnight.

Before serving, toss to mix the salad, adjust the seasonings with kosher salt and freshly ground black pepper. Whisk the oil and vinegar together, sprinkle into the salad, and toss. Top with shavings of Parmigiano-Reggiano.

Try Sangiovese, a fruity red Italian wine that will complement the balsamic vinaigrette.

Sliced
Country Ham

Orecchiette
with
Wild and Brown
Mushrooms in a
Balsamic Vinaigrette

Warm Focaccia

Sweet Peaches
and Figs

Fresh Tomato, Ricotta, and Chopped Basil Salsa Cruda on Penne

This stir-together sauce is great in the summer made with the ripest tomatoes from your garden. The penne pasta is shaped like a quill and holds the sauce quite effectively.

PREPARATION TIME: 10 MINUTES
COOKING TIME: 15 MINUTES

MAKES 4 SERVINGS

All the Trimmings

Start with the olives and breadsticks served informally in the living room. Then move to the dinner table for the pasta course. Because this pasta dish waits for no one, serve the salad after the pasta course. Dessert could be at the table or back in the living room.

8 QUARTS WATER

3 TABLESPOONS SALT

1 POUND PENNE PASTA

3—4 VERY RIPE, LARGE TOMATOES, CHOPPED

1½ CUPS RICOTTA CHEESE

½ RED ONION, FINELY CHOPPED

1 CLOVE GARLIC, FINELY CHOPPED

¼ CUP EXTRA-VIRGIN OLIVE OIL

1 CUP LOOSELY PACKED BASIL LEAVES, STEMS REMOVED, COARSELY CHOPPED (RESERVE SOME WHOLE LEAVES FOR GARNISH)

In a 10-quart pot, bring the water to a brisk boil. Add the salt and stir in the pasta. When the water returns to a boil, begin timing and cook until al dente according to the package directions. Remove and reserve ½ cup of the pasta cooking water. Drain the pasta, but do not rinse it. Return the drained pasta to the pot in which it was cooked. Stir in the reserved cooking water to keep the pasta from sticking to itself. (The pasta will continue to cook and absorb water even after it has been drained.) Stir in the remaining ingredients. Serve warm on warmed dinner plates with a sprig of basil in the center of each plate.

How to select tomatoes:

Summer is the best time to get really fine tomatoes. A good tomato should have some greenish or yellowish marks on it and be bright red. This indicates that it was allowed to ripen mostly on the vine. Perfectly red tomatoes usually come from a greenhouse. The better the tomato, the better this and other dishes turn out. If you are making the dish in a no-tomato season such as early spring, use plum tomatoes. Obviously you will need more. Plum tomatoes are the most dependable for flavor off season. Leave the hothouse tomatoes at the store. They aren't worth it.

Olives
and
Bread Sticks

Fresh Tomato, Ricotta,
and
Chopped Basil Salsa Cruda
on Penne

Romaine Lettuce Salad
with
Lemon Vinaigrette
and
Shavings of Parmesan

Pound Cake
with
Berries

**An earthy Sauvignon Blanc
is the obvious choice for basil.
Or, if you are in the mood for a red wine, try a
Cabernet Franc or a Cabernet Franc blend from
the Lombardy region. We have had good luck with
wines from Guido Berlucchi, a Franciacorta estate.**

Warm Penne and Pistachio Vegetable Salad

This colorful salad can be made any time of year. It is a must-not-miss.

PREPARATION TIME: 15 MINUTES
COOKING TIME: 10 MINUTES

MAKES 4 SERVINGS

All the Trimmings

Serve the sliced apples and cheese in the living room. The cheese is great on tart varieties of apple such as Macoun or Granny Smith. Serve the salad on either a large platter or individual plates. Serve the ice cream at the table and pass the bowls family style. The cookies can go on a pretty plate and be passed as well. This makes for a wonderfully casual dinner.

8 QUARTS WATER

3 TABLESPOONS SALT,
PLUS ADDITIONAL TO TASTE

1 POUND PENNE PASTA

2 MEDIUM CARROTS,
CUT INTO JULIENNE

2 MEDIUM YELLOW SQUASH,
CUT INTO JULIENNE

1 CUP SLICED MUSHROOMS

12 CHERRY TOMATOES, HALVED

4 GREEN ONIONS WITH TOPS,
CUT INTO 1-INCH LENGTHS

3/4 CUP SHELLED AND COARSELY
CHOPPED PISTACHIOS
(RESERVE A HANDFUL OF
WHOLE NUTS FOR GARNISH)

1/2 CUP LOOSELY PACKED
PARSLEY LEAVES

1/4 CUP WHITE WINE VINEGAR

1/2 CUP EXTRA-VIRGIN OLIVE OIL

FRESHLY GROUND BLACK PEPPER
TO TASTE

In a large pasta pot, bring the water to a boil. Add the 3 tablespoons of salt, the penne, and cook for 6 minutes. Add the carrots, squash, and mushrooms to the pot and boil for 2 minutes. Drain and transfer the pasta and cooked vegetables to a bowl along with the cherry tomatoes, green onions, chopped pistachios, parsley leaves, vinegar, olive oil, and salt and pepper to taste. Toss well and garnish with whole pistachios. Serve at once.

How to make marsala ice cream:

In the food processor, combine a quart of best-quality vanilla ice cream and ¾ cup marsala cooking wine. Mix and return to the freezer. The marsala and vanilla are perfect flavor complements. If you'd like to really wow your guests, toss in a cup of just-toasted walnuts before freezing.

A nutty Pouilly-Fumé
is a great choice, as it will
pick up the pistachio flavor.

Sliced
Apples and
Explorateur
or
St. Andre Cheese

Warm Penne
and
Pistachio Vegetable
Salad

Ciabatta Bread

Marsala Ice Cream
and
Butter Cookies

Warm Lima Bean, Mint, and Parsley Salad

This light salad combines the astringent flavors of lemon and mint! Great for summer.

PREPARATION TIME: 10 MINUTES
COOKING TIME: 15–18 MINUTES

MAKES 4 SERVINGS

All the Trimmings

Start with the pita, hummus, and babaganoush in the living room. Serve the lima bean salad on dinner plates preset at the table. Serve the cheese, dried fruits, and nuts on little bread plates set at each place. Finish with baklava, which is available at most Greek or Middle Eastern grocery stores. The honey flavor of the baklava will be the perfect finish to this brightly flavored meal.

1 (1-POUND) BAG FROZEN
   LIMA BEANS

2 STALKS CELERY,
   COARSELY CHOPPED

1 RED BELL PEPPER, SEEDED AND
   COARSELY CHOPPED

1/2 RED ONION, CHOPPED

1 CUP COARSELY CHOPPED
   FRESH MINT LEAVES

1 CUP COARSELY CHOPPED FRESH
   FLAT-LEAF PARSLEY

JUICE OF 1 LEMON

2 TABLESPOONS CIDER VINEGAR

1/4 CUP EXTRA VIRGIN OLIVE OIL

1/2 TEASPOON SALT

FRESHLY GROUND BLACK PEPPER
   TO TASTE

Bring a large pot of water to a boil and cook the lima beans for 15 to 18 minutes. Drain, and combine the beans in a large salad serving bowl with the remaining ingredients. Toss and serve.

How to cook frozen lima beans:

For a salad like this, the beans should not be overcooked. They should still have some substance. That's why we suggest only 15 to 18 minutes of cooking. The beans should not fall apart as they are being tossed. This salad can be served hot or cold.

**We love the taste of a good lager beer with mint.
It just says summer.**

Pita Bread
Hummus
and
Babaganoush

Warm Lima Bean,
Mint, and Parsley Salad

Manchego Cheese

Assortment
of
Dried Fruits
and Nuts

Baklava

Grilled Marinated Chicken and Vegetable Salad with Pine Nuts

This is the essence of summer. The final result depends upon the best farmers' market produce you can find. Cover that grill with balsamic olive oil–bathed summer vegetables and poultry, and soon you'll have a one-dish dinner that you can serve now or later. Ideal for those long summer evenings when people seem to straggle in from outdoor activities happy, ravenous, and tan.

PREPARATION TIME: 30 MINUTES
MARINATING TIME: AT LEAST 1
HOUR UP TO 24 HOURS

COOKING TIME: 15 MINUTES
MAKES 8 SERVINGS

Make as much as 1 day ahead, covering and refrigerating the finished dish, then remove it from the refrigerator about an hour before serving, since the flavors are most intense at room temperature.

MARINADE:

- ½ cup extra-virgin olive oil
- ¼ cup balsamic vinegar
- ½ teaspoon kosher salt, or to taste
- ½ teaspoon cracked peppercorns
- ½ teaspoon red pepper flakes

FOR THE GRILL

- 4 boneless, skinless chicken thighs, or use breasts if you prefer
- 1 large portobello mushroom, thickly sliced
- 1 red bell pepper, seeded and cut into thick wedges
- 1 medium sweet (Walla Walla or Vidalia type) onion, cut into thick wedges
- 1 small zucchini, cut into thick, lengthwise pieces
- 1 small Japanese eggplant, cut into thick, lengthwise pieces
- 1 ear sweet corn, shucked

FOR THE SALAD

- 1 large beefsteak tomato, finely chopped
- 4 cloves garlic, minced
- ½ cup chopped fresh flat-leaf parsley leaves, plus whole sprigs for garnish
- ½ cup chopped fresh basil leaves, plus whole sprigs for garnish
- Salt and freshly ground black pepper, to taste
- 8 cups mixed baby greens
- ½ cup pine nuts

In a bowl, whisk together the marinade ingredients. Divide the mixture between 2 large bowls.

Place the chicken between sheets of wax paper and flatten it with a mallet or rolling pin. Add the chicken to 1 bowl of marinade and turn the pieces to coat all sides. Cover and refrigerate for at least 1 hour.

Place the mushroom, pepper, onion, zucchini, eggplant, and corn in the second bowl of marinade. Cover and set aside for 1 hour.

In a small bowl, combine the chopped tomato, garlic, parsley, and basil. Season with salt and pepper, cover, and set aside.

Preheat a gas or charcoal grill. Grill the chicken, sliced vegetables, and corn on the cob until crisp-tender, 5 to 9 minutes per side. Save the marinade from the vegetables but discard the marinade that held the raw chicken. Remove the chicken and vegetables from the grill after they're done, and transfer them to the large bowl with the vegetable marinade.

When cool, slice the cooked chicken and vegetables into a rough julienne. Cut the corn off the cob. Now mix all the ingredients together: the cooked and julienned meat and vegetables, the reserved marinade, and the tomato-garlic mixture. Cover and set aside until you are ready to eat. If you hold the salad for more than 2 hours, refrigerate it and bring it back to room temperature before eating.

To serve, place the salads in the kitchen and serve restaurant style with small bowls of olives and almonds on the side.

Mixed Olives
and
Toasted
Salted Almonds

Grilled Marinated
Chicken and Vegetable
Salad with Pine Nuts

Hot Pita Bread
and
Sweet Butter

Peach
Cobbler

How to handle and prepare chicken safely:

Food safety when handling chicken is imperative. Since unwanted bacteria are found on uncooked poultry but are killed by heat, you should never save the marinade in which you have soaked raw chicken. Always discard it after you've put the bird on the grill. And while you are marinating chicken, keep it covered and refrigerated.

If you place uncooked poultry on a cutting board, or cut it, take care to wash the board and knives with hot, soapy water before using them again. When you're cooking chicken, take care to get it cooked through. That's why we recommend pounding the chicken pieces to a uniform thickness so that they will cook evenly and quickly over the high heat.

Once the chicken and vegetables are grilled and cut, it's safe to leave them at room temperature for no more than 2 hours, after which they should be covered and refrigerated for maximum safety.

**Chicken always presents
a good opportunity to show off a subtle wine.
Try a nice white Burgundy from the Côte d'Or.**

Clam and Cheese Tortellini Salad

Cooking out of the pantry is easy if you keep canned clams on hand and packages of tortellini in the freezer. If you happen to have made a pass through the fish section of the grocery store, you can make this meal with fresh clams. Cook the clams, and the rest of the directions remain the same.

PREPARATION TIME: 15 MINUTES   CHILLING TIME: 30 MINUTES

COOKING TIME: 10 MINUTES   MAKES 6 SERVINGS

All the Trimmings

The fennel and blood oranges can be served just to the side of the pasta salad. After the main course, peel and chop the peaches. Place them in a dessert bowl, drizzle with marsala, and pass them with the cookies.

Make this salad as much as 1 day ahead, refrigerate covered, and serve chilled.

3 LARGE EGGS

8 QUARTS WATER

3 TABLESPOONS SALT

12 OUNCES FRESH
    CHEESE TORTELLINI

2 (6½-OUNCE) CANS
    MINCED CLAMS, DRAINED

2 STALKS CELERY,
    FINELY CHOPPED

6 GREEN ONIONS WITH TOPS,
    FINELY CHOPPED

1 LARGE RED BELL PEPPER,
    SEEDED AND FINELY CHOPPED

1 HEAD BUTTER LETTUCE

DRESSING:

    Juice and zest of ½ lemon

    2 tablespoons extra-virgin
      olive oil

    ½ teaspoon dried oregano

    ½ teaspoon dried
      crushed sage

    Salt and freshly ground
      black pepper to taste

12 leaves romaine lettuce

Place the eggs in a large sauce pot. Add the cold water and salt, and bring to a boil. Add the tortellini to the same pot and cook al dente, following the package directions, about 3 minutes. Drain. Remove and shell the cooked eggs. Chop the eggs and combine them with the cooked pasta, clams, celery, green onions, and bell pepper in a large salad bowl.

In a small bowl, whisk the dressing ingredients together and pour the dressing over the tortellini mixture. Toss, cover, and chill for up to 1 hour.

To serve, place 2 romaine lettuce leaves on each dinner plate and top with a portion of tortellini.

How to cook pasta:

For every pound of pasta, pick a pot big enough to hold 8 quarts of water with enough space for the pasta to roll around freely. Add salt to the water *after* it comes to a boil. For best flavor, use about 3 tablespoons per pound of dried pasta. Add the pasta all at once to the boiling water and stir hard from the bottom of the pot to prevent the pasta from sticking to itself or the pot. Once the water returns to a boil, begin timing. To determine doneness, scoop up a piece with a slotted spoon. Blow on it so you don't burn your mouth, then bite down on it. You'll soon learn to identify al dente, or firm to the bite. Don't cook the pasta to mush. Finish by draining the pasta into a large colander set in the sink. Keep your head up out of the steam, and use mitts to protect your hands. Rinse pasta only if you plan to use it in a salad.

Clam
and Cheese
Tortellini Salad

Grilled Italian Bread

Fennel and
Blood Orange Slices
Drizzled with
Extra-Virgin Olive Oil

Peaches with Marsala
and
Butter Cookies

Espresso

Shellfish is best served with dry wines.
New Zealand Sauvignon Blanc is excellent.

Crab with Vegetable Confetti Salad and a Lemon-Mustard Vinaigrette

This light vegetable salad is colorful and satisfying. Buy fresh crabmeat the day you're making the salad and check the pull-date. Crab is precious, and fragile.

All the Trimmings

Preset the table with ice cold gazpacho (bought, if possible). Serve the salad from a large platter in the middle of the table. Pass the bread and butter. A bakery vanilla pudding cake with fresh whipped cream is a great ending, and mints clean the palate after this fine summer meal.

PREPARATION TIME: 15 MINUTES
COOKING TIME: 10 MINUTES

MAKES 6 SERVINGS

4 QUARTS WATER

3 TABLESPOONS SUGAR

VINAIGRETTE:

    ¼ cup white wine vinegar

    Juice of 1 lemon

    ¼ cup extra-virgin olive oil

    1 teaspoon seeded mustard

    ½ teaspoon sugar

    Salt and freshly ground
      black pepper to taste

1 CUP GREEN BEANS

1 CUP YELLOW WAX BEANS

12 BABY CARROTS, JULIENNED

1 MEDIUM ZUCCHINI,
    PEELED AND JULIENNED

1 MEDIUM YELLOW
    SQUASH, JULIENNED

1 MEDIUM RED BELL PEPPER,
    SEEDED AND JULIENNED

2 STALKS CELERY, CHOPPED

½ RED ONION, CHOPPED

2 HEADS BOSTON LETTUCE,
    TORN INTO BITE-SIZE PIECES

1 POUND COOKED CRAB MEAT,
    PICKED OVER

PAPRIKA, FOR GARNISH

In a large pot, bring the water and sugar to a rolling boil.

Meanwhile, in a large salad bowl, combine the dressing ingredients.

When the water is boiling, throw in the green beans, yellow wax beans, carrots, zucchini, and yellow squash. When the water almost returns to a boil, drain the vegetables and refresh them under running cold water. Add the blanched vegetables to the bowl with the salad dressing and add the red bell pepper, celery, red onion, and lettuce. Toss thoroughly. Arrange on a platter and top with the cooked crab. Garnish with a little paprika.

How to blanch vegetables:

Blanching vegetables in water with a little sugar is a wonderful trick for a salad like this. Not only does it soften the vegetables, it brings out the natural sugars, which act in opposition to the lemony dressing. It is important not to overcook them. Watch closely after you put the vegetables in the water. When you see the first bubbles, remove the vegetables. A cold water bath helps stop the cooking and set the glorious color. Some cooks even plunge the vegetables into a sink full of ice water.

Gazpacho

Crab
with a Vegetable
Confetti Salad
and Lemon-Mustard
Vinaigrette

Crusty French Bread
and Butter

Vanilla Pudding Cake
with
Fresh Whipped Cream

Chocolate
Mints

Using the shellfish-with-dry-white-wine rule, we recommend an Albarino from the Galician region of Spain. The vines for this grape are grown on the sea cliffs and you can almost smell the saltwater spray in the wine. Perfect for a crab salad.

Poached Salmon and Carrot Salad
with a Blueberry Vinaigrette

The flavors of carrots, salmon, and blueberry vinaigrette make a perfect blend.

All the Trimmings

This meal can be served either on individual plates or on a large platter, with the 4 salmon steaks in the middle surrounded by the ring of carrots. For the bread and cheese course, provide a bread plate or saucer. Of course, buy a beautiful fruit tart from a great bakery.

PREPARATION TIME: 10 MINUTES
COOKING TIME: 10 MINUTES

MAKES 4 SERVINGS

6 CUPS WATER

3 TABLESPOONS CIDER VINEGAR

1 POUND CARROTS, PEELED AND JULIENNED

4 SALMON STEAKS

1/3 CUP EXTRA-VIRGIN OLIVE OIL

1/4 CUP BLUEBERRY VINEGAR

1/2 CUP FINELY CHOPPED FRESH FLAT-LEAF PARSLEY

2 TEASPOONS BLUEBERRY JAM

1/2 TEASPOON SALT

FRESHLY GROUND BLACK PEPPER TO TASTE

4 CUPS BABY GREENS

In a 12-inch skillet or flameproof gratin pan, combine the water and cider vinegar. Bring to a boil over high heat and place the carrots in the water. Boil for 5 minutes, or just until the carrots are blanched. Remove them from the water and set aside. Reduce the heat to medium and gently place the salmon steaks in the pan. Simmer on medium-low for 5 minutes. Carefully remove the salmon from the water and set them on a plate to cool for about 5 minutes. Cover and refrigerate until ready to serve.

In the bottom of a salad bowl, whisk together the olive oil, blueberry vinegar, parsley, blueberry jam, salt, and pepper. Taste and adjust the seasoning.

Toss the lettuce with the blueberry vinaigrette and divide it equally among 4 dinner plates. Top with the salmon steaks and surround the steaks with the poached carrots. The carrots and salmon may be served warm or cold on top of the greens. Serve immediately.

How to select and prepare salmon:

Poaching salmon is one of the finest ways to cook this rich and beautiful fish. Salmon in general will be moister and tastier when cooked over low, controlled heat. When buying salmon, or any fish, always look for one that is not grown on a farm. Beware of inexpensive Atlantic salmon or Alaskan Pink. It is often farmed and quite fishy. As with all fish, a good fishmonger will let you smell it. If it smells really fishy or ammonia-like, do not buy it. Good, fresh fish will never smell fishy.

Dry Salami
and Mustard
with
Baguette Slices

Poached Salmon
and Carrot Salad
with a
Blueberry Vinaigrette

Cheese Course
and
Dark Walnut
Raisin Bread

Fruit Tart

Try a nice buttery, non-oaked Chardonnay to complement the rich flavor of the salmon. Or, if you are in the mood for a red wine, try a Pinot Noir.

Skewered Tomatoes and Shrimp with Roasted Red Peppers and Corn Salad on a Bed of Mesclun

This warm salad is a cold knockout. The flavors of Boursin cheese and shrimp are natural together.

PREPARATION TIME: 20 MINUTES
COOKING TIME: 4 MINUTES

MAKES 4 SERVINGS

All the Trimmings

Set up your guests' palates with the tart olives—a great beginning to this rich salad. End with a simple bowl of coffee ice cream and a few cookies. This is a great summer meal.

VINAIGRETTE:

- ¼ cup cider vinegar
- 1 clove garlic, minced
- 2 teaspoons sugar
- ½ teaspoon mustard
- ¼ teaspoon dried oregano
- ¼ teaspoon dried basil
- ½ teaspoon salt
- ½ teaspoon freshly ground black pepper
- ¾ cup olive oil

SALAD:

- 1½ cups frozen corn kernels
- 1 (16-ounce) jar roasted red peppers
- ¼–½ red onion, finely chopped
- 1 pound raw shrimp, peeled and deveined
- 10 cherry tomatoes, halved
- 4 cups mesclun
- 4 (¼-inch-thick) slices Herbed Boursin cheese (see Note)

Preheat the grill. In a large bowl, toss together the cider vinegar, garlic, sugar, mustard, oregano, basil, salt, and pepper. Stirring constantly with a whisk, dribble in a very slow stream of olive oil. Remove some of the vinaigrette and set it aside to paint on the shrimp and tomatoes. Toss in the frozen corn, roasted red peppers, and red onion with the remaining dressing.

On metal skewers (we figure 2 skewers per person), alternate the shrimp and cherry tomato halves, making sure the cut side of the tomatoes are all facing the same direction. Brush the shrimp and tomatoes with the reserved vinaigrette.

Arrange the mesclun on 4 individual plates. In the center of each plate, mound a portion of the corn and red pepper mixture. Top each with a slice of Boursin cheese.

Place the shrimp and tomato skewers on the preheated grill turned to medium-low. Cook for 1½ to 2 minutes per side. Do not overcook or you will have shrimp leather. Arrange 2 skewers

How to roast red peppers:

We buy roasted red peppers fresh in the deli section of the grocery store. They seem much better than the ones in a jar. If you feel ambitious, roast them yourself for the very best. Preheat the oven to 450°F. Place the peppers on a baking sheet and roast until the skins blacken, turning them a time or two, about 20 minutes. Pop the peppers into a paper bag to steam for a few minutes, then rub off the skins between your fingers. Cut the peppers into slivers. Cover and refrigerate or freeze until ready to use.

across each plate. The cheese will melt slightly. Serve at once. This meal waits for no one.

NOTE: Boursin is a brand of herbed French cream cheese. Most stores with a gourmet section carry it. You can substitute an herbed or vegetable American cream cheese, but the texture is not as good.

Kalamata
Olives

Skewered Tomatoes
and Shrimp
with
Roasted Red Peppers
and Corn Salad
on a Bed of Mesclun

Ciabatta
and/or Focaccia Bread

Coffee Ice Cream
with
Chocolate Syrup
and
Cookies

Try a nice buttery Chardonnay, non-oaked, of course. The buttery flavor of the Chardonnay will work well with the cheese and the rich, sweet flavor of the shrimp.

Bay Shrimp, Tomato, and Basil Salad

Here's a peppy, pungent, puckery, sweet-sour salad that tastes best made with shrimp that have never been frozen. If you can't buy fresh bay shrimp, choose small, fresh cooked shrimp. Rock shrimp are also lovely in this dish.

PREPARATION TIME: 20 MINUTES   MAKES 6–8 GENEROUS SERVINGS
COOKING TIME: 10 MINUTES

All the Trimmings

Arrange the shrimp salad on a platter. Pass around the baguette. End with the berries. This light dinner will satisfy even the hungriest guest.

Make this as much as one day ahead, then cover, refrigerate, and serve it cold.

1 POUND COOKED BAY SHRIMP

8 QUARTS WATER

3 TABLESPOONS SALT

1/2 POUND SMALL PASTA SHELLS

4 LARGE ROMA TOMATOES

1/2 GREEN BELL PEPPER, SEEDED

2 SMALL SHALLOTS, PEELED

1 CLOVE GARLIC, PEELED

1/4 CUP FRESH BASIL LEAVES

1/4 CUP EXTRA-VIRGIN OLIVE OIL

JUICE OF 1 LEMON

1/2 TEASPOON KOSHER SALT, OR TO TASTE

1/2 TEASPOON FRESHLY GROUND BLACK PEPPER, OR TO TASTE

1 HEAD BUTTER LETTUCE, WASHED AND SPUN DRY

Place the shrimp in the bottom of a large salad bowl.

Bring the water to a boil, add the 3 tablespoons of salt, and cook the pasta until al dente, stirring frequently.

Meanwhile, in a food processor fitted with the steel blade, combine the tomatoes with the pepper, shallots, garlic, and basil. Pulse 5 or 6 times to reduce to a rough puree. (Alternatively, finely chop the vegetables on a cutting board.) Add the tomato mixture to the salad bowl with the shrimp, then add the cooked and rinsed pasta, stir in the olive oil and lemon juice, and season with kosher salt and the pepper. Cover and refrigerate 30 minutes or up to 24 hours. Serve on a bed of butter lettuce.

How to choose and cook salad pasta:

Choosing and cooking pasta for salads is simple. First of all, choose only imported Italian pastas made from durum wheat. Dried pastas seem less delicate than fresh and are likely to stand up better in a salad. No need to get stingy here. Even the most expensive, imported pastas are a bargain.

Bring 8 quarts water to a rolling boil, then throw in 3 tablespoons salt (water comes to a boil quicker without the salt). Now throw in the pasta all at once and cook it just until *al dente*, "to the bite," stirring a time or two to prevent sticking. For salads, rinse it in a colander under cold, running water until the pasta is cold. Now, the pasta won't stick together and can be combined with other salad ingredients and served later.

Okay, so you still don't have the faintest idea what "al dente" (firm but tender) means. Spear a piece of pasta from the water after a couple of minutes and cut it in two. Look at the cut piece. You'll notice the center of the pasta still looks white and hard. Keep cooking and cutting. The moment the pasta is cooked through it will no longer have anything but the faintest white core. Take a bite. Now you'll notice it's kind of springy in the mouth. Whisk it off the heat and into the colander before it overcooks and becomes mushy.

Grissini
and Slivered
Pepper Cheese

Bay Shrimp,
Tomato, and
Basil Salad

Crusty Baguette

Mixed Berries
and Peaches
Drizzled with Honey
and Lemon Juice

Iced
Cappuccino

**Basil and shrimp call
for a Vouvray from the Loire valley.
The herbal note to this dry wine will
nicely complement the flavors of this salad.**

Artichokes, Capers, Olives, Lemon Zest, and Italian Tuna on Pasta Shells

In Italy a no-cook pasta sauce is known as salsa cruda, and makes a wonderful one-dish dinner. In this version, the combination of artichokes, olives, capers, and lemon zest is not only beautiful, but bold in flavor.

All the Trimmings

Start with the slivers of fennel and celery in the living room. Serve this sumptuous pasta dish family style, either on a large platter or in a bowl. The bread plates can double for the cheese course. End with biscotti and amaretto in the backyard or in the living room.

PREPARATION TIME: 10 MINUTES
COOKING TIME: 15 MINUTES

MAKES 4 SERVINGS

8 QUARTS WATER

3 TABLESPOONS SALT

1 POUND SMALL PASTA SHELLS

SALSA CRUDA:

　1 (6-ounce) jar artichoke hearts, drained

　¼ cup drained and rinsed capers

　½ cup pitted and chopped Kalamata olives

Juice and zest of 1 lemon

2 (6½-ounce) cans imported Italian tuna in olive oil, drained

½ cup extra-virgin olive oil

Freshly ground black pepper to taste

½ cup chopped fresh flat-leaf parsley leaves

In a 10-quart pot, bring the water to a brisk boil. Add salt and stir in the pasta shells. When the water returns to a boil, begin timing and cook al dente according to the package directions. Reserve ½ cup of the pasta cooking water. Drain the pasta, but do not rinse. Transfer the shells to a large serving bowl. Stir in the reserved pasta water to keep the pasta from sticking to itself. Pasta continues to cook and absorb water even when it has been drained. Add in the salsa cruda ingredients and toss. Garnish with the chopped parsley leaves.

What's a Kalamata Olive?

These medium-size, purply-black Greek olives are oblong in shape and have pointy ends. They've been cured in vinegar and brined. You'll find them sold in bulk or in jars, and in restaurants in "Greek" salads with feta. Can't find them? Substitute other black, ripe olives. *Nicoise* olives, tiny, brown-and purply-colored, make a good substitute. *Piquees*, those shriveled black olives you see that have been salted to draw out the juices, also work well. If you shop in a store that sells a variety of olives in bulk, by all means taste before buying. Avoid any olives that are too bitter or too strongly flavored for your dish.

Slivers
of Fennel
and Celery

Artichokes, Capers,
Olives, Lemon Zest,
and Italian Tuna
on Pasta Shells

Italian Semolina Bread

Selection of Italian
Cheeses and Grapes

Biscotti

Amaretto
Over Ice

**Try a citrusy Albarino, from Spain.
This wine will not only complement
the lemon, but will go with the capers and tuna.**

Seared Tuna with a Black and White Sesame Seed Crust on a Bed of Greens

This elegant preparation is best served by candlelight.

All the Trimmings

This is a wonderful meal for plate service. The black and white sesame seeds are beautiful against the red tuna flesh. The Japanese snack crackers are a great non-filling starter. And easy too. The main dish is very filling. In keeping with the black and white theme, finish with dark and white chocolate mousse—bought, of course. Wow, what an easy meal.

PREPARATION TIME: 10 MINUTES
COOKING TIME: 10 MINUTES

MAKES 6 SERVINGS

½ CUP BLACK SESAME SEEDS
½ CUP WHITE SESAME SEEDS
6 MEDIUM TUNA STEAKS
3 TABLESPOONS PEANUT OIL
2 TABLESPOONS
    RICE WINE VINEGAR

3 TABLESPOONS EXTRA-VIRGIN
    OLIVE OIL
½ TEASPOON SESAME OIL
½ TEASPOON SOY SAUCE
½ TEASPOON SUGAR
6 CUPS MESCLUN

Combine the sesame seeds on a large piece of wax paper. Bread each tuna steak with the seeds, pressing the seeds into the fish with the heel of your hand. In a large skillet, heat the peanut oil for 2 minutes, add the tuna steaks and cook on each side for 3 to 5 minutes, depending on how well done you like your fish. The steaks will be rare in the middle after 5 minutes per side. If you want them better done, leave them in longer. Once cooked, remove the steaks from the skillet and set them aside.

In a large salad bowl, combine the rice wine vinegar, olive oil, sesame oil, soy sauce, and sugar. Gently toss in the mesclun greens. Arrange the greens in the middle of individual plates. Now slice the room temperature tuna steaks. Fan out the slices on top of the greens. Serve at once.

How to cook tuna steaks:

When cooking tuna steaks, the great sin is to overcook them. Most better fish markets will give you 3- to 4-inch-thick tuna steaks. The rule of thumb is 2 to 3 minutes per inch for tuna. You should check the doneness before slicing. Also check with your guests. Some people hate rare tuna and some people, such as pregnant women, simply shouldn't eat rare meat, period. In those cases, remove some of the steaks early for those who want them rare and simply continue to cook the rest for folks who want theirs well done. The point is for guests to enjoy themselves without having to adhere to someone else's sense of food correctness.

Wasabi
Peas and
Japanese
Snack Crackers

Seared Tuna
with a Black and White
Sesame Seed Crust
on a Bed of Greens

Crusty Bread

Dark and White
Chocolate
Mousse

**Try a dry
Italian Prosecco
served in champagne flutes.**

Sun-Dried Tomatoes, Pancetta, Mushrooms, and Wilted Lettuce Salad

We love wilted lettuce salads. The pancetta here is a natural complement to the sun-dried tomatoes and mushrooms.

PREPARATION TIME: 15 MINUTES
COOKING TIME: 10–15 MINUTES

MAKES 4 SERVINGS

All the Trimmings

This salad is best served out of a big salad bowl or on a large platter and passed around. Bring out the soup and the salad at once and serve very casually. Buy the cheesecake from a good bakery. Serve it in a pool of the sauce for a beautiful presentation.

½ CUP SUN-DRIED TOMATOES, RECONSTITUTED IN HOT WATER, DRAINED, AND SOAKED IN OLIVE OIL; SLICED

8 CUPS CURLY GREEN LEAF LETTUCE

¼ CUP OLIVE OIL (MAY USE THE OIL FROM THE TOMATOES)

½ POUND PANCETTA, FINELY CHOPPED

1 PINT MUSHROOMS, STEMS REMOVED, QUARTERED

¼ CUP RED WINE VINEGAR

½ TEASPOON SALT

FRESHLY GROUND BLACK PEPPER, TO TASTE

Combine the tomatoes with the lettuce in a large bowl or on a large platter. In a 12-inch skillet over medium heat, heat the olive oil for 2 minutes, add the pancetta and cook for 4 to 5 minutes. Add the mushrooms and cook for another 4 to 5 minutes. Add the vinegar and boil the mixture for 2 minutes, stirring constantly. Pour the hot vinaigrette, mushrooms, and pancetta over the lettuce, season with the salt and pepper, and serve immediately.

How to soup up tomato soup:

Of course the tomato soup starts in a can. Add a handful of Italian parsley, use part milk and part cream instead of water to thin it, and top it with slivers of Parmigiano-Reggiano cheese. To make perfect slivers, use a potato peeler on a cold chunk of the cheese. The parsley will wilt and the cheese slivers will look great against the red soup.

For dessert, make the raspberry brandy sauce by combining 1 cup raspberry jelly with ½ cup brandy. Microwave on high (100% power) for 1 minute, or heat on the stovetop for 3 minutes, then pour it over the cheesecake.

Cream
of Tomato
Souped-up Soup

Sun-Dried Tomatoes,
Pancetta, Mushrooms,
and
Wilted Lettuce Salad

Italian Baguette
with Chèvre

Cheesecake
with
Raspberry
Brandy
Sauce

Try a Dolcetto d'Alba.
This versatile Italian red wine
from the Piedmont region is fruity with
soft tannins, and will complement the mushrooms.

Fresh Figs, Nectarines, and Ham Tossed in a Red Wine Reduction

This menu works on the principle of opposites. The peppery breadsticks set up the palate perfectly for the sweet salad, which is foiled by the blue cheese and French baguette. If you think you don't like blue cheese, try it with this meal. It is the natural complement to the figs and nectarines. This is strictly a summer dish, when the fruits are at their peak.

All the Trimmings

This is a plate service meal. Serve the fig, nectarine, ham mixture on individual dinner plates over a bed of mesclun. Serve the bread and cheese on side plates.

PREPARATION TIME: 20 MINUTES
COOKING TIME: 5 MINUTES

MAKES 4 SERVINGS

1 CUP DRY RED WINE

$1/2$ CUP SUGAR

8 TO 10 FRESH FIGS, THINLY SLICED

4 NECTARINES, PITTED, QUARTERED, AND SLICED

$1/2$ POUND SLICED BLACK FOREST HAM, CUT INTO $1/4$-INCH JULIENNE STRIPS

2 CUPS MESCLUN

4 SPRIGS FRESH MINT, FOR GARNISH

In a medium saucepan, stirring every so often, bring the wine and sugar to a boil and cook until the wine is reduced by half, about 5 minutes. Remove the pan from the heat and set it aside to cool.

Toss the figs, nectarines, and ham together in a bowl and add half the wine reduction, reserving the other half.

Divide the mesclun equally among 4 dinner plates. Using a large mug, scoop up a portion of the ham mixture and pat it into the mug. In the center of each dinner plate, invert the mug on top of the mesclun so that you get a mound of the ham mixture. Repeat for the remaining 3 portions. Drizzle each serving with some of the remaining wine sauce and garnish each plate with a sprig of mint.

How to choose a ham:

"Some pigs are created more equal than others."—*Animal Farm*, George Orwell.

It's true, hams vary a great deal. Prosciutto is a cured ham that is intensely flavored and salty (in a good way). Black Forest ham is smoked, and a good one is rather lean. Canned ham and pressed ham, available at many delis, are pure hog slop. What is that congealed stuff around the meat? Please don't ruin this salad with a cheap cut of ham. Buy only the best smoked ham. Prosciutto can also be used, but make sure it is fresh.

About blue cheese:

There are many varieties of blue cheese. They can be made with sheep's, goat's, or cow's milk. Some are made with a combination of different milks. A blue cheese has a very complex flavor. You literally should be able to get several flavors at once when you take a small bite of cheese: tobacco, beef, berries, and a distinct tanginess. With this meal, we serve a French Roquefort. Steve Jenkins in his *Cheese Primer* says that Roquefort is too good for salad dressing and should be served beside a salad. We couldn't agree more.

Other major types of blue cheese include American Maytag Blue, English Stilton, Italian Gorgonzola, and Spanish Cabrales. They are each wonderful and offer different qualities. Buy Steve Jenkins's book and become an expert through tasting and comparing. Poor quality blue cheese will be overly salty. Bad cheese will have a grayish color.

Peppery
Bread Sticks

Fresh Figs,
Nectarines, and
Ham
Tossed in a
Red Wine Reduction

Blue Cheese
and
French Baguette

Butter
Cookies

**This salad
screams dry Riesling.
Check out the Alsace wines for a change.**

Couscous Summer Deli Salad

Golden couscous tossed with ham and turkey comes alive with the addition of bright green peas and sage. We like it for lunch on a bed of greens. Couscous is a Berber pasta from Morocco in northern Africa that resembles small grains of golden semolina. Moroccan women must be able to steam a perfect couscous. As for Americans, we buy it instant—presteamed—in a box. Stir it with boiling water and let it stand for 5 minutes. Fluff with a fork. It's perfect.

PREPARATION TIME: 10 MINUTES

COOKING TIME: 5 MINUTES

MAKES 6 SERVINGS

All the Trimmings

To serve, place a handful of mixed baby greens on a plate and top with a portion of the couscous mixture. Garnish with additional sprigs of parsley, if you wish. Pass the pita bread, hummus, and babaganoush. Blood oranges and radicchio are on the side. Brownies and fresh berries complete the meal.

Make this 1 day ahead, cover, and refrigerate. Serve at room temperature.

2 CUPS COOKED COUSCOUS (COOKED ACCORDING TO PACKAGE DIRECTIONS)

1 STALK CELERY, FINELY CHOPPED

1 SHALLOT, FINELY CHOPPED

1 CUP CHOPPED BLACK FOREST DELI HAM

1 CUP CHOPPED DELI TURKEY BREAST

3/4 CUP FROZEN PEAS, THAWED

1/2 TEASPOON MINCED FRESH SAGE LEAVES, OR 1/4 TEASPOON DRIED

1/2 CUP BEST-QUALITY MAYONNAISE

1/4 CUP SOUR CREAM

1 TEASPOON DIJON MUSTARD

1/4 CUP CHICKEN BROTH

1/2 TEASPOON KOSHER SALT, OR TO TASTE

1/2 TEASPOON CRACKED PEPPER, OR TO TASTE

CHOPPED FRESH FLAT-LEAF PARSLEY FOR GARNISH

6 CUPS MIXED BABY GREENS

Place the couscous in a large salad bowl and toss it with the celery, shallot, ham, turkey, peas, and sage.

In a small bowl, whisk together the mayonnaise, sour cream, mustard, and broth. Season to taste with salt and pepper, then toss the dressing with the salad. Sprinkle with the parsley, cover, and refrigerate until serving time, or for up to 24 hours. Bring the salad back to room temperature before serving on a bed of baby greens.

How to select couscous:

Couscous is made by removing both bran and germ from durum wheat berries. The semolina (endosperm) is steamed and pressed to form tiny pellets, then dried. You can buy it in varying degrees of coarseness, but a medium-fine grade is the most common. While the traditional couscous is steamed over broth for up to an hour in a traditional clay pot called a "couscousier," your supermarket will probably carry the American instant kind, which simply requires fluffing up in boiling broth or water. So easy. Serve it as you would rice, either hot or cold in salads. Its lovely golden color and nutty flavor make a fine addition to many Middle Eastern dinners.

Couscous
Summer Deli Salad

Hot Pita Pockets
with Hummus and
Babaganoush

Blood Oranges
and Radicchio
with Mint Leaves

Brownies
and
Fresh Raspberries

**A nice fizzy Prosecco
from the Vento region of Italy
will complement this light meal.
What a way to dress up cold cuts!**

Roast Peppered Beef with Pears and Apples

Think of this as a cross between a Thai beef salad and Pacific Rim cooking from California. Using the best provender the West Coast provides, along with an Asian method, you'll get a glorious-looking and -tasting one-dish dinner with thin slices of Asian-spiced, rare roast tenderloin slices fanned out over pears, apples, and mixed baby greens.

All the Trimmings

This menu is made for entertaining a few good friends for a weekend lunch. Plate up the salad in the kitchen and set it out atop your best-looking chargers. Who will know you didn't have to cook much? The table can look glorious, with lots of fresh fruit for a centerpiece, bread and butter on the side, and a dessert that is nothing more than assorted bakery treats and ice creams set in the middle of the table on a chilled marble square (that you bought at the tile store). Send around the dessert spoons and little plates. Now your guests can have a taste of everything. Isn't that all you want anyway?

PREPARATION TIME: 15 MINUTES

MARINATING TIME: 30 MINUTES

COOKING TIME: 35–45 MINUTES

MAKES 8 SERVINGS

Designed for cooking and eating at once, the recipe, nevertheless, offers the leftovers that make a great next-day lunch eaten cold right out of the refrigerator.

MARINADE:

3 tablespoons honey

3 tablespoons fish sauce (nam pla)

1 tablespoon soy sauce

¼ cup mirin, or rice wine

2 teaspoons dark sesame oil

TRIPLE GINGER DRESSING:

½ cup rice wine vinegar

2 tablespoons vegetable oil

2 tablespoons water

1 tablespoon minced fresh chives, plus additional for garnish

1 tablespoon grated fresh ginger

1 teaspoon ginger powder

1 tablespoon chopped crystallized ginger

1 teaspoon honey

½ teaspoon kosher salt

1 (2½-POUND) BEEF TENDERLOIN ROAST

1 TABLESPOON CRACKED BLACK PEPPERCORNS

4 CUPS MIXED BABY GREENS

2 RIPE COMICE OR BOSC PEARS, EACH CORED AND CUT INTO 8 WEDGES

2 RIPE MCINTOSH APPLES, EACH CORED AND CUT INTO 8 WEDGES

JUICE AND ZEST OF 1 LEMON

In a large bowl, combine the marinade ingredients. Combine the dressing ingredients in a jar, shake well, and set aside.

Place the meat in the marinade, turning to coat all sides, then cover and refrigerate for at least 30 minutes. Remove the roast from the marinade and pat it dry. Discard the marinade.

Preheat the oven to 425°F. Press the peppercorns into the surface of the roast with the heel of your hand. Place the roast on a rack in a shallow roasting pan. Insert a meat thermometer so that the bulb is centered in the thickest part, not resting in fat. Roast for 35 to 45 minutes. The thermometer should read 135° for rare, or 155° for medium. The temperature will continue to rise about 5° after removal from the oven. Let the meat stand for about 10 minutes while you compose the plates. Then carve the roast into ¼-inch slices.

To serve, toss the greens with the dressing then divide them among 8 plates. After cutting the fruit, toss it with the lemon juice and zest to prevent it from browning. Fan out 2 pear and 2 apple slices on each plate. Add a portion of sliced meat, and garnish each serving with minced chives. Serve with additional dressing passed in a pitcher.

Assorted
Cheeses
and
Good Breads

Roast
Peppered Beef
with
Pears and Apples

Dessert Tray:
Tarts, Tortes,
and
Ice Creams

**A white Bordeaux
will go nicely with this salad.
The earthy flavor of the Bordeaux
will work with the beef and complement
the sweetness of the apples and pears.**

PART IV

Out of the Oven

Roasts, Casseroles, Pizza,
Quiches, and Stratas

Roasts, Fast and Slow

Slow-Roasted Barbecued Brisket and Southwestern Vegetables

Real Texas barbecue takes 18 hours over a cool hardwood fire, but you can create an easy approximation if you have a big, heavy-weight Dutch oven and 4 to 5 hours. Slow roasting creates meltingly delicious brisket, and all you have to do is turn it over a few times. Set on a bed of Southwestern vegetables, this dish makes its own punched-up au jus. It's dinner fit for company in one pot. Perfect for a cool, rainy summer evening.

PREPARATION TIME: 10 MINUTES   MAKES 6–8 SERVINGS
COOKING TIME: 4–5 HOURS

All the Trimmings

Serve the meat and vegetables on a platter, slicing the meat thin, on an angle. Pour the sauce into a gravy boat and pass it. This meal is best served family style. For a truly authentic Texas-style meal, serve the white bread stacked on a plate, followed by a mixture of buttered honey.

The brisket can be made at your convenience, covered, and refrigerated, then reheated right in the pan over medium heat until it bubbles. If you have a large enough Dutch oven, you can double this recipe and feed twice as many people with no extra work.

1/4 CUP BARBECUE DRY RUB (COMMERCIAL OR SEE BELOW FOR HOMEMADE)

1 (3- TO 5-POUND) BRISKET OF BEEF

4–6 LARGE EARS OF CORN, SHUCKED

1 LARGE SWEET YELLOW ONION, QUARTERED

4 LARGE ROMA TOMATOES

1 LARGE GREEN OR RED BELL PEPPER, SEEDED AND QUARTERED

2 JALAPEÑOS PEPPERS, SEEDED AND HALVED, OR TO TASTE

Preheat the oven to 300°F. Rub dry seasonings into the meat on all sides and place the brisket in a large porcelain-clad cast-iron Dutch oven. Place it in the preheated oven and roast uncovered for 1 hour, then turn and roast for another hour, uncovered.

How to cook brisket:

The brisket is a cut of meat that is full of flavor but needs your tender, loving care to yield its all. Like the chuck roast, or pot roast, it benefits by long, slow cooking so that the meat relaxes and becomes so tender you can stab it with a fork and easily twirl the fork in the meat.

This preparation yields its own pan juices, which, once you cover the pan, begin to braise the meat and vegetables. Braising works on the principle that the meat is first browned—perhaps in hot fat on top of the stove, or in the oven in an open pan, as in this slow roasted recipe—then finished in a covered pan with a small amount of liquid until it becomes tender. You can braise in a "slow" oven, about 300°, or on top of the stove over low heat.

How to make a dry rub:

If you can't find a commercial dry rub for your barbecue, you can easily make one yourself. Simply stir together 3 tablespoons each salt, black pepper, and paprika, with ½ teaspoon cayenne, ⅓ cup sugar, and 2 tablespoons each garlic powder and chili powder. Store the mixture in a clean jar in your cupboard. Massage it generously into meats you plan to barbecue or cook in the oven.

You'll notice a good bit of pan juices at this point. That's good. After the second hour, remove the meat from the pan, make a "bridge" or "rack" with the ears of corn, nestle the remaining vegetables around the corn, and set the brisket on top of this improvised corn-cob rack. The meat will now continue to cook out of the pan juices. Put the lid on the pan and cook it for 2 to 3 hours more, turning the meat every hour or so, until it is meltingly tender. Hold in the Dutch oven until you're ready to serve.

Chips
and Salsa

Slow-Roasted
Barbecued Brisket
with
Southwestern Vegetables

Sliced White Onions
and Pickled Jalapeños

Country White Bread,
Butter, and Honey

Fresh Peach and
Nectarine Slices
over Vanilla
Ice Cream

**Barbecue always says beer to us.
Why mess with success?**

Roasted Lemon Chicken
with Fingerling Potatoes, Tomatoes, and Olives

Make and serve this in a black skillet, and the presentation will be so mouthwatering that your guests will practically fall upon it. Never mind that it goes together in a flash, is as easy to make as a box cake, and still tastes like you cooked all day. Just take your compliments. You've earned them.

PREPARATION TIME: 15 MINUTES   MAKES 4–6 SERVINGS
COOKING TIME: 1 HOUR

All the Trimmings

One of those eat-with-your-eyes dinners, this works best if you preset the table with the salad course. The brilliant red of whole radicchio leaves, fanned out orange slices, and bright green mint will make your guests hungry immediately. Bring the black skillet full of chicken and vegetables to the table for the host to make up plates. Remember to light the candles, and use bright linens and casual flowers. Now's a good time for summer flowers in a quart mason jar. This dinner is about comfort and ease, for both cook and diners.

This tastes as good reheated as when it's first cooked, so feel free to make it at your convenience, cover and refrigerate, then pop it back in the oven to heat through, about 10 minutes at 450°F.

1/4 CUP EXTRA-VIRGIN OLIVE OIL

2 LARGE LEMONS, 1 CUT INTO THIN SLICES, THE OTHER ZESTED AND JUICED

SALT AND FRESHLY GROUND BLACK PEPPER TO TASTE

1/2 TEASPOON CAYENNE

6 CLOVES GARLIC, SMASHED

8 LARGE CHICKEN THIGHS WITH SKIN AND BONES, OR USE BREASTS IF YOU PREFER

1 TABLESPOON CHOPPED FRESH ROSEMARY LEAVES

10 SMALL ROMA TOMATOES, HALVED

20 KALAMATA OLIVES

16 SMALL FINGERLING YUKON GOLD POTATOES

ROSEMARY SPRIGS, FOR GARNISH

Preheat the oven to 450°F. Coat a 10- to 12-inch cast-iron or cast iron–clad ovenproof skillet with 1 tablespoon olive oil. Arrange the lemon slices in a single layer in the bottom of the skillet.

In a large bowl, combine 2 tablespoons of the remaining oil with the lemon juice and zest, salt and ground pepper, the cayenne, and half the smashed garlic. Add the chicken and rub this mixture into all the surfaces. Arrange the chicken pieces one layer deep in the skillet.

Now add the remaining oil to the bowl, along with additional salt and pepper, the rosemary, tomatoes, olives, potatoes, and the remaining garlic. Toss to coat, then arrange on top of the chicken. Roast in the preheated oven for 1 hour, or until the

How to oven-roast to perfection:

Oven-roasting concentrates flavors, seals in juices, and caramelizes foods so that you get the best flavor for the least amount of effort. Remember to let the oven preheat completely before you place the skillet inside. If you put the pan in too soon, the surfaces won't seal quickly enough and liquids will boil away, leaving a dry, unappetizing one-dish dinner. We keep a thermometer in the oven at all times and check to make sure the oven is truly at the temperature called for in the recipe before we add the food. Also, remember that every time you open the oven door, you're losing about 5 minutes cooking time because of the cold air rushing into the oven, so keep those peeks to a minimum.

chicken is cooked through. Well-cooked chicken will yield clear juices when pierced. If the juices have a pink tinge, return the chicken to the oven for 10 minutes, then retest.

Serve on warmed dinner plates garnished with a sprig of rosemary.

Radicchio, Blood Oranges, and Mint with Pine Nuts and Three-Citrus Vinaigrette (page 25)

Roasted Lemon Chicken with Fingerling Potatoes, Tomatoes, and Olives

Hot Olive Bread with Extra-Virgin Olive Oil and Balsamic Vinegar

Salty Blue Cheese and Sweet Grapes with Butter Cookies

Espresso

Roast chicken is always a good opportunity to show off a fine wine. Try a Burgundy from the Côte d'Or, Premier Cru. Treat yourself to a good bottle. This dinner is worth it, and so are you.

Roasted Duck
with Sweet Potatoes, Sage, Fruit, and Port

There is nothing more dramatic and celebrant than bringing a whole duck to the table. Add the fruit to the roasting pan during the last 10 minutes.

PREPARATION TIME: 5 MINUTES
COOKING TIME: 55 MINUTES

MAKES 4 SERVINGS

All the Trimmings

This rather formal dinner is very rich. For that reason, we start off with crudités and a simple dip. Serve the crudités with before-dinner wine in the living room. Designate a duck carver and have your guests pass their plates to be filled. Pass the salad to be added to the plate with the duck. The walnut bread can be served with dinner if you like, but be sure to save some for the cheese course.

The cheeses should be out of the refrigerator for at least 3 hours prior to serving. This allows the cheese to come to room temperature, which enhances the flavor. The French would eat this with a knife and fork, but most Americans like it with a little bit of bread.

Finally, buy the crème brûlées if you can. Remove them from the refrigerator just before serving dinner so that they can also begin to warm up. Run them under the broiler just before serving.

Best if made and served promptly, although we do admit leftovers are wonderful when warmed in the microwave for a minute or two.

1 (3-POUND) DUCK, WINGS FOLDED AND LEGS TRUSSED UP WITH COOKING STRING, ALL FAT TRIMMED FROM THE CAVITY AREA

1 TABLESPOON VEGETABLE OIL

½ CUP RED PLUM JAM

½ CUP PORT WINE

3 SWEET POTATOES, PEELED AND QUARTERED

2 MEDIUM, TART UNPEELED COOKING APPLES, CORED AND COARSELY CHOPPED (GRANNY SMITH, JONATHAN, OR RED DELICIOUS)

2 PEARS, CORED AND COARSELY CHOPPED

2 KIWI FRUIT, PEELED AND COARSELY CHOPPED

¾ CUP DRIED CRANBERRIES OR CHERRIES

¼ CUP CHOPPED FRESH SAGE, PLUS SPRIGS OF SAGE FOR GARNISH

Preheat the oven to 450°F. Remove and discard the duck giblets. Rinse and thoroughly dry the duck. Lightly oil the duck and place it in a roasting pan, breast side up. Roast uncovered for 25 minutes.

Meanwhile, in a small bowl, combine the red plum jam and port. Reduce the heat to 350°, surround the bird with the sweet potato quarters, spoon the port mixture over the bird, and continue roasting uncovered for 25 minutes more. Add the chopped apples, pears, and kiwis, the dried cranberries, and the chopped sage to the pan, surrounding the duck, and cook for an additional 10 minutes. Cut the strings and remove the duck to a warmed plate and surround with potatoes and fruit.

How to make an impromptu hors d'oeuvre from a bowling ball of bread:

A classic sour cream dip can be served in a hollowed-out loaf of bread purchased from a good bakery. Choose a small, round loaf, cut off the top, and hollow out the middle. You can cut up the bread from the middle into chunks and serve it with the dip along with crudités. To make a simple dip, combine 1 pint sour cream with chopped red onions, frozen and thawed spinach, herbes de Provence, and salt and pepper to taste. Serve the dip in the hollowed-out bread. When it's time for clean-up, just discard the hollowed-out bread.

Crudités with
Spinach Sour
Cream Dip Served
in a Loaf of Bread

Roast Duck
with Sweet Potatoes,
Sage, Fruit, and Port

Romaine Lettuce with Fennel
and Sherry Wine Vinaigrette

Whole-Wheat
Walnut-Raisin Bread

Assorted Cheeses: Aged
Gouda, Explorateur, and
Saga Blue Sauterne

Crème Brûlée

A Shiraz from South Australia or Petite Sirah from California or France (the same grape) are the classic game wines. The fruity quality of the wine will complement the fruit in this dish.

Roasted Monkfish with Garlic and Ginger on a Bed of Root Vegetables

By roasting the vegetables, not only do all of the flavors intensify but so do all the colors. The red, orange, yellow, and white are really dazzling.

PREPARATION TIME: 20 MINUTES
COOKING TIME: 45 MINUTES

MAKES 6 GENEROUS SERVINGS

All the Trimmings

Start with red pepper hummus (bought of course) and crackers in the living room. Serve the main course on a large platter to be passed, family style. Arrange the colorful, roasted root vegetables on the platter and top them with the fish fillets and chopped fresh chives. Serve the salad course with the cheese course on small plates with the walnut bread. Morbier is a mild cow's milk cheese made in the Comité region of France. It's a great cheese to serve with the stronger, more complex, aged Gouda. We serve the Morbier whole so that people can serve themselves, and we precut the Gouda into strips. Remember to arrange your cheese platter before dinner, cover it with plastic wrap, and leave the cheese out at room temperature. Finish with a vanilla mousse or pudding (store-bought). The vanilla will soothe the palate after these intense flavors.

2 LEEKS, WHITE AND PALE GREEN PARTS ONLY, CUT IN HALF LENGTHWISE

2 MEDIUM RED POTATOES, CUT INTO STRIPS EQUAL IN THICKNESS TO THE LEEKS

1 SWEET POTATO, PEELED AND CUT INTO STRIPS EQUAL IN THICKNESS TO THE LEEKS

2 CARROTS, PEELED, CUT IN HALF BOTH ACROSS AND LENGTHWISE

2 BEETS, PEELED AND QUARTERED

1 YELLOW ONION, CHOPPED

1/4 CUP OLIVE OIL

4 CLOVES GARLIC, PEELED

1 (2-INCH) PIECE FRESH GINGER, PEELED

1/2 TEASPOON SALT

1 TEASPOON FRESHLY GROUND BLACK PEPPER

2 TABLESPOONS TAWNY PORT

1 TABLESPOON SOY SAUCE

2 POUNDS SKINNED AND FILLETED MONKFISH

3 TABLESPOONS BUTTER, MELTED

1 TEASPOON CHOPPED FRESH CHIVES

Preheat the oven to 475°F. In a 14-inch glass baking dish, toss the leeks, red potatoes, sweet potato, carrots, beets, and onion with the olive oil. In a food processor, chop the garlic and ginger together. Remove half the garlic and ginger mixture and toss the other half with the vegetables and the salt and pepper. Roast for 30 minutes, or until the vegetables are tender, then add the port and soy sauce and turn the vegetables.

Thoroughly dry the monkfish fillets. Top the vegetables with the fillets. Brush the fillets with the melted butter and sprinkle them with the remaining garlic and ginger mixture. Return the pan to the oven and roast for 15 minutes more, or just until the fish flakes. Sprinkle the monkfish with the chopped fresh chives just before serving.

How to prepare leeks:

To clean the leeks, cut off the dark green parts of the stem. Trim off the roots as if you were trimming a beard. Leaving the stubs of the root intact will hold the leek together as it cooks. Run the cut leeks under cold running water to remove all the sand from between the leaves. Our rule of thumb to be sure all the sand is out is to wash once, then wash again.

Red
Pepper Hummus
and Crackers

Roasted Monkfish
with Garlic and Ginger
on a Bed of Root Vegetables

Baby Greens
with Honey Mustard
Vinaigrette

Morbier Cheese
and
Aged Gouda

Raisin-Walnut Bread

Vanilla Mousse

The rich flavor of the monkfish marries well with a rich, buttery Chardonnay. Try a David Wynn from South Australia.

Roasted Root Vegetables with Sirloin

Next time you're planning to entertain a crowd, but barely have time to run the vacuum and set the table, make this glamorous roasted dinner all in one pan. Roast the meat and the vegetables together, then carve luscious slices of steak on the bias and let your guests pick and choose from among their favorite vegetables. This is a win-win menu that requires little besides scrubbing a lot of vegetables and using a meat thermometer to check on the internal temperature of that steak.

All the Trimmings

This is a terrific buffet presentation. Compose the platter, grouping like vegetables together and fanning the beef slices out from a center bowl containing the horseradish sauce. Compose the grapefruit and avocado wedges in a bowl and drizzle the salad with the vinaigrette. Decorate the table with seasonal fruits and nuts: whole pears and apples, walnuts and pecans, colorful leaves. Be sure there's plenty of golden candlelight and your favorite music playing. This is too easy.

PREPARATION TIME: 15 MINUTES MAKES 12 SERVINGS
COOKING TIME: 1 HOUR OR LESS

You are going to pray for leftovers from this meal. Roasted vegetables reheat beautifully in the microwave and those thin slices of beef are great cold the next day with more horseradish-mayo sauce.

2 TEASPOONS DRIED ROSEMARY LEAVES, CRUSHED

3/4 TEASPOON KOSHER SALT

1/2 TEASPOON CRACKED PEPPERCORNS

1 (3-POUND) BONELESS TOP SIRLOIN OF BEEF, CUT 2 INCHES THICK

1/4 CUP EXTRA-VIRGIN OLIVE OIL, PLUS 2 TABLESPOONS FOR THE PAN

2 MEDIUM BEETS, SCRUBBED AND QUARTERED

2 MEDIUM PARSNIPS, SCRUBBED AND HALVED LENGTHWISE

2 MEDIUM CARROTS, SCRUBBED AND HALVED LENGTHWISE

2 MEDIUM TURNIPS, SCRUBBED AND QUARTERED

2 MEDIUM SWEET POTATOES, PEELED AND CUT INTO CHUNKS

2 CUPS WHOLE FINGERLING YUKON GOLD POTATOES, SCRUBBED

1 WHOLE HEAD GARLIC, ROUGH OUTER HUSK REMOVED

2 LEEKS, WHITE AND LIGHT GREEN PARTS, WASHED THOROUGHLY AND CUT IN HALF LENGTHWISE

2 LARGE RED ONIONS, QUARTERED

1/2 CUP CHICKEN BROTH

Preheat the oven to 425°F. Rub half the rosemary, salt, and pepper into both sides of the beef. Combine the remaining rosemary, salt, and pepper with the oil.

Coat a 10-×-15-inch roasting pan with 2 tablespoons olive oil, then arrange the vegetables in a single layer in the pan. Toss them with the rosemary-pepper scented oil. Pour the broth into the bottom of the pan. Place a rack over the vegetables and place the

How to roast vegetables and meat:

When you are preparing vegetables for roasting, cut them to uniform size so that they'll cook evenly. We prefer large chunks so that the vegetables have plenty of surface for crisp bites, but creamy centers for all the comfort that brings.

High heat will successfully roast both the meat and the vegetables in one pan. Place an oven thermometer in your oven to be sure it is heated to the temperature you have set. It's important to get the oven plenty hot so that when the pan of food is placed inside, everything goes POW and the surfaces are sealed up tight. In the end, you should have gorgeous caramelized vegetables, their sugars having transformed them into golden glistening bites, and perfectly roasted beef, caramelized to a deep mahogany on the outside, yet still pink and rare in the middle. And remember to lift that meat out of the pan with tongs if it cooks to the temperature you want before the vegetables are ready.

steak on the rack. Insert a meat thermometer into the meat so that the bulb is centered in the thickest part, not resting in fat.

Roast the steak and vegetables for 45 to 50 minutes, or until the steak is rare (135° on the meat thermometer) to medium (155°) and the vegetables are tender. If the meat is cooked before all the vegetables are done, remove it to a cutting board, tent it with foil, and let it rest while the vegetables continue to roast.

Let the steak rest for 10 minutes before carving. (Thick-cut steaks will continue to rise in temperature about 5° after removal from the oven.)

Carve the steak into thin, crosswise slices. Serve the meat and vegetables on a large, flat platter.

NOTE: Horseradish-Mayonnaise Sauce is just what it says: about ½ cup best-quality mayo tuned up with a heaping tablespoon of horseradish. Taste and adjust to suit you.

Grand Cru Burgundies are called for here.

Grapefruit Sections
and Avocado with a
Three-Citrus Vinaigrette
(page 25)

Roasted Root Vegetables
with Sirloin

Horseradish-Mayonnaise
Sauce (see Note)

Hot Crusty French Bread
and Sweet Butter

Apple Pie and
Vanilla
Ice Cream

Casseroles and Other Comfortable Dinners from One Pot

Chipotle Chicken con Queso on a Bed of Lima Beans

Here's a layered dish that nearly jumps off the plate. The flavors are bright, the colors are intense, the result is satisfying, and it's cooked in under an hour.

PREPARATION TIME: 20 MINUTES   MAKES 6 SERVINGS

COOKING TIME: 45 MINUTES

All the Trimmings

Casual is the operative word here. We like to bring the casserole dish to the table that's been preset with the salads. Serve each diner from a stack of plates at the head of the table and pass the hot rolls. Be sure there's plenty of beer, and it's dinner.

Make this a day or so ahead, then cover and refrigerate it. Re-heat the casserole in the oven or microwave and serve it hot. You may decide, as we did, that it's even better the second time around.

1½ POUNDS CHICKEN TENDERS (BONED, SKINNED CHICKEN BREAST STRIPS)

1 (20-OUNCE) PACKAGE FROZEN FORDHOOK LIMA BEANS

1 DRIED CHIPOTLE PEPPER

1 QUART WATER

1 TEASPOON SALT

1 TABLESPOON OLIVE OIL

4 (6-INCH) CORN TORTILLAS

1 YELLOW BELL PEPPER, SEEDED AND FINELY CHOPPED

1 (4-OUNCE) CAN CHOPPED GREEN CHILES, DRAINED

1 LARGE PLUM TOMATO, MINCED

1 CUP SHREDDED CHEDDAR CHEESE

½ CUP SOUR CREAM

How to poach chicken:

You'll notice this recipe calls for cooking lima beans and chicken tenders in barely salted water to begin. This is simply poaching, and you'll get the tenderest results if you don't just go crazy and let the water boil vigorously. Gently boiling water will not toughen the chicken or the beans, so that at the end of the cooking time, you can tear the chicken into strips between 2 forks. Cooking the beans and chicken together makes both ingredients taste better, and adding a chipotle to the cooking water zips up the flavor. If you can't find chipotles (a dried, smoked jalapeño), substitute a scant ½ teaspoon dried chile flakes.

Preheat the oven to 350°F.

In a large flameproof casserole, combine the chicken, lima beans, chipotle, water, and salt. Bring the mixture to a boil on top of the stove, then lower the heat and simmer until the chicken and beans are tender, about 18 minutes. Drain the mixture into a colander. Preheat the oven to 350°. Brush the casserole dish with the olive oil and line the bottom with the corn tortillas. Add a layer of lima beans. Shred the chicken and add a layer of shredded chicken. Now layer in the peppers and tomato. Combine half the cheese with the sour cream and layer it on top of the peppers. Sprinkle the remaining cheese over all. Bake for about 25 minutes, or until the cheese is bubbly and brown. Serve hot.

To complement the smoky chipotle, try an icy cold Mexican beer.

Pineapple
Slices with
Red Chile Flakes

Chipotle
Chicken con Queso
on a
Bed of Lima Beans

Hot Bolillos
and
Sweet Butter

Butter Cookies
and
Vanilla Bean
Ice Cream

Duck Sausage on a Bed of Lentils

In the United States, far too often lentils are relegated to a soup. In fact, they are terrific as a side dish or as a bed for the main course. They are different in texture and flavor from other legumes, being smaller and more subtle than their coarser cousins. With the proliferation of available sausage varieties, you could make many variations of this dish.

All the Trimmings

This meal is best served informally at the table. We suggest that the host stack all the plates at his/her place and serve the lentils, since the pot can be heavy and hard to pass around. Then pass the salad and bread. The pineapple can be run under the broiler just before serving dessert.

PREPARATION TIME: 15 MINUTES   MAKES 6 SERVINGS
COOKING TIME: 1½ HOURS

This dish can be made a day in advance. Refrigerate it covered, then reheat on the stovetop to just under the boil.

2 TABLESPOONS OLIVE OIL

1 TABLESPOON BUTTER

1 GREEN BELL PEPPER, SEEDED AND FINELY CHOPPED

2 LARGE CARROTS, FINELY CHOPPED

2 STALKS CELERY, FINELY CHOPPED

1 ONION, FINELY CHOPPED

1 POUND DUCK SAUSAGE OR OTHER GOURMET LINK SAUSAGE

½ TEASPOON DRIED MARJORAM

1 TEASPOON DRIED SAGE

½ TEASPOON DRIED THYME

1 BAY LEAF

1 (1-POUND) CAN TOMATOES, DRAINED

3½ CUPS HOT WATER

1¾ CUPS DRIED LENTILS, RINSED

1 TEASPOON SALT

FRESHLY GROUND BLACK PEPPER TO TASTE

1 CUP GRATED EMMENTALER OR SWISS CHEESE

Preheat the oven to 350°F.

Preheat a large Dutch oven on top of the stove over medium-high heat for 1 minute. Add the olive oil and butter and heat for 1 minute. Add the green pepper, carrots, celery, onion, sausage, marjoram, sage, thyme, and bay leaf, and sauté on high for 5 minutes. Add the tomatoes and water and scrape up any browned bits from the bottom of the pan. Add the lentils, season with salt and pepper, cover, and bake for 1 hour. Remove from the oven, taste, adjust the salt and pepper to taste, and remove the bay leaf. Cover with the cheese and return the pan to the oven to bake uncovered for 15 minutes more. Serve piping hot.

How to broil a pineapple:

Slice the pineapple lengthwise into quarters from stem end to core, leaving the top and bottom attached. Lay the slices out on cookie sheets. With a sharp paring knife, cut away and discard the core, then slice the flesh away from the skin. Cut the flesh into bite-size diamonds, leaving the flesh in the skin as a sort of bowl. Mix 1 cup white wine with ¼ cup honey and brush the flesh of the pineapple with the honey-wine mixture. The pineapple can be prepared up to this point 4 hours ahead. Run it under the broiler until the sugar in the pineapple begins to brown, 3 to 5 minutes. Remove and serve at once with butter pecan ice cream.

The spicy yet earthy flavor of the sausage will go nicely with a fruity Shiraz from South Australia, or a Petite Sirah from California or France.

St. Andre
Cheese and
Tart Apple Slices

Duck Sausage
on a Bed of Lentils

Romaine Lettuce
with Dried Cranberries
in a Honey Mustard
Vinaigrette

Broiled Pineapple
with White Wine
and Honey

Butter Pecan
Ice Cream

Melinda's Sweet Hot Ham Balls with Yams and Red Onion

Put this on the buffet or take it to the potluck. It's easy to put together and easy to eat. We call Linda's husband, Joe, "the mustard man." We notice that if we put out several different flavors of mustard, he likes to slather different mustards on different bites. Offer a variety. You'll be surprised. People like every kind and class of mustard with their ham and sweet potatoes. Give them a choice.

PREPARATION TIME: 20 MINUTES
COOKING TIME: 1 HOUR

MAKES 28 (2-INCH) HAM BALLS
PLUS VEGETABLES
(56 COCKTAIL-SIZE PIECES)

All the Trimmings

Get out that old-fashioned tablecloth. Grab a bunch of sunflowers. Make a big pitcher of sweet iced tea. Serve the ham balls in the middle of the table, whether a buffet or a dinner table, and add the traditional Southern side dishes. You might even want to play the Willie Nelson music. It's that kind of day.

Make and bake this dish, then cover and freeze it for up to a month. To serve, simply thaw, then reheat in the microwave a few moments or in a hot oven until it bubbles, about 15 minutes.

2 POUNDS LEAN, BONELESS HAM

1 POUND LEAN GROUND PORK LOIN

1/4 CUP SWEET HOT MUSTARD

1/2 TEASPOON CAYENNE

1 CUP SEASONED BREAD CRUMBS

1/2 CUP MINCED FRESH FLAT-LEAF PARSLEY LEAVES, PLUS WHOLE PARSLEY SPRIGS FOR GARNISH

3 LARGE EGGS, BEATEN

1 CUP HALF AND HALF

3 LARGE YAMS OR SWEET POTATOES, PEELED AND CUT INTO BITE-SIZE CHUNKS

1 LARGE RED ONION, CUT INTO BITE-SIZE WEDGES

SAUCE:

    2 cups dark brown sugar

    1 cup water

    1 cup cider vinegar

Preheat the oven to 350°F. Put about a third of the ham in the bowl of a food processor fitted with the steel blade. Process until the meat is finely minced, then transfer it to a large bowl. Repeat until you have minced all the ham. Now, combine the ham and ground pork with the mustard, cayenne, bread crumbs, parsley, eggs, and half and half. Stir to mix. Scoop up 1/4 cup of the mixture, and form it into a 2-inch ball. Repeat until all the mixture is used and arrange the ham balls 1 layer deep in a large baking pan. Nestle the yam and onion pieces around the ham balls, laying the potatoes flat so they can be covered in liquid.

    In a large microwavable bowl or a pan, combine the sauce ingredients and heat to boiling. Stir to dissolve the sugar, then pour

How to caramelize meats in the oven:

Because we have started with a flavorful mixture of ham and pork, we can skip the usual step of browning the meat before we cook it in the sweet sauce. Simply leave the top half of the meat exposed to the hot oven air by not submerging the ham balls completely in sauce, and you'll get a lovely caramelization with the blended flavors from the sauce. All cooked in one pan and in one step. It's easy and we like it.

in just enough of the mixture to half cover the ham balls. Try to submerge the vegetables.

Bake for 1 hour in the preheated oven. Lift the ham balls and vegetables out of the liquid, arrange them on a platter, and garnish with the parsley sprigs. Serve warm or at room temperature with an assortment of mustards.

Sweet Pickles,
Celery Sticks,
Deviled Eggs,
and Black Olives

Coleslaw

Melinda's Sweet Hot
Ham Balls with Yams
and Red Onion

Assorted Mustards

Biscuits, Butter, and
Strawberry Jam

Chocolate Cake
and Vanilla
Ice Cream

For a taster's delight, try an assortment of microbrew beers to go along with the assortment of mustards.

Joann's Spicy East Texas Pork Chop and Rice Casserole

This recipe is based on one given to Katherine's father by a long-time friend and colleague Joann Griggs, City Manager of Jacinto City, Texas. Joann is a hard-working executive who knows the benefit of a fast and good supper. We've added a dry rub to spice up this Texas classic.

PREPARATION TIME: 10 MINUTES
SAUTÉING TIME: 10 MINUTES

BAKING TIME: 45 MINUTES
MAKES 4 SERVINGS

All the Trimmings

Serve the nachos, pickled okra, and pickled jalapeños in the living room. At suppertime, arrange some rice on the side of each dinner plate with a pork chop slightly overlapping the rice. Sprinkle with chopped fresh parsley to add color. Serve at once. Pass Brown and Serve dinner rolls with room-temperature butter and honey, a fine Texas tradition. Finally, pass the sweet onions. They will probably not last through the meal. And don't forget the ice cream. Those who must rely on Häagen-Dazs can substitute butter pecan for a close approximation to Texas's own Blue Bell brand ice cream.

DRY RUB:

- ¼ cup chili powder
- ¼ cup paprika
- ⅛ teaspoon cayenne
- ½ teaspoon ground cumin
- ½ teaspoon sugar
- ¾ teaspoon salt

4 THICK-CUT PORK CHOPS, THOROUGHLY DRIED

3 TABLESPOONS PEANUT OIL

1 LARGE YELLOW ONION, COARSELY CHOPPED

1 GREEN BELL PEPPER, SEEDED AND COARSELY CHOPPED

2 CUPS LONG-GRAIN RICE

1 (15-OUNCE) CAN CHICKEN BROTH

2½ CUPS WATER

SALT AND FRESHLY GROUND BLACK PEPPER TO TASTE

FRESH FLAT-LEAF PARSLEY, FINELY CHOPPED, FOR GARNISH

Preheat the oven to 350°F. In a plate or flat bowl, combine the dry rub ingredients. Pat the pork chops dry and rub both sides with the mixture.

Preheat a non-reactive, ovenproof 12-inch skillet over medium heat for 1 minute. Add the peanut oil to the hot skillet and continue to heat until the oil just begins to smoke. Add the pork chops to the skillet and cook for 2 minutes on each side. The chops do not need to be cooked through at this point, as they will finish cooking in the oven. Remove the chops from the skillet and set them aside. Stir the onion and bell pepper into the pan and cook for 3 to 5 minutes, until the onion becomes translucent. Add the rice and cook for 2 minutes. Add the chicken stock and water and scrape up the browned bits from the bottom of the pan.

How to prepare onions:

Vidalia, Walla Walla Sweet, or Texas 1015 onions are sweet and mild and available all summer and into the fall. To marinate, simply slice 4 Vidalia, Walla Walla, or Texas 1015 sweet onions thin, and stir them together with 1 cup rice wine vinegar and ¼ cup sugar. Cover and refrigerate for 30 minutes. Lift the onions out of the liquid and serve. You can add cucumbers if you wish. We have been known to keep one of these marinated onion bowls going for weeks during high summer.

Taste the stock and adjust the seasonings, adding salt and pepper. Lay the pork chops on top of the rice mixture and bake in the preheated oven for 45 minutes. Chops should be cooked through, with no pink at the center when done. Garnish with freshly chopped parsley.

In East Texas, the teetotalers would have iced tea while the rest of us sinners had a nice cold beer with this meal.

Cheese Nachos

Pickled Okra and
Jalapeño Peppers

Joann's Spicy
East Texas Pork Chop
and Rice Casserole

Dinner Rolls with
Butter and Honey

Texas 1015 Onions
in Rice Wine Vinegar

Texas Praline
Ice Cream

Aunt Mary's Green Rice Custard

Used as a part of the Easter celebration dinner when our cousin Kaki was growing up, this savory rice custard makes a comforting one-dish dinner all by itself. Yes, we may add a few slices of deli Black Forest ham and cantaloupe on the side, but basically the rice itself makes a meal. Think of it as Alabama's answer to risotto.

All the Trimmings

This is ideal take-it-to-the-park food. Think about it. You make the rice custard, you pack up all the side dishes, and you whisk yourself off to the park with a checkered tablecloth, real wine flutes, and a roll of paper towels for catastrophes. Listen to great music under the stars. Comfort yourself with this savory custard. What more could you ask?

PREPARATION TIME: 15 MINUTES   MAKES 6 SERVINGS
COOKING TIME: 1½ HOURS

This is an ideal make-ahead. Cover the cooked dish and refrigerate it until serving time. Then simply reheat it in the microwave a few moments, or in a hot oven for up to 10 minutes.

½ CUP LONG-GRAIN RICE

1¼ CUPS WATER

¼ TEASPOON KOSHER SALT

1 TABLESPOON BUTTER

1½ CUPS HALF AND HALF

2 LARGE EGGS, BEATEN

½ POUND SHARP WHITE CHEDDAR CHEESE, GRATED

1 CUP CHOPPED FRESH FLAT-LEAF PARSLEY LEAVES

2 SHALLOTS, MINCED

2 CLOVES GARLIC, MINCED

SALT AND FRESHLY GROUND BLACK PEPPER TO TASTE

½ TEASPOON CAYENNE

Place a large pan filled with 1 inch of water on the bottom rack of the oven. Preheat the oven to 325°F.

In the bottom of a large soufflé or casserole dish, combine the rice, water, kosher salt, and butter. Cover with plastic wrap and cook in the microwave on high (100% power) for 15 minutes, or until the rice is cooked and the water is absorbed. Alternatively, cook the rice, covered on the stovetop over medium heat for about 15 minutes.

Whisk the half and half and eggs together in a 2-cup glass measure. Add the cheese, parsley, shallots, garlic, and salt, pepper, and cayenne to the cooked rice. Pour the cream mixture over all. Whisk to mix thoroughly, then set the dish in the pan with the water, and bake until the custard sets, about 1 to 1¼ hours.

What the heck is a bain marie?

Old-fashioned cookbooks, especially those written by people who went to fancy, French-influenced cooking schools, often referred to a bain marie. All this means is a pan of water into which you set another baking dish to cook something gently—usually something with eggs—like a custard. This hot water bath is not only useful for cooking custards so that they have a silky texture, it is also helpful for reheating foods, provided you don't put a refrigerator-cold crockery dish inside a hot water bath. We've cracked a good dish or two trying to hurry it up.

Cantaloupe,
Pepato Cheese,
and Black Forest
Ham Slices

Aunt Mary's
Green Rice Custard

Deviled Eggs
with Capers

Hot Biscuits
and Sweet Butter
with Fig Preserves

Strawberry
Shortcake

**Aunt Mary,
being from the Panhandle of Texas,
would only approve of iced tea for this meal.**

Not June Cleaver's Tuna Noodle, But Linguine with Sautéed Tuna and Mixed Peppers

What do you suppose June Cleaver would have thought if she'd ever tried a tuna noodle casserole made with fresh tuna? This dish is only a distant but distinctly aristocratic cousin of the original.

PREPARATION TIME: 20 MINUTES   MAKES 6 SERVINGS
COOKING TIME: 35 MINUTES

All the Trimmings

Warmed dinner plates make all the difference when you're serving one-dish dinners. You can warm them in one of several ways. Sometimes we drizzle a little water on the plates, stack them, and nuke 'em in the microwave a couple minutes, then tilt them to drain off the water, wipe them dry, and add the cooked food. If you can plan ahead, place the plates in the oven and heat them more slowly.

Make this a day ahead, cover and refrigerate, then reheat, covered, for about 15 minutes in a 350°F oven before serving.

8 QUARTS WATER

3 TABLESPOONS SALT, PLUS ADDITIONAL TO TASTE

12 OUNCES FRESH LINGUINE

3 TABLESPOONS OLIVE OIL

1 POUND FRESH TUNA STEAKS

FRESHLY GROUND BLACK PEPPER TO TASTE

2 LARGE BELL PEPPERS, PREFERABLY 1 RED AND 1 GREEN, SEEDED AND JULIENNED

4 CLOVES GARLIC, FINELY CHOPPED

$1/2$ TEASPOON CRUSHED RED PEPPER

$3/4$ CUP CHICKEN BROTH

JUICE AND ZEST OF 1 LEMON

$3/4$ CUP SNIPPED FRESH FLAT-LEAF PARSLEY LEAVES

2 TABLESPOONS DRAINED CAPERS

In a large pot, bring the water and the 3 tablespoons of salt to a boil. Add the pasta and cook until al dente, according to the package directions, about 2 minutes for fresh pasta. Drain and place the pasta in a warmed bowl, cover, and set aside.

Reheat the same pot over medium heat and add 1 tablespoon of the olive oil. Sauté the tuna steaks until done through, about 3 to 4 minutes per side. Season to taste with salt and pepper. Remove them to a cutting board to cool. Sauté the peppers and garlic in an additional tablespoon of the oil with the crushed red pepper until they're beginning to brown, about 5 minutes. Remove the peppers to the linguine bowl. Add the chicken broth and lemon juice and zest to the pot and scrape up the browned bits from the bottom. Bring to a boil, then return the pasta and peppers to the pan and toss to mix the ingredients. Cut the tuna into bite-size

How to cook fish without overcooking it:

This is really too easy. Just remember the 10-minutes-to-the-inch rule. Whether you're cooking on the stove-top or in the oven, or even out on the barbecue, measure the thickness of the fish and cook it no more than 10 minutes per 1 inch of thickness. For example, these tuna steak fillets, which are most likely going to be about ¾ inch thick, will be done in about 7 minutes, and that's counting both sides. Say 4 minutes for side one and 3 minutes for the other. What could be simpler? Plenty of heat to sear the surface, then a short cooking time, and you'll have a fish dinner to remember.

pieces, and add it to the pot to heat through. Toss with the parsley and capers and serve.

Linguine
with
Sautéed Tuna
and Mixed Peppers

Mixed Bitter Greens
with a
Sesame Vinaigrette

Breadsticks

Mangoes
in Heavy Cream
Dusted with
Cinnamon

Try a rich, yet dry Pinot Blanc from Alsace, France. These wines will not overwhelm the tuna and will marry exceedingly well with the sautéed peppers.

A Pizza, a Tart, a Couple of Quiches, and a Strata

Onions, Onions, and More Onions Pizza

A golden spring pizza with white, green, and golden onions as well as sun-dried tomatoes—this homemade version tastes so much better than anything you can buy—with a few notable exceptions—that we believe there's nothing better you could make for family or friends.

Make the dough in the food processor, gather the onions from the garden (or the farmers' market), roll out and top the dough, then pop it into the oven. What could be easier? Think of it as a one-dish dinner on a crust. And if you're really pressed for time or inspiration, skip the dough step and buy a pizza crust from your local pizzeria or even a Boboli crust from the grocery store.

PREPARATION TIME: 20 MINUTES   COOKING TIME: 20 MINUTES
RESTING TIME: 30 MINUTES   MAKES 4 SERVINGS

Start the dough at your convenience early in the day, form it into a ball, and refrigerate it until time to roll out, cover, and bake. Store leftovers wrapped in plastic for a great pizza breakfast the next day. Warm it in the toaster oven if you wish.

**FOOD PROCESSOR
CORNY PIZZA CRUST:**

- 2 cups bread flour
- 2 tablespoons yellow cornmeal
- 1 teaspoon salt

- 2 teaspoons Rapid Rise instant yeast
- 2 tablespoons extra-virgin olive oil
- ⅞ cup warm tap water

TOPPING:

3 tablespoons extra-virgin
   olive oil

¼ cup Mediterranean feta
   spread with sun-dried
   tomato and basil
   (see Note page 145)

2 cups thinly sliced, mixed
   spring onions: Vidalia,
   green, cipolline,
   and leeks

10 sun-dried tomatoes
   in oil, patted dry and
   roughly chopped

1 teaspoon dried oregano,
   OR 1 tablespoon fresh
   minced leaves

½ teaspoon kosher salt

2 tablespoons grated
   Asiago cheese

2 tablespoons freshly
   grated Parmesan cheese

In a food processor fitted with the steel blade, combine the flour, 1 tablespoon of the cornmeal, the salt, and the yeast. Pulse 3 times to aerate, then add the oil and water. Process until the dough forms a ball that rides the blade—this takes only a moment—then process 45 seconds longer. Remove the lid and blade, lift out the dough, and knead by hand a moment (it should be quite soft). Form the dough into a donut shape and replace it in the food processor bowl. Put the lid back on and let the dough rest for 30 minutes.

Preheat the oven to 425°F. On a lightly floured board, roll out the dough into a 14-inch irregular circle. Sprinkle the remaining tablespoon of cornmeal onto a pizza pan, screen, or peel. Flop the dough over the rolling pin, transfer it to the pan, and spread it with a little of the olive oil, then the feta.

Combine the onions and sun-dried tomatoes in a large bowl and sprinkle them with the oregano, salt, and the remaining olive oil. Toss to mix. Arrange the topping on the pizza crust in a uniform single layer, then sprinkle with the Asiago and Parmesan cheeses.

Bake in the preheated oven for 15 to 20 minutes, or until the topping is brown and bubbly. Let the pizza cool a few moments, then cut into wedges. Serve warm.

How to make pizza dough in the food processor:

Making pizza dough in the food processor is so simple. Start with good 14 percent protein bread flour and fast-acting Rapid Rise yeast, and you're sure to have good results. When making any kind of yeast dough, you need to know a couple basic principles: Flour takes up water from the air, so you'll have to exercise some judgment about exactly how much liquid to add to make a soft dough. Just give that dough a quick pinch after it's formed a ball that rides the blade of the food processor. The dough should feel like baby fat, soft, nearly sticky, but silky and smooth as a baby's back. If the dough is hard as a fist, or crumbly, add more water, a tablespoon at a time. If the dough is more like cake batter, add a tablespoon or so more of flour until the dough sets up, soft and supple. Once you get the hang of it, you'll wonder why you ever bought a pizza crust in the first place. Think about it. You've got about 25 cents worth of flour, yeast, oil, salt, and water. Learn a skill and you're on your way to a fabulous new bread that you can top as you wish.

All the Trimmings

We think of pizza as Friday night food. Casual, pull-up-the-chairs-around-the-television-for-the-big-game food. We like to keep it simple, serve on straw mats, pour the wine into short barrel glasses, and pass the brownies from a basket. It's a real spur-of-the-moment dinner that we can make out of the refrigerator if we have to. It's no-fuss cooking that should be reflected in the way you set the stage. Light the candles if you want, play the music, but whatever you do, relax.

NOTE: The Mozzarella, Tomato, and Basil Tower is just what it says: a stack of thick slices of fresh mozzarella and tomato, separated by basil leaves and finished by drizzling it with a vinaigrette.

With Italian food we always suggest Italian wines. Try an Italian Merlot. These light red wines will complement the onion and tomatoes in this dish.

Antipasti:
Mortadella,
Salami, Peperoncini

Fresh Mozzarella,
Tomato, and Basil Tower
with Balsamic Vinaigrette
(see Note)

Onions, Onions,
and More Onions Pizza

Brownies and
Vanilla Bean
Ice Cream

Espresso

Shrimp and Crabmeat Quiche

Whether you are a pastry champ and can turn out a pie shell by hand in a hurry, or the queen of the grocery-store version, once you have a baked pie shell, this is one quick and easy entrée for a celebratory lunch. Actually, if you bake up 2 or 3 pie shells, you can make a variety of savory party pastries all at once: one with crab and shrimp, another with chicken, another with 3 cheeses, for example. Make a classic quiche Lorraine by substituting 4 strips of crisp-cooked bacon for the shrimp and crab in this recipe. Use your imagination.

PREPARATION TIME: 15 MINUTES   MAKES 1 (10-INCH) PIE, 6 SERVINGS
COOKING TIME: 1 HOUR

All the Trimmings

When our friend Diana has friends in for holiday lunch, she presets the table using a bright charger, a dinner plate, then a clear glass plate on that, preset with a wedge of quiche, and a big serving of salad. She decorates the table with little presents and holiday ornaments. Wine flutes are ready for wine or bubbly cranberry fizzle made by mixing equal parts cranberry juice and fizzy water. Pass the hot bread. Lift off the glass plates after the main course, and there's a good-looking dinner plate ready to receive a generous serving of chocolate cake and fresh fruit. Pour the coffee or tea. It's an easy lunch with nothing more than a dishwasher full of plates after it's done to remind you of your efforts.

Make this early on the day you plan to serve it, then refrigerate it, covered. Remove it from the refrigerator and warm it in the oven before serving.

1 UNBAKED PREPARED
    PASTRY SHELL

1 TABLESPOON FLOUR

2 TABLESPOONS BUTTER

2 SHALLOTS, MINCED

4 LARGE EGGS, LIGHTLY BEATEN

2 CUPS HALF AND HALF

1/2 TEASPOON WORCESTERSHIRE
    SAUCE

1/2 TEASPOON SALT

1/2 TEASPOON CAYENNE

1 CUP COARSELY SHREDDED SWISS
    OR GRUYÈRE CHEESE

1/2 POUND COOKED WHITE LUMP
    CRABMEAT, PICKED OVER

1/2 POUND COOKED, SHELLED, AND
    DEVEINED BAY SHRIMP

Preheat the oven to 425°F. Open the prepared crust onto a work surface and rub it with the flour, pressing out any cracks. Transfer it to a 10-inch quiche or pie pan. Press the dough into the pan, folding under any excess border to form double-thick sides. Pierce the dough all over with a fork. Bake until golden, 10 to 12 minutes. Cool in the pan on a rack. Reduce the oven temperature to 350°.

In a small skillet, melt the butter and sauté the shallots until golden, about 2 minutes, then set them aside.

In a bowl, whisk together the eggs, half and half, Worcestershire sauce, salt, and cayenne, then stir in the cheese, crab, shrimp, and sautéed shallots. Pour the mixture into the baked pie shell and bake for 45 to 55 minutes, or until the custard is set and a skewer inserted near the center comes out clean. Serve warm or at room temperature.

How to prepare a tender piecrust:

After more years than we'd care to remember of making piecrusts, Marion Cunningham taught us a technique—over the phone—that forever demystified the art of the perfect piecrust. This is the technique Marion uses in her California children's classes. All you need are your own 2 hands and a rolling pin. For a large single-crust pie, pour 1¾ cups all-purpose flour and 1 teaspoon salt and 1 teaspoon sugar into a large bowl. Toss it with your hands to mix. Then add 1 stick (½ cup) unsalted butter and 2 tablespoons vegetable shortening, cut into bits. Rub the fat into the flour with your fingers, lifting the flour and fat, and letting it fall "like snowflakes," as Marion says, back into the bowl. Put an ice cube in ½ cup water and drizzle it into the flour and fat mixture, mixing gently just until the dough holds together. Don't overmix and don't add more water than needed. Gather the dough into a disk, wrap it in plastic, and put it in the freezer for 10 minutes or so. Now roll it out on a lightly floured board to about ½-inch thickness and about 2 inches larger than the pan (about 12 inches for a 10-inch tart). Flop the rolled dough onto the rolling pin and transfer it to the pan, rolling it out into the pan. Press the dough down into the pan and trim the edges as necessary. If this seems hard to you, just try to think about those seven-year-olds at the Y in Walnut Creek turning out lovely piecrusts under the patient tutelage of Marion Cunningham. Still don't get it? Buy a piecrust from the refrigerator case at the grocery store. Works quite well, actually.

Tossed
Baby Greens
with
Three-Citrus Vinaigrette
(page 25)

Shrimp and Crabmeat
Quiche

Hot Italian
Olive Bread

Fresh Fruit of the Season
and a Great Bakery
Chocolate Cake

Hot Coffee
and Tea

Try a dry white Spanish Albarino or Vinho Verde from Portugal. The Spanish and Portuguese vintners like their wines very dry, perfect for seafood.

Tortilla and Cilantro Quiche

This recipe uses corn tortillas for a quick and delicious crust. No pastry rolling required.

PREPARATION TIME: 15 MINUTES

COOKING TIME: 45 MINUTES

MAKES 6 SERVINGS

All the Trimmings

Serve the chips and salsa casually in the living room. Move to the table where the salads have been preset. For drama, the host should have a stack of dinner plates next to where he/she is sitting. Bring out the tortilla quiche in the black skillet and compose each guest's plate adding a dollop of sour cream and cilantro. This type of table service is warm and cozy and helps slow the pace of dinner. It also helps build anticipation as each piece is passed around the table. End with individual flans. We buy really good ones in the Hispanic grocery section of the market. Set them on individual plates in the kitchen, disposing of the containers. You take all of the credit for a beautiful meal!

8 CORN TORTILLAS

3 TABLESPOONS BUTTER, CUT INTO 6 CHUNKS

8 EGGS, BEATEN

1 CUP GRATED CHEDDAR CHEESE

1 SMALL TOMATO, CHOPPED (ABOUT 1/2 CUP)

1/2 GREEN BELL PEPPER, SEEDED AND CHOPPED

5 GREEN ONIONS WITH TOPS, CHOPPED

1/4 CUP FINELY CHOPPED FRESH CILANTRO, PLUS SEVERAL SPRIGS FOR GARNISH

1/2 TEASPOON SALT

3/4 TEASPOON FRESHLY GROUND BLACK PEPPER

3 PICKLED JALAPEÑO PEPPERS, STEMMED, SEEDED, AND SLICED

SOUR CREAM FOR GARNISH.

Preheat the oven to 300°F. In a 10-inch dry black skillet over the highest heat, cook the tortillas one at a time, turning once, for 15 seconds, just to soften. Set the tortillas aside. When finished cooking all 6 tortillas, remove the black skillet from the flame and fan the tortillas out onto the bottom, going up the sides of the skillet like the petals of a flower. Dot the tortilla crust with the butter.

In a bowl, combine the eggs, Cheddar cheese, tomato, green pepper, green onions, chopped cilantro, salt, and pepper. Pour the mixture into the tortilla-lined skillet. Arrange the jalapeño strips on top of the egg mixture in a sunburst pattern. Bake for 45 minutes. A skewer inserted into the middle will come out clean. Serve warm or at room temperature, sliced into wedges with a dollop of sour cream and a sprig of cilantro on top.

How to make a simple Southwestern salad:

This classic south-of-the-border salad has wonderful flavor combinations. Toss the romaine in a plain vinaigrette, then arrange it on individual plates. Top the lettuce with slices of orange and avocado and a sprinkling of pomegranate seeds. The only way to remove the pomegranate seeds is by hand. Cut the fruit in half, and begin peeling with a paring knife. Then dig your fingers in and remove the seeds. Don't worry. The pomegranate juice will eventually wash off.

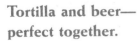

**Tortilla and beer—
perfect together.**

Chips
and Salsa

Romaine Lettuce
with
Avocado,
Orange Slices,
and
Pomegranate Seeds

Tortilla and Cilantro
Quiche

Flan

Italian Country Strata

Having people over for Sunday brunch makes a nice punctuation point for the weekend. Foods for kids are easy. You'll have a terrific opportunity to invite other families whose lives are as rushed as yours. All you have to do by way of preparation is to remember to put the strata in the refrigerator on Saturday night so that all that lovely custard can set up before the morning.

PREPARATION TIME: 15 MINUTES   MAKES 10 SERVINGS
COOKING TIME: 1 HOUR

All the Trimmings

Serve this brunch on a sideboard so that people feel free to take what they like from the available choices. You could add boxed cereals along with the yogurt for the diehard Wheaties crowd. If you've included the little folks in this party, stack up non-breakable bowls for them to use so that neither you nor their parents have to worry about breakage.

Complete the recipe up until the final baking on the day before serving. If you have leftovers, cover and refrigerate, then reheat in the oven or microwave and serve hot.

8 THICK SLICES ITALIAN COUNTRY BREAD, CRUSTS REMOVED

10 LARGE EGGS

4 CUPS HALF AND HALF

1 TEASPOON DRY MUSTARD

1 CUP COTTAGE CHEESE

1½ CUPS FRESHLY GRATED PARMIGIANO-REGGIANO CHEESE

4 CLOVES GARLIC, MINCED

½ TEASPOON BLACK PEPPER

1 CUP CHOPPED FRESH FLAT-LEAF PARSLEY

1 TABLESPOON CHOPPED FRESH ROSEMARY

4 GREEN ONIONS WITH TOPS, MINCED

1 CUP BROCCOLI FLORETS

1 CUP CAULIFLOWER FLORETS

1 CUP BABY CARROTS

1 (10-OUNCE) BOX FROZEN SPINACH, THAWED, DRAINED, AND SQUEEZED DRY

Lightly butter a 9-×-13-inch casserole dish and add the bread slices, overlapping them slightly.

In a large bowl, whisk together the eggs, half and half, and mustard. Add the cottage cheese, ½ cup of the Parmigiano-Reggiano, the garlic, pepper, parsley, and rosemary. Stir to mix, then pour over the bread. Use a spatula to press the mixture into the bread. Cover and refrigerate overnight.

One and a half hours before serving time, remove the strata mixture from the refrigerator. Preheat the oven to 375°F. Add the vegetables to the strata and push them into the egg mixture so that they're covered by custard. Top with the remaining 1 cup of Parmesan cheese. Bake for 1 hour, uncovered, until the strata is browned and a knife inserted in the center comes out clean. Cut into squares and serve hot.

How to poach fruit in the microwave:

Count on 1 piece of fruit per diner, plus 1 for the pot, and peel and deseed the fruit, cutting it into equal-size pieces. Choose apples, pears, quinces, peaches, or plums. Place it in a microwavable dish and add 1 inch of fruit juice or water. Season to taste with cinnamon, a little brown sugar, and/or butter. Cover and cook on high (100% power) at a rate of 3 minutes per cup of fruit. In other words, for 2 cups of fruit, microwave for 6 minutes. Cool and serve in small bowls, at room temperature, hot, or cold.

Warm
Poached Pears
and Apples
in
Cranberry Juice

Italian Country Strata

Vanilla or Maple
Yogurt with Fresh Berries

Fresh Squeezed
Orange Juice

Cappuccino

Try a Sangiovese or Sangiovese blend from Italy. This fruity red wine will complement the eggs and herbs in this dish.

Asparagus-Tarragon Tart

A golden tart flecked with tarragon and accented by a wheel of roasted asparagus, this is mouthwatering to look at and delicious for a light, glamorous lunch. Use a piecrust from the grocery store's refrigerated case— we like the ones in the red box—or make and bake your own.

All the Trimmings

Here's a preset ladies' lunch where the food makes the decorations. Start out with snowy white linens, add a twist of pastel ribbons, then mark each place with a colorful charger and 2 plates—a dinner plate with a clear glass plate over it. Onto the glass plate preset a wedge of asparagus tart and a serving of tomato salad. Pass the hot bread and enjoy. Comes time for dessert, remove the glass plates and pass a tray of huge Driscoll strawberries with brown sugar and crème fraîche for your guests to arrange on the dinner plates. Pass the butter cookies. Make the coffee. It's a party.

PREPARATION TIME: 20 MINUTES   MAKES 4 LUNCHEON SERVINGS
COOKING TIME: 45 MINUTES TOTAL

Make this tart early on the day you plan to serve it, cover, and reserve. Serve it warm or at room temperature. Refrigerate leftovers for a heavenly breakfast the next day.

1 PREPARED, UNBAKED PIECRUST

1 TEASPOON ALL-PURPOSE FLOUR

1 POUND FRESH ASPARAGUS, SNAPPED INTO ABOUT 3½-INCH LENGTHS, STEMS DISCARDED

⅔ CUP HALF AND HALF

2 LARGE EGGS

2 TABLESPOONS FRESH LEMON JUICE

GRATED ZEST OF ½ LEMON

½ CUP FRESHLY GRATED PARMESAN CHEESE

1 TEASPOON DRIED TARRAGON, OR 1 TABLESPOON MINCED FRESH TARRAGON LEAVES

½ TEASPOON KOSHER SALT

Preheat the oven to 450°F. Place the prepared crust on a work surface and rub it with the flour, pressing out any cracks. Transfer the crust to a 9-inch pie or quiche pan and press the dough into the pan, folding the excess border under to form double-thick sides. Pierce the dough all over with a fork. Bake until golden, 10 to 15 minutes. Cool in the pan on a rack. Reduce the oven temperature to 375°.

Bring a pot of water to a boil and steam the asparagus tips just until crisp-tender, 3 to 4 minutes. Lift the steamer out of the pan and run the asparagus under cold water to set the color. Drain on paper towels.

Make the custard by whisking together the half and half, eggs, lemon juice and zest, the Parmesan, and the tarragon. Arrange the asparagus in a spoke pattern in the baked crust, alternating tip ends and midsections, with the cut ends meeting in the center. Pour the custard over the asparagus. Sprinkle with the salt. Bake until the tart puffs and the top browns, 30 to 35 minutes. Cool and cut into 6 wedges.

Vine-Ripened
Cherry Tomatoes
and Cucumbers on a
Bed of Baby Greens
with a Touch of
Balsamic Vinaigrette

Asparagus-Tarragon Tart

Hot French Bread
and Sweet Butter

Strawberries,
Brown Sugar,
and
Crème Fraîche

Butter Cookies

Espresso

**The herbal note of a Pouilly-Fumé
will nicely complement the tarragon.**

How to select and prepare asparagus:

Choosing tender asparagus is half the battle. There are those who prefer the pencil-thin stalks, and those who like them fat-as-your-thumb, but the deal with asparagus is that it pushes up out of the ground and what you see is what you get. The thin ones aren't younger, or necessarily more tender than the thick ones. They're just thinner. You can find asparagus not only in a range of sizes, but also from pale cream through violet, to deepest sea green. The cream-colored ones were grown by farmers who mounded the earth around them to keep the chlorophyll from developing. Highly prized in France, these pale beauties are usually quite expensive, and may be tough besides. You'll find English and Italian purple varieties, but in the United States, you'll mostly find green ones.

So there you are in the market looking at spring's bounty. How to choose? First, note the bud top. It should be tightly closed. If you see any hint of flowering, pass those by, because they'll be woody as toothpicks. Note the color. If the green is bright and clear, that means it's fresh and you should grab it and cook it that day. If the color seems more like army green, pass on by. It's probably old and tough and might even be bitter and stringy. For best results, pick and cook asparagus the same day. If you have to store it, wrap it in plastic and refrigerate it for no more than a couple days.

Just when you're ready to cook it, snap off the woody ends and discard them. This is easy. Hold the asparagus by both ends and snap, it will break naturally where the tender shoot ends. Now you'll have long ones and short ones, but that's okay. If you've chosen thick asparagus, you may wish to give the ends a quick peel—the way the French do—but actually, if you've chosen wisely and well, this is a step that's quite unnecessary.

When you cook the asparagus, don't overdo it or you'll lose the bright color and the ideal crisp-tender texture. Whether cooking in water, or steaming, time it so you cook it just right: 1 to 2 minutes for pencil-thin stalks, 3 to 5 minutes for mediums, 5 to 8 minutes for thicker ones, and 10 to 12 minutes for the really giant ones. If you're cooking a lot, bundle them loosely with cotton string and stand them in water.

To test for doneness, poke a stalk with a knife. Remove it from the heat while there's still a little resistance. Either run to the table with a mountain of asparagus and sweet butter, or—if you plan to use the asparagus in another recipe—run it under cold water to set the color and stop the cooking. Drain, then use in the recipe of choice.

Index

A

Almond slivers, toasting, 143
Appetizer, quick, 75. *See also* Hors
    d' oeuvre, impromptu
Apples
    Beer-Braised Pork Chops with
        Onions, Apples, Cabbage, and
        Currants, 50–51
    Risotto with Apples and Sausage,
        76–77
    Roast Peppered Beef with Pears and
        Apples, 182–83
    selecting, 77, 183
    Warm Poached Pears and Apples in
        Cranberry Juice, 217
Apricots, stewing dried, 134
Artichokes
    Artichokes, Capers, Olives, Lemon
        Zest, and Italian Tuna on Pasta
        Shells, 172–73
    Braised Chicken with
        Artichokes and Greek Olives, 48–49
    Seafood Paella with Artichoke
        Hearts, 38–39
Asian pickles, 11
Asparagus
    Asparagus, Ham, and Rice Casserole,
        72–73
    selecting and preparing, 220

B

Babaganoush, 26, 27, 100, 101, 180,
    181
Bacon: Red Beans and Rice, 130–31
Bain marie, 205
Balsamic Vinaigrette, 151
Bananas
    Sautéed Bananas with Rum and Ice
        Cream, 127
    Tamarind Beef and Bean Stew with
        Pineapple and Bananas, 88–89
Barbecued food
    dry rub for, 187
    Slow-Roasted Barbecued Brisket and
        Southwestern Vegetables, 186–87
Bean sprouts, cold marinated, 21
Beans
    Black Bean Sauce, 14–15
    cooking, 129
    Debra Pucci's Super-Quick White
        Bean and Escarole Soup, 128–29
    lima. *See* Lima beans
    Mesclun Salad with Black Beans, Red
        Bell Pepper, and Red Onion
        Vinaigrette, 121
    Red Beans and Rice, 130–31
    Refried Beans, 45
    Rice and Refried Beans, 31, 45
    Tamarind Beef and Bean Stew with
        Pineapple and Bananas, 88–89
Beef
    Barbara Bradley's Green Chile Stew
        with Beef and Pork, 90–91
    Beef and Tomato Stir-Fry with
        Whiskey and Black Bean Sauce,
        14–15
    Beef Bigos, 94–95
    Braised Herbes de Provence Beef in
        Burgundy Wine, 56–57
    choosing and cooking ground, 59
    Cincinnati-Style Chili, 84–85
    flank steak, 15
    German Spiced Beef with Root
        Vegetables, 96–97
    Peppery Italian Beef Stew on Grilled
        Polenta Rounds, 92–93
    Real Texas Chili, 82–83
    Roasted Root Vegetables with
        Sirloin, 194–95
    Roast Peppered Beef with Pears and
        Apples, 182–83
    Slow-Roasted Barbecued Brisket and
        Southwestern Vegetables, 186–87
    Spanish Steak with Sautéed Peppers
        and Walnuts, 28–29
    Stir-Fried Sirloin and Bitter Greens,
        12–13
    Stracotto (Parma Pot Roast with
        Pasta), 54–55
    Tamarind Beef and Bean Stew with
        Pineapple and Bananas, 88–89
    Zucchini Beef Bow-ties, 58–59
Beverages
    Mimosa, 63
    Mint julep, 131
    Sangria, 39
Black Beans, Spicy, 61
Black Bean Sauce, 14–15

Blue cheese, 179
    Blue Cheese Dip, 85
Blueberry Chicken, 22–23
Blueberry Vinaigrette, 166
Bok choy: Braised Bok Choy and
    Chicken in a Ginger Sauce, 46–47
Bouillabaisse, Oregon, 108–9
Braised dishes, 46–61
    Beer-Braised Pork Chops with
        Onions, Apples, Cabbage, and
        Currants, 50–51
    Braised Bok Choy and Chicken in a
        Ginger Sauce, 46–47
    Braised Chicken with Artichokes and
        Greek Olives, 48–49
    Braised Herbes de Provence Beef in
        Burgundy Wine, 56–57
    Broccoli Rabe with Italian Sausage,
        Tortellini, and Fresh Cherry
        Tomatoes, 52–53
    Stracotto (Parma Pot Roast with
        Pasta), 54–55
    Tequila-Braised Chicken with Two
        Kinds of Peaches, 60–61
    Zucchini Beef Bow-ties, 58–59
Breads
    corn, 83
    Sesame Seed Crust, 174–75
    See also Grains; Sandwiches; Tortillas
Brisket, cooking, 187
Broccoli
    Broccoli Rabe with Italian Sausage,
        Tortellini, and Fresh Cherry
        Tomatoes, 52–53
    Stir-Fried Chicken Thighs with
        Sugar Snaps, Shiitakes, Carrots,
        and Broccoli, 2–4
Bulgur
    Bulgur, Chick-pea, and Tomato Pilaf,
        146–47
    Bulgur, Tomato, and Feta Salad,
        144–45
    preparing, 145
Butter, compound, 73

C

Cabbage
    Beer-Braised Pork Chops with
        Onions, Apples, Cabbage, and
        Currants, 50–51
    Korean (kim chee), 2
Cajun food
    Louisiana Swampland Shellfish
        Gumbo, 114–15
    Red Beans and Rice, 130–31
Cake, Chinese yellow sponge, 9
Caribbean food, 127
Carmelizing
    meats, 201
    vegetables, 118, 195
Carrots
    Poached Salmon and Carrot Salad
        with a Blueberry Vinaigrette, 166
    Stir-Fried Chicken Thighs with
        Sugar Snaps, Shiitakes, Carrots,
        and Broccoli, 2–4
    See also Root vegetables
Casseroles
    Asparagus, Ham, and Rice Casserole,
        72–73
    Chipotle Chicken con Queso on a
        Bed of Lima Beans, 196–97
    Joann's Spicy East Texas Pork Chop
        and Rice Casserole, 202–3
    Not June Cleaver's Tuna Noodle, But
        Linguine with Sautéed Tuna and
        Mixed Peppers, 206–7
Catsup Sauce, 20–21
Chayote, 127
Cheese
    blue, 179
    Blue Cheese Dip, 85
    Broccoli Rabe with Italian Sausage,
        Tortellini, and Fresh Cherry
        Tomatoes, 52–53
    Bulgur, Tomato, and Feta Salad,
        144–45
    Cheese Ravioli with Butter and
        Parmigiano-Reggiano, 54–55
    Clam and Cheese Tortellini Salad,
        162–63

feta, about, 145
    Fresh Figs, Red Pepper Flakes, and
        Lemon Zest with Freshly Grated
        Parmigiano-Reggiano Cheese,
        13
    Fresh Mozzarella, Tomato, and Basil
        Tower with Balsamic Vinaigrette,
        211
    Fresh Tomato, Ricotta, and Chopped
        Basil Salsa Cruda on Penne,
        152–53
    Italian Cheese Plate, 53
    Polenta with Chicken Apple
        Sausage, Apples, and Fontina
        Cheese, 74
    Quesadillas Primavera, 44–45
    Ripe Pears with Shaved Parmigiano-
        Reggiano and Balsamic Vinaigrette
        on a Bed of Baby Greens, 59
    Spinach and Sugar Snap Risotto with
        Parmigiano-Reggiano, 132–33
    Stracotto (Parma Pot Roast with
        Pasta), 54–55
Chick-peas: Bulgur, Chick-pea, and
        Tomato Pilaf, 146–47
Chicken
    Berkeley Panned Chicken with
        Polenta, Peppers, and Corn,
        24–25
    Blueberry Chicken, 22–23
    Braised Bok Choy and Chicken in a
        Ginger Sauce, 46–47
    Braised Chicken with Artichokes and
        Greek Olives, 48–49
    broth, 118
    Chicken apple sausage. See Sausage
    Chicken Pot-au-Feu, 116–18
    Chicken-Walnut Stir-Fry, 6–7
    Chipotle Chicken con Queso on a
        Bed of Lima Beans, 196–97
    Grilled Marinated Chicken and
        Vegetable Salad with Pine Nuts,
        158–59
    handling and preparing, 160
    Jerry Thompson's Costa Rican
        Tropical Stew, 126–27
    Kaki's White Chicken Chili for
        Sissies, 86–87

Paprika Chicken with Saffron
    Dumplings, 136–37
poaching, 47, 197
Roasted Lemon Chicken with
    Fingerling Potatoes, Tomatoes,
    and Olives, 188–89
Seafood Paella with Artichoke
    Hearts, 38–39
selecting, 124
Stir-Fried Chicken Thighs with
    Sugar Snaps, Shiitakes, Carrots,
    and Broccoli, 2–4
Tarragon-Smothered Chicken with
    Pearl Onions and Mushrooms,
    122–23
Tequila-Braised Chicken with Two
    Kinds of Peaches, 60–61
Tortilla Chicken Soup, 120–21
Chilequiles, Poblano Pepper, 70–
    71
Chili
    Cincinnati-Style Chili, 84–85
    Kaki's White Chicken Chili for
        Sissies, 86–87
    Real Texas Chili, 82–83
Chinese cleaver, 15, 118
Chinese food
    bakery, 9
    Beef and Tomato Stir-Fry with
        Whiskey and Black Bean Sauce,
        14–15
    Braised Bok Choy and Chicken in a
        Ginger Sauce, 46–47
    cake, 9
    Cantonese, 14
    Chinese Sweet and Sour Pork with
        Eggplant, 10–11
    cooking meat for, 15
    curry powder, 16
    dumplings, 9, 106–7
    pastries, 9
    poaching chicken for, 49
    Stir-Fried Shrimp and Onions in a
        Catsup Sauce, 20–21
    See also Stir-fry
Chipotles, 113
Chowder, Gulf, 110–11
Cinnamon Lamb Sauté, 26–27

Clams
    buying and cooking, 39
    Clam and Cheese Tortellini Salad,
        162–63
    Fennel and Pernod Shellfish Stew,
        104–5
    Seafood Paella with Artichoke
        Hearts, 38–39
Coffee, making strong, 101
Cooking methods
    beans, 129
    blanching vegetables, 165
    braising, 49
    brisket, 187
    broiling pineapple, 199
    broth, 113, 118
    bulgur, 145
    canned tomatoes, 111
    carmelizing, 201
    Chinese cleaver, 15, 118
    coffee, strong, 101
    compound butter, 73
    concentrating flavors, 33
    deglazing, 49
    Dutch oven, 57
    fish, 207
    flour, 137
    French, 49, 57
    French chef's knife, 15
    frittata, 67
    ground beef, 59
    hard-cooked eggs, 147
    lima beans, 157
    meat, 95
    mollusks, 39
    noodles, 35
    omelets, 63
    panned meats, 25
    pasta, 151, 163
    poaching chicken, 47, 197
    pressure cookers, 55
    rice/risotto, 7, 37, 79, 133
    roasting meats/vegetables, 189, 195
    roasting red peppers, 169
    salmon, 19
    sautéeing, 19, 29, 49
    searing meat, 93
    stewing dried apricots, 134

stir-fry, 3, 5, 6, 13, 19
toasting almond slivers and sesame
    seeds, 143
tortellini, 53
tortillas, 71
tuna steaks, 175
wok, 3, 5, 6
Corn
    Berkeley Panned Chicken with
        Polenta, Peppers, and Corn,
        24–25
    Cornbread, 83
    Cornmeal, 74. See also Polenta;
        Posole
    Corn Salad, 168–69
    Mexican roasting ears, 31
    Risotto with Ham, Corn, and Red
        Pepper, 78–79
    Skewered Tomatoes and Shrimp
        with Roasted Red Peppers and
        Corn Salad on a Bed of Mesclun,
        168–69
Costa Rican Tropical Stew, 126–27
Couscous
    Cinnamon Lamb Sauté, 26–27
    Couscous Summer Deli Salad,
        180–81
    selecting, 181
    Turkey and Cranberry Couscous,
        40–41
Crab
    Crab with a Vegetable Confetti
        Salad and a Lemon-Mustard
        Vinaigrette, 164–65
    Louisiana Swampland Shellfish
        Gumbo, 114–15
    Shrimp and Crabmeat Quiche,
        212–13
Cream cheese, French (Boursin), 169
Cucumber Ribbons in Rice Wine
    Vinegar, Sugar, and Red Pepper
    Flakes, 11
Currants: Beer-Braised Pork Chops
    with Onions, Apples, Cabbage,
    and Currants, 50–51
Curried food
    Lamb and Sweet Potato Curry Stew,
        102–3

Lemon Madras Egg Curry, 68–69
Thai Curried Coconut Salmon and
    Spinach Stir-Fry with Basil, 16–17
Curry powder, 16, 19
Custard
    Asparagus Tarragon Tart, 218–19
    Aunt Mary's Green Rice Custard,
        204–5
    Italian Country Strata, 216–17

D

Deglazing, 49
Desserts
    Broiled Pineapple with White Wine
        and Honey, 198, 199
    Cheesecake with Raspberry Brandy
        Sauce, 177
    Chopped Mango over Pineapple
        Sherbet, 11
    Mango Slices with Lime Wedges,
        17
    Marsala Ice Cream, 155
    Sautéed Bananas with Rum and Ice
        Cream, 127
    strawberry. See Strawberries
    Tangerine Sections Drizzled with
        Honey, Fresh Mint, and Crushed
        Pistachios, 49
Dips
    Blue Cheese Dip, 85
    Shrimp Dip, 15
    Sour Cream Dip, 191
    Spinach Sour Cream Dip, 191
Duck
    Duck Sausage on a Bed of Lentils,
        198–99
    Roasted Duck with Sweet Potatoes,
        Sage, Fruit, and Port, 190–91
Dumplings
    Chinese Dumplings, 9, 106–7
    Saffron Dumplings, 136–37
Dutch oven meals, cooking, 57

E

Eastern European food, 94–95
Egg dishes, 62–71
    cooking eggs for, 147
    Herbes de Provence Lettuce Frittata,
        64
    Lemon Madras Egg Curry, 68
    Lox-Tarragon Omelet, 62–63
    Poblano Pepper Chilequiles, 70–71
    Spring Frittata with Flat-Leaf Parsley,
        Baby Leeks, Green Onions, and a
        Touch of Balsamic Vinegar, 66–67
Eggplant
    Chinese Sweet and Sour Pork with
        Eggplant, 10–11
    Japanese Eggplant, Bell Pepper, and
        Lamb Stir-Fry, 8–9
Eggs, hard-cooked, 147
Escarole: Debra Pucci's Super-Quick
    White Bean and Escarole Soup,
    128–29

F

Figs
    Fresh Figs, Nectarines, and Ham
        Tossed in a Red Wine Reduction,
        178–79
    Fresh Figs, Red Pepper Flakes, and
        Lemon Zest with Freshly Grated
        Parmigiano-Reggiano Cheese, 13
Filé: Louisiana Swampland Shellfish
    Gumbo, 114–15
Fish
    Artichokes, Capers, Olives, Lemon
        Zest, and Italian Tuna on Pasta
        Shells, 172–73
    California Hot Pot, 138–39
    cooking, 207
    Grouper Veracruz, 30–31
    Mustard Salmon with Buttered Egg
        Noodles, 34–35
    Roasted Monkfish with Garlic and
        Ginger on a Bed of Root
        Vegetables, 192–93

salmon, buying and cooking, 19
    Seafood Paella with Artichoke
        Hearts, 38–39
    Thai Curried Coconut Salmon and
        Spinach Stir-Fry with Basil, 16–17
    See also Seafood
Flour, choosing and using, 137
French chef's knife, 15
French cooking, 49, 57, 118, 205
French food
    Braised Herbes de Provence Beef in
        Burgundy Wine, 56–57
    Chicken Pot-au-Feu, 116–18
    cream cheese (Boursin), 169
    Shrimp and Crabmeat Quiche,
        212–13
    Tarragon-Smothered Chicken with
        Pearl Onions and Mushrooms,
        122–23
Frittata
    Herbes de Provence Lettuce Frittata,
        64
    preparing, 67
    Spring Frittata with Flat-Leaf Parsley,
        Baby Leeks, Green Onions, and a
        Touch of Balsamic Vinegar, 66–67
Fruit, poaching, 217

G

Game. See Duck
Gazpacho, Impromptu, 143
Grains. See Bulgur; Couscous; Polenta
Green Chile Stew with Beef and Pork,
    90–91
Greens
    Cherry Tomatoes and Cucumbers on
        a Bed of Baby Greens with
        Balsamic Vinaigrette, 219
    Mixed Bitter Greens with Sesame
        Vinaigrette, 207
    Ripe Pears on a Bed of Greens with
        Gorgonzola, Hazelnuts, and
        Three-Citrus Vinaigrette, 24, 25
    Ripe Pears with Shaved Parmigiano-
        Reggiano and Balsamic Vinaigrette
        on a Bed of Baby Greens, 59

Seared Tuna, with a Black and White Sesame Seed Crust on a Bed of Greens, 174–75

Stir-Fried Sirloin and Bitter Greens, 12–13

Tossed Baby Greens with Three-Citrus Vinaigrette, 213

Tossed Greens, Edible Flowers, and Herb Salad, 67

Grouper Veracruz, 30–31

Gumbo, Louisiana Swampland Shellfish, 114–15

Gumbo filé, 115

H

Ham
  Asparagus, Ham, and Rice Casserole, 72–73
  choosing, 170
  Fresh Figs, Nectarines, and Ham Tossed in a Red Wine Reduction, 178–79
  Melinda's Sweet Hot Ham Balls with Yams and Red Onion, 200–1
  Risotto with Ham, Corn, and Red Pepper, 78–79

Hazelnuts: Ripe Pears on a Bed of Greens with Gorgonzola, Hazelnuts, and Three-Citrus Vinaigrette, 24, 25

Hors d'oeuvre, impromptu, 191. See also Appetizer, quick

Horseradish Mayonnaise Sauce, 193

Hungarian food, Pork Paprikash over Rice, 98–99

I

Ice Cream, Marsala, 155

Italian food
  Artichokes, Capers, Olives, Lemon Zest, and Italian Tuna on Pasta Shells, 172–73
  Broccoli Rabe with Italian Sausage, Tortellini, and Fresh Cherry Tomatoes, 52–53

cheese plate, 53

Cheese Ravioli with Butter and Parmigiano-Reggiano, 54–55

Fresh Mozzarella, Tomato, and Basil Tower with Balsamic Vinaigrette, 211

Italian Country Strata, 216–17

Onions, Onions, and More Onions Pizza, 208–11

Orecchiette Puttanesca, 148–49

Peppery Italian Beef Stew on Grilled Polenta Rounds, 92–93

Stracotto (Parma Pot Roast with Pasta), 54–55

See also Pasta

J

Jamaican food, PickaPepper Sauce, 43

Japanese Eggplant, Bell Pepper, and Lamb Stir-Fry, 8–9

K

Kim chee (Korean cabbage slaw), 2

L

Lamb
  Cinnamon Lamb Sauté, 26–27
  Japanese Eggplant, Bell Pepper, and Lamb Stir-Fry, 8–9
  Lamb and Mint Paella, 36–37
  Lamb and Sweet Potato Curry Stew, 102–3
  Uzbekistan Lamb Stew with Cilantro, Dried Fruit, and Pine Nuts, 100–1

Latin American food, 127

Leeks, preparing, 193

Lemon-Mustard Vinaigrette, 164–65

Lemon-pecan butter, 73

Lima beans, cooking, 157
  Chipotle Chicken con Queso on a Bed of Lima Beans, 196–97

Warm Lima Bean, Mint, and Parsley Salad, 156–57

M

Madras curry powder, 16

Mango-Pineapple Salsa, 127

Marsala Ice Cream, 155

Meat
  carmelizing, 201
  pan-broiling, 29
  panned, 25
  roasting, 189, 195. See also Roasted dinners
  sautéeing, 29. See also Sautéed dishes
  searing, 93
  stir-frying. See Stir-fry
  See also Bacon; Beef; Chicken; Duck; Ham; Lamb; Pork; Sausage; Turkey and Cranberry Couscous

Mexican food
  Caldo Mariscos y Chipotle, 112–13
  Poblano Pepper Chilequiles, 70–71
  Quesadillas Primavera, 44–45
  Refried Beans, 45
  Rice and Refried Beans, 31, 45
  roasting ears of corn, 31
  See also Tortillas

Microwave, poaching fruit in, 217

Microwave meals, 72–79
  Polenta with Chicken Apple Sausage, Apples, and Fontina Cheese, 74
  Risotto with Apples and Sausage, 76–77
  Risotto with Ham, Corn, and Red Pepper, 78–79

Mimosa, 63

Mint julep, 131

Mollusks, buying and cooking, 39

Mongolian Sauce, 139

Mussels: Seafood Paella with Artichoke Hearts, 38–39

N

Nectarines: Fresh Figs, Nectarines, and Ham Tossed in a Red Wine Reduction, 178–79

O

Oils, for stir-fry, 19
Okra: Louisiana Swampland Shellfish Gumbo, 114–15
Onions, preparing, 203
Oriental food. *See* Stir-fry
Oysters: Louisiana Swampland Shellfish Gumbo, 114–15

P

Paella
    cooking, 37
    Lamb and Mint Paella, 36–37
    Seafood Paella with Artichoke Hearts, 38–39
Pan-broiling, 29
Panned meats, 25
Paprikash, 98–99
Pasta
    Artichokes, Capers, Olives, Lemon Zest, and Italian Tuna on Pasta Shells, 172–73
    Broccoli Rabe with Italian Sausage, Tortellini, and Fresh Cherry Tomatoes, 52–53
    Buttered Egg Noodles, 35
    Cheese Ravioli with Butter and Parmigiano-Reggiano, 54–55
    choosing and cooking for salad, 171
    Clam and Cheese Tortellini Salad, 162–63
    cooking, 151, 163, 171
    Fresh Tomato, Ricotta, and Chopped Basil Salsa Cruda on Penne, 152–53
    Not June Cleaver's Tuna Noodle, But

Linguine with Sautéed Tuna and Mixed Peppers, 206–7
    Orecchiette Puttanesca, 148–49
    Orecchiette with Wild and Brown Mushrooms in a Balsamic Vinaigrette, 150–51
    Stracotto (Parma Pot Roast with Pasta), 54–55
    Warm Penne and Pistachio Vegetable Salad, 154–55
    Zucchini Beef Bow-ties, 58–59
Pastries, Chinese, 9
Peaches: Tequila-Braised Chicken with Two Kinds of Peaches, 60–61
Peanut oil, 19
Pears
    Ripe Pears on a Bed of Greens with Gorgonzola, Hazelnuts, and Three-Citrus Vinaigrette, 24, 25
    Ripe Pears with Shaved Parmigiano-Reggiano and Balsamic Vinaigrette on a Bed of Baby Greens, 59
    Roast Peppered Beef with Pears and Apples, 182–83
    selecting and serving, 99, 183
    Warm Poached Pears and Apples in Cranberry Juice, 217
Peas
    Bulgur, Chick-pea, and Tomato Pilaf, 146–47
    Hot Dried Wasabi Peas, 11, 16, 17, 47
    Spinach and Sugar Snap Risotto with Parmigiano-Reggiano, 132–33
    Stir-Fried Chicken Thighs with Sugar Snaps, Shiitakes, Carrots, and Broccoli, 2–4
    Sugar Snap Peas with Curried Mayonnaise, 35
Peppers, roasting red,' 169
PickaPepper Sauce, 43
Pico de Gallo, 91
Piecrust, 213
Pilaf: Bulgur, Chick-pea, and Tomato Pilaf, 146–47
Pineapple
    broiling, 199
    Mango-Pineapple Salsa, 127

Tamarind Beef and Bean Stew with Pineapple and Bananas, 88–89
Pine nuts
    Grilled Marinated Chicken and Vegetable Salad with Pine Nuts, 158–59
    Uzbekistan Lamb Stew with Cilantro, Dried Fruit, and Pine Nuts, 100–1
Pistachios
    Pistachio Vegetable Salad, 154–55
    Tangerine Sections Drizzled with Honey, Fresh Mint, and Crushed Pistachios, 49
    Warm Penne and Pistachio Vegetable Salad, 154–55
Pizza
    making dough for, 210–11
    Onions, Onions, and More Onions Pizza, 208–11
Poaching
    chicken, 47
    fruit, 217
Poblano Pepper Chilequiles, 70–71
Polenta
    Berkeley Panned Chicken with Polenta, Peppers, and Corn, 24–25
    Grilled Polenta Disks with Olive Oil and Red Pepper Flakes, 57
    Grilled Polenta Rounds, 93
    Polenta with Chicken Apple Sausage, Apples, and Fontina Cheese, 74
Pork
    Barbara Bradley's Green Chile Stew with Beef and Pork, 90–91
    Beer-Braised Pork Chops with Onions, Apples, Cabbage, and Currants, 50–51
    Chinese Sweet and Sour Pork with Eggplant, 10–11
    Joann's Spicy East Texas Pork Chop and Rice Casserole, 202–3
    Melinda's Sweet Hot Ham Balls with Yams and Red Onion, 200–1
    Pork Paprikash over Rice, 98–99

See also Bacon; Ham; Sausage
Posole, Barbara Bradley's, 134–35
Potatoes
    Red New Potatoes Tossed in Butter
        and Seeded Mustard, 51
    Roasted Lemon Chicken with
        Fingerling Potatoes, Tomatoes,
        and Olives, 188–89
    See also Root vegetables
Pumpkin Soup, 41

Q

Quesadillas
    Kaki's White Chicken Chili for
        Sissies, 86–87
    making, 87
    Quesadillas Primavera, 44–45
Quiche
    Shrimp and Crabmeat Quiche,
        212–13
    Tortilla and Cilantro Quiche,
        214–15

R

Raspberry Brandy Sauce, 177
Red peppers, roasting, 169
Rice
    Arborio, 79, 144
    Asparagus, Ham, and Rice Casserole,
        72–73
    Aunt Mary's Green Rice Custard,
        204–5
    cooking, 7, 37, 79, 133
    Dave's Yankee Dirty Rice, 42–43
    Joann's Spicy East Texas Pork Chop
        and Rice Casserole, 202–3
    Pork Paprikash over Rice, 98–99
    Red Beans and Rice, 130–31
    Rice and Refried Beans, 31, 45
    serving, 20
    Spanish, 37
    See also Risotto
Risotto
    cooking, 37

Risotto with Apples and Sausage,
    76–77
Risotto with Ham, Corn, and Red
    Pepper, 78–79
Spinach and Sugar Snap Risotto with
    Parmigiano-Reggiano, 132–33
Roasted dinners, 186–95
    Roasted Duck with Sweet Potatoes,
        Sage, Fruit, and Port, 190–91
    Roasted Lemon Chicken with
        Fingerling Potatoes, Tomatoes,
        and Olives, 188–89
    Roasted Monkfish with Garlic and
        Ginger on a Bed of Root
        Vegetables, 192–93
    Roasted Root Vegetables with
        Sirloin, 194–95
    Slow-Roasted Barbecued Brisket and
        Southwestern Vegetables, 186–87
Roasting
    meat and vegetables, 195
    oven, 189
Root vegetables
    German Spiced Beef with Root
        Vegetables, 96–97
    Roasted Root Vegetables with
        Sirloin, 194–95
Russian food (of the former Soviet
    Union), Uzbekistan Lamb Stew
    with Cilantro, Dried Fruit, and
    Pine Nuts, 100–1

S

Salad dressing
    Annie's Salad Dressing, 23
    See also Vinaigrettes
Salads
    avocado, 71, 89, 195
    Baby Spinach and Strawberry Salad
        with Goat Cheese Disks, 142–43
    Bay Shrimp, Tomato, and Basil Salad,
        170–71
    Belgian Endive Salad with Three-
        Citrus Vinaigrette, 63
    Bulgur, Tomato, and Feta Salad,
        144–45

cabbage slaw (kim chee), 2
Celery and Black and Green Olive
    Salad in a Vinaigrette, 32, 33
Cherry Tomatoes and Cucumbers on
    a Bed of Baby Greens with
    Balsamic Vinaigrette, 219
choosing and cooking pasta for,
    171
Clam and Cheese Tortellini Salad,
    162–63
Cold Marinated Bean Sprouts, 21
Corn Salad, 168–69
Couscous Summer Deli Salad,
    180–81
Crab with a Vegetable Confetti
    Salad and a Lemon-Mustard
    Vinaigrette, 164–65
Cucumber Ribbons in Rice Wine
    Vinegar, Sugar, and Red Pepper
    Flakes, 11
Fennel Slices and Celery, 22, 23
Fresh Figs, Nectarines, and Ham
    Tossed in a Red Wine Reduction,
    178–79
Grilled Marinated Chicken and
    Vegetable Salad with Pine Nuts,
    158–59
mesclun, 75, 93, 105, 107, 121,
    168–69
Mixed Bitter Greens with Sesame
    Vinaigrette, 207
oranges in, 30, 31, 105, 133, 149,
    163, 181, 189, 215
Orecchiette with Wild and Brown
    Mushrooms in a Balsamic
    Vinaigrette, 150–51
Pickled Beets and Toasted Walnuts
    in Vinaigrette, 57
Ripe Pears on a Bed of Greens with
    Gorgonzola, Hazelnuts, and
    Three-Citrus Vinaigrette, 24, 25
Ripe Pears with Shaved Parmigiano-
    Reggiano and Balsamic Vinaigrette
    on a Bed of Baby Greens, 59
romaine, 27, 49, 73, 103, 153, 191,
    199, 215
Salad of Jicama and Tangerines with
    Cilantro, 113

Seared Tuna, with a Black and White Sesame Seed Crust on a Bed of Greens, 174–75
simple Southwestern, 215
Skewered Tomatoes and Shrimp with Roasted Red Peppers and Corn Salad on a Bed of Mesclun, 168–69
sliced tomatoes in, 17, 35, 43, 79, 211
Spinach and Bacon Salad, 77
Spinach and Bacon Salad with Hot Vinaigrette, 109
Sun-Dried Tomatoes, Pancetta, Mushrooms, and Wilted Lettuce Salad, 176–77
Tossed Baby Greens with Three-Citrus Vinaigrette, 213
Tossed Greens, Edible Flowers, and Herb Salad, 67
Warm Lima Bean, Mint, and Parsley Salad, 156–57
Warm Penne and Pistachio Vegetable Salad, 154–55
Salmon
    Mustard Salmon with Buttered Egg Noodles, 34–35
    Poached Salmon and Carrot Salad with a Blueberry Vinaigrette, 166
    selecting and preparing, 19, 167
    Thai Curried Coconut Salmon and Spinach Stir-Fry with Basil, 16–17
Salsa, 91
    Mango-Pineapple Salsa, 127
    Quesadillas Primavera, 44–45
    tropical, 127
Salsa cruda
    Artichokes, Capers, Olives, Lemon Zest, and Italian Tuna on Pasta Shells, 172–73
    Fresh Tomato, Ricotta, and Chopped Basil Salsa Cruda, 152–53
Sandwiches, Mexican. See Quesadillas
Sangria, 39
Sauces
    Black Bean Sauce, 14–15
    Catsup Sauce, 20–21

cutting board, 149
Ginger Sauce, 46–47
Horseradish Mayonnaise Sauce, 193
Horseradish Sauce, 97
Mongolian Sauce, 139
PickaPepper Sauce, 43
Pico de Gallo, 91
Raspberry Brandy Sauce, 177
See also Salsa; Salsa cruda
Sausage
    Broccoli Rabe with Italian Sausage, Tortellini, and Fresh Cherry Tomatoes, 52–53
    Dave's Yankee Dirty Rice, 42–43
    Duck Sausage on a Bed of Lentils, 198–99
    Polenta with Chicken Apple Sausage, Apples, and Fontina Cheese, 74
    Red Beans and Rice, 130–31
    Risotto with Apples and Sausage, 76–77
    Seafood Paella with Artichoke Hearts, 38–39
Sautéed dishes, 22–45
    Berkeley Panned Chicken with Polenta, Peppers, and Corn, 24–25
    Blueberry Chicken, 22–23
    Cinnamon Lamb Sauté, 26–27
    cooking methods for, 19, 29, 49
    Dave's Yankee Dirty Rice, 42–43
    Grouper Veracruz, 30–31
    Lamb and Mint Paella, 36–37
    Martini Scallops on a Bed of Spinach, 32–33
    Mustard Salmon with Buttered Egg Noodles, 34–35
    Quesadillas Primavera, 44–45
    Spanish Steak with Sautéed Peppers and Walnuts, 28–29
    stir-fry compared to, 19
    Turkey and Cranberry Couscous, 40–41
Scallops
    Fennel and Pernod Shellfish Stew, 104–5

Martini Scallops on a Bed of Spinach, 32–33
Sea bass
    Caldo Mariscos y Chipotle, 112–13
    Seafood Paella with Artichoke Hearts, 38–39
Seafood
    Bay Shrimp, Tomato, and Basil Salad, 170–71
    Caldo Mariscos y Chipotle, 112–13
    Clam and Cheese Tortellini Salad, 162–63
    Crab with a Vegetable Confetti Salad and a Lemon-Mustard Vinaigrette, 164–65
    Fennel and Pernod Shellfish Stew, 104–5
    Gulf Chowder, 110–11
    Louisiana Swampland Shellfish Gumbo, 114–15
    Martini Scallops on a Bed of Spinach, 32–33
    methods for cooking, 39
    Not June Cleaver's Tuna Noodle, But Linguine with Sautéed Tuna and Mixed Peppers, 206–7
    Oregon Bouillabaisse, 108–9
    Poached Salmon and Carrot Salad with a Blueberry Vinaigrette, 166
    Seafood Paella with Artichoke Hearts, 38–39
    Seared Tuna, with a Black and White Sesame Seed Crust on a Bed of Greens, 174–75
    Shrimp and Crabmeat Quiche, 212–13
    Shrimp and Ginger Soup, 106–7
    Skewered Tomatoes and Shrimp with Roasted Red Peppers and Corn Salad on a Bed of Mesclun, 168–69
    Stir-Fried Shrimp and Onions in a Catsup Sauce, 20–21
Sesame seeds, toasting, 143
Shrimp
    Fennel and Pernod Shellfish Stew, 104–5

Louisiana Swampland Shellfish
Gumbo, 114–15
Seafood Paella with Artichoke
Hearts, 38–39
Shrimp and Crabmeat Quiche,
212–13
Shrimp and Ginger Soup, 106–7
Skewered Tomatoes and Shrimp
with Roasted Red Peppers and
Corn Salad on a Bed of Mesclun,
168–69
Stir-Fried Shrimp and Onions in a
Catsup Sauce, 20–21
Shrimp Dip, 15
Sirloin
choosing and cooking, 59
Roasted Root Vegetables with
Sirloin, 194–95
Stir-Fried Sirloin and Bitter Greens,
12–13
Zucchini Beef Bow-ties, 58–59
Skillet dinners
Beer-Braised Pork Chops with
Onions, Apples, Cabbage, and
Currants, 50–51
Braised Chicken with Artichokes and
Greek Olives, 48–49
See also Braised dishes
Slaw, cabbage (kim chee), 2
Soups
Ad Lib Pumpkin Soup, 41
Caldo Mariscos y Chipotle, 112–13
California Hot Pot, 138–39
Cream of Tomato Souped-up Soup,
177
Debra Pucci's Super-Quick White
Bean and Escarole Soup, 128–29
Gulf Chowder, 110–11
Impromptu Gazpacho, 143
Louisiana Swampland Shellfish
Gumbo, 114–15
making broth for, 113, 118
Oregon Bouillabaisse, 108–9
Shrimp and Ginger Soup, 106–7
Tarragon-Smothered Chicken with
Pearl Onions and Mushrooms,
122–23
Tortilla Chicken Soup, 120–21

Spanish rice, 37
Spanish Steak with Sautéed Peppers
and Walnuts, 28–29
Spinach
Baby Spinach and Strawberry Salad
with Goat Cheese Disks, 142–43
Caldo Mariscos y Chipotle, 112–13
Martini Scallops on a Bed of
Spinach, 32–33
Spinach and Bacon Salad, 77
Spinach and Bacon Salad with Hot
Vinaigrette, 109
Spinach and Sugar Snap Risotto with
Parmigiano-Reggiano, 132–33
Spinach Sour Cream Dip, 191
Steak
flank, 15
Spanish Steak with Sautéed Peppers
and Walnuts, 28–29
See also Sirloin
Stews
Barbara Bradley's Green Chile Stew
with Beef and Pork, 90–91
Beef Bigos, 94–95
Braised Herbes de Provence Beef in
Burgundy Wine, 56–57
Chicken Pot-au-Feu, 116–18
Fennel and Pernod Shellfish Stew,
104–5
German Spiced Beef with Root
Vegetables, 96–97
Jerry Thompson's Costa Rican
Tropical Stew, 126–27
Lamb and Sweet Potato Curry Stew,
102–3
Peppery Italian Beef Stew on Grilled
Polenta Rounds, 92–93
Pork Paprikash over Rice, 98–99
Tamarind Beef and Bean Stew with
Pineapple and Bananas, 88–89
Uzbekistan Lamb Stew with
Cilantro, Dried Fruit, and Pine
Nuts, 100–1
Stir-fry, 2–21
Beef and Tomato Stir-Fry with
Whiskey and Black Bean Sauce,
14–15
Chicken-Walnut Stir-Fry, 6–7

Chinese Sweet and Sour Pork with
Eggplant, 10–11
Japanese Eggplant, Bell Pepper, and
Lamb Stir-Fry, 8–9
method for, 3, 5, 6, 13, 19
oils for, 19
Stir-Fried Chicken Thighs with
Sugar Snaps, Shiitakes, Carrots,
and Broccoli, 2–4
Stir-Fried Shrimp and Onions in a
Catsup Sauce, 20–21
Stir-Fried Sirloin and Bitter Greens,
12–13
Thai Curried Coconut Salmon and
Spinach Stir-Fry with Basil, 16–17
See also Sautéed dishes
Strawberries
Baby Spinach and Strawberry Salad
with Goat Cheese Disks, 142–43
Fresh Strawberries Dipped in
Chocolate Sauce, 78, 79
Sliced Strawberries with Pepper and
Grand Marnier, 37
Strawberries Dipped in Crème
Fraîche and Brown Sugar, 72, 73,
218, 219
Strawberries Romanoff, 27
Sweet and Sour Pork with Eggplant,
10–11
Sweet potatoes
Lamb and Sweet Potato Curry Stew,
102–3
Roasted Duck with Sweet Potatoes,
Sage, Fruit, and Port, 190–91

T

Tamarind paste, 88, 89
Tangerines
Salad of Jicama and Tangerines with
Cilantro, 113
Tangerine Sections Drizzled with
Honey, Fresh Mint, and Crushed
Pistachios, 49
Tart, Asparagus Tarragon, 218–19
Thai Curried Coconut Salmon and
Spinach Stir-Fry with Basil, 16–17

Thai curry paste, 16
Tomatoes
Bay Shrimp, Tomato, and Basil Salad,
170–71
Beef and Tomato Stir-Fry with
Whiskey and Black Bean Sauce,
14–15
Broccoli Rabe with Italian Sausage,
Tortellini, and Fresh Cherry
Tomatoes, 52–53
Bulgur, Chick-pea, and Tomato Pilaf,
146–47
Bulgur, Tomato, and Feta Salad,
144–45
Cherry Tomatoes and Cucumbers on
a Bed of Baby Greens with
Balsamic Vinaigrette, 219
Fresh Mozzarella, Tomato, and Basil
Tower with Balsamic Vinaigrette,
211
Fresh Tomato, Ricotta, and Chopped
Basil Salsa Cruda on Penne,
152–53
Onions, Onions, and More Onions
Pizza, 208–9
Roasted Lemon Chicken with
Fingerling Potatoes, Tomatoes,
and Olives, 188–89
selecting, 153
Skewered Tomatoes and Shrimp
with Roasted Red Peppers and
Corn Salad on a Bed of Mesclun,
168–69
sliced, 17, 35, 43, 79
Sun-Dried Tomatoes, Pancetta,
Mushrooms, and Wilted Lettuce
Salad, 176–77
Tomato Souped-up Soup, 177
See also Salsa; Salsa cruda
Tortillas
preparing, 71. See also Quesadillas
Tortilla Chicken Soup, 120–21
Tortilla and Cilantro Quiche,
214–15

Tuna
Artichokes, Capers, Olives, Lemon
Zest, and Italian Tuna on Pasta
Shells, 172–73
cooking, 175
Not June Cleaver's Tuna Noodle, But
Linguine with Sautéed Tuna and
Mixed Peppers, 206–7
Seared Tuna, with a Black and White
Sesame Seed Crust on a Bed of
Greens, 174–75
Turkey and Cranberry Couscous,
40–41

U

Uzbekistan Lamb Stew with Cilantro,
Dried Fruit, and Pine Nuts, 100–1

V

Vegetables
blanching, 165
carmelizing, 118, 195
dip for. See Dips
German Spiced Beef with Root
Vegetables, 96–97
Grilled Marinated Chicken and
Vegetable Salad with Pine Nuts,
158–59
Italian Country Strata, 216–17
Oriental. See Stir-fry
Quesadillas Primavera, 44–45
Roasted Monkfish with Garlic and
Ginger on a Bed of Root
Vegetables, 192–93
Roasted Root Vegetables with
Sirloin, 194–95
roasting, 195
Slow-Roasted Barbecued Brisket and
Southwestern Vegetables, 186–87
stir-fry. See Stir-Fry

Vegetable Confetti Salad, 164–65
Warm Penne and Pistachio
Vegetable Salad, 154–55
See also specific vegetables
Vinaigrettes
Balsamic Vinaigrette, 151
Blueberry Vinaigrette, 166
Hot Vinaigrette, 109
Lemon-Mustard Vinaigrette, 164–65
Lemon Vinaigrettes, 103
Red Onion Vinaigrette, 121
Three-Citrus Vinaigrette, 25, 63, 93,
149
types of vinegar for, 23
Vinegar, using, 23

W

Walnuts
Chicken-Walnut Stir-Fry, 607
Pickled Beets and Toasted Walnuts
in Vinaigrette, 57
Spanish Steak with Sautéed Peppers
and Walnuts, 28–29
Wasabi peas, 11, 16, 17, 47
Whitefish: Seafood Paella with
Artichoke Hearts, 38–39

Y

Yams: Melinda's Sweet Hot Ham Balls
with Yams and Red Onion, 200–1
Yucca, 127

Z

Zucchini Beef Bow-ties, 58–59